DISTRIBUTED BLACKNESS

CRITICAL CULTURAL COMMUNICATION

General Editors: Jonathan Gray, Aswin Punathambekar, Adrienne Shaw

Founding Editors: Sarah Banet-Weiser and Kent A. Ono

Dangerous Curves: Latina Bodies in the Media
Isabel Molina-Guzmán

The Net Effect: Romanticism, Capitalism, and the Internet
Thomas Streeter

Our Biometric Future: Facial Recognition Technology and the Culture of Surveillance
Kelly A. Gates

Critical Rhetorics of Race
Edited by Michael G. Lacy and Kent A. Ono

Circuits of Visibility: Gender and Transnational Media Cultures
Edited by Radha S. Hegde

Commodity Activism: Cultural Resistance in Neoliberal Times
Edited by Roopali Mukherjee and Sarah Banet-Weiser

Arabs and Muslims in the Media: Race and Representation after 9/11
Evelyn Alsultany

Visualizing Atrocity: Arendt, Evil, and the Optics of Thoughtlessness
Valerie Hartouni

The Makeover: Reality Television and Reflexive Audiences
Katherine Sender

Authentic™: The Politics of Ambivalence in a Brand Culture
Sarah Banet-Weiser

Technomobility in China: Young Migrant Women and Mobile Phones
Cara Wallis

Love and Money: Queers, Class, and Cultural Production
Lisa Henderson

Cached: Decoding the Internet in Global Popular Culture
Stephanie Ricker Schulte

Black Television Travels: African American Media around the Globe
Timothy Havens

Citizenship Excess: Latino/as, Media, and the Nation
Hector Amaya

Feeling Mediated: A History of Media Technology and Emotion in America
Brenton J. Malin

The Post-Racial Mystique: Media and Race in the Twenty-First Century
Catherine R. Squires

Making Media Work: Cultures of Management in the Entertainment Industries
Edited by Derek Johnson, Derek Kompare, and Avi Santo

Sounds of Belonging: U.S. Spanish-Language Radio and Public Advocacy
Dolores Inés Casillas

Orienting Hollywood: A Century of Film Culture between Los Angeles and Bombay
Nitin Govil

Asian American Media Activism: Fighting for Cultural Citizenship
Lori Kido Lopez

Struggling For Ordinary: Media and Transgender Belonging in Everyday Life
Andre Cavalcante

Wife, Inc.: The Business of Marriage in the Twenty-First Century
Suzanne Leonard

Homegrown: Identity and Difference in the American War on Terror
Piotr Szpunar

Dot-Com Design: The Rise of a Useable, Social, Commercial Web
Megan Sapnar Ankerson

Postracial Resistance: Black Women, Media, and the Uses of Strategic Ambiguity
Ralina L. Joseph

Netflix Nations: The Geography of Digital Distribution
Ramon Lobato

The Identity Trade: Selling Privacy and Reputation Online
Nora A. Draper

Media & Celebrity: An Introduction to Fame
Susan J. Douglas and Andrea McDonnell

Fake Geek Girls: Fandom, Gender, and the Convergence Culture Industry
Suzanne Scott

Locked Out: Regional Restrictions in Digital Entertainment Culture
Evan Elkins

The Digital City: Media and the Social Production of Place
Germaine R. Halegoua

Distributed Blackness: African American Cybercultures
André Brock Jr.

Distributed Blackness

African American Cybercultures

André Brock Jr.

NEW YORK UNIVERSITY PRESS
New York

NEW YORK UNIVERSITY PRESS
New York
www.nyupress.org

Library of Congress Cataloging-in-Publication Data

Names: Brock, André L., Jr., author.
Title: Distributed blackness : African American cybercultures / André Brock, Jr.
Description: New York : New York University Press, [2019] | Series: Critical cultural communication | Includes bibliographical references and index.
Identifiers: LCCN 2019012037 | ISBN 9781479820375 (cloth ; alk. paper) | ISBN 9781479829965 (paperback ; alk. paper)
Subjects: LCSH: African Americans—Communication. | African Americans and mass media. | African Americans—Intellectual life—21st century. | Internet—Social aspects—United States. | Online social networks—United States.
Classification: LCC P94.5.A37 .B76 2019 | DDC 302.23089/96073—dc23
LC record available at https://lccn.loc.gov/2019012037

New York University Press books are printed on acid-free paper, and their binding materials are chosen for strength and durability. We strive to use environmentally responsible suppliers and materials to the greatest extent possible in publishing our books.

Manufactured in the United States of America

10 9 8 7 6 5 4 3 2

Also available as an e-book

To my grandmother, Mrs. Florence Elaine Paris Scott Brock,

House Hollis, First of Her Name

I finally finished it, Grandma

CONTENTS

Introduction

> Race can be ontological without being biological, metaphysical without being physical, existential without being essential, shaping one's being without being one's shape.
>
> —Charles Mills (1998, p. xiv)

The Black body has long been a feature—and shibboleth—of articulations and theorizations of Black culture.[1] The materiality of the Black body is easily understood as a benighted canvas for the iniquities and oppressions levied upon it, but its materiality has also led to elaborate, strained, scientific rationales about the legitimacy of race as a social construct. When scholars first sought to understand information technology use by Black folk, the Black body was only legible through its perceived absence: absence from the material, technical, and institutional aspects of computers and society. Over the last half decade, however, Black digital practice has become very much a mainstream phenomenon, even if its expert practitioners rarely receive economic compensation for their brilliance or political compensation for their activism.[2] But online identity has long been conflated with whiteness, even as whiteness is itself signified as a universal, raceless, technocultural identity. By this I mean that whiteness is what technology does to the Other, not the technology users themselves. The visibility of online Blackness can be partially attributed to the concentration of Black folk in online spaces that are not exclusively our own; we are finally present online in ways that the mainstream is unable to disavow. Imagine, if you will, millions of Black people interacting through networked devices—laptops, computers, smartphones—at once separate and conjoined. This online aggregation and coherence of Blackness online, absent Black bodies, is what inspired this book.

I titled this book *Distributed Blackness* to evoke how Blackness has expertly utilized the internetwork's capacity for discourse to build out a social, cultural, racial identity. Black online culture and sociality are more easily visualized today thanks not only to the hashtag and other algorithmic means but also to the near infrastructural use of social networking services as well as older online artifacts, such as messaging services, blogs, and bulletin boards, where one could see articulations of Black identity across digital networks. My subtitle, *African American Cybercultures*, speaks to this text's theoretical and rhetorical thinking about how and why Blackness and Black culture are easily and pungently performed, absent embodiment, when mediated by technologies—specifically information technologies, the online, and the digital.

Distributed Blackness is also a reference to the methodology used throughout this text: critical technocultural discourse analysis (CTDA). I devised CTDA as a corrective to normative and analytic research on cultural digital practice. It decenters the Western deficit perspective on minority technology use to instead prioritize the epistemological standpoint of underrepresented groups of technology users. CTDA pulls together multiple disparate data points to conduct a holistic analysis of an information technology artifact and its practices. *Distributed* here refers not only to CTDA's analysis of discourses across websites, services, and platforms—published by the technology's users about their wielding of the technology—but also to its holistic approach to analyzing technology as discourse, practice, and artifact. This approach lends CTDA analytic power to understand how digital practitioners filter their technology use through their cultural identity rather than through some preconceived "neutral" perspective.

Finally, *Distributed Blackness* is a callback to one of the first cultural networked informational Black artifacts: *The Negro Motorist Green Book* (Green, 1941). On first glance, the *Green Book* is just a book—a directory of Black businesses published by Blacks for Blacks long before the internet. Hall (2014) argues for the *Green Book* as a tool to resist postcolonial and postbellum legacies of white racial violence and hegemony (pp. 307–319). I agree but insist that the *Green Book* should also be viewed as one of the first cultural network browsers. The network in this instance was the US highway system—a developing infrastructure tailored for the exponentially growing numbers of automobile owners. As early as the 1910s, Black drivers saw automobile ownership as a pathway to personal mobility and technological expertise and as a signal of belonging to the middle class, with the attendant properties of racial uplift ideology (Franz, 2004, pp. 131–153). Moreover, one of the hallmarks of post–World War II life in the United States was the spread of "leisure" as an outlet for relaxation, and Blacks were just as eager to share in it as any other American. Like many whites, Blacks began to consider cross-country driving as not only a pathway to leisure activities but also a way to return to their ancestral homes in the South following the Great Migration's dispersal of Black families across the United States.

In doing so, however, they had to traverse entire states—particularly in the Midwest, where "sundown towns" were most prevalent (Loewen, 2005), but also in the West and Northeast, where local Blacks were mired in state-sanctioned Jim Crow violence and customs. Imagine, then, in spaces where Blacks were already discriminated against, the arrival of affluent "foreign" and unfamiliar Blacks looking for sustenance, fuel, or just a chance to rest. *The Negro Motorist Green Book* was precisely designed to provide these highway "browsers" with a guide to safe spaces that would welcome weary Black travelers and vacationers.

First published in 1936 by Victor Green and continuing through 1967 (albeit under a different name), the *Green Book* featured information garnered from those who drove across the country by necessity: salesmen, athletes, clergy, and entertainers. This singular Jim Crow–era periodical helped Black folk navigate America's roads by annotating safe waypoints and destinations. It was distributed in part by the United States Travel Bureau and, crucially, by the Standard Oil Company, lending the *Green Book* a national audience. Eventually, the book listed resources available to traveling Blacks across the continental United States as well as locations in Canada, Alaska, the Caribbean, and Mexico.

Arguing for the *Green Book* as an example of distributed Blackness—an informational artifact linking Black information seekers to Black cultural resources across a network—then, seems like a no-brainer. The *Green Book* was the Google (or more appropriately, the Yahoo! Open Directory Project of Black information, since the directory was human-reviewed rather than algorithmically determined) of its time, a search engine for those seeking culturally vital information. These resources, catering to the needs and wants of a technologically enabled mobile Black community, were distributed unequally across the network. Even as highways and driving were increasingly promoted as "quintessential American" activities, Blacks were often excluded from enjoying them in the same way. The *Green Book* imagined the US highway system as a Black technological network—not as an Afrofuture but as a present-day marvel containing possibilities for joy and for violence—that performed resistance alongside Blackness as the capacity to enjoy leisure even as urban renewal projects used the construction of interstate highways as a means to destroy vibrant Black urban communities. While the internet doesn't offer the same physical potential for discrimination and racist violence against Black folk, there is still a pressing need for the curation of digital and online resources for Black folk seeking information and "safe spaces." These spaces range from portal websites like Everything Black, to bulletin board websites like Nappturality, to the pioneering gossip blogs Crunk and Disorderly and Concrete Loop, to the Blackbird browser, to upcoming efforts to create mobile apps. In short, networked information—in the form of resources for identification, community, self-defense, joy, resistance, aesthetics, politics, and more—is essential to Black online identity. How, then, do the internet and digital media mediate Blackness?

The possibilities of Black digital identity, Black digital practices, and Black digital artifacts first came to me upon reading Miller and Slater's (2000) ethnographic study of Trinidadian internet users. Trinidad and Tobago—a polyglot former English colony in the Caribbean inhabited by people of African, indigenous, Indian, Chinese, and white descent—while tiny, has an immense diasporic population across North America and Europe, yet this has done little to diminish the diaspora's national and ethnic identity. Over the course of their eleven-year study, Miller and Slater found that the internet became an expression of Trinidadian identity. This finding was (and still is) in direct contrast to bromides about technology forcing users to adapt to mainstream culture and also counters long-standing deficit-based beliefs about people of color and information technologies. Instead, the Trinidadians found ways to make the internet Trinidadian in thought and in deed. Miller and Slater write, "Trinidadians have a 'natural affinity' for the internet. They apparently take to it 'naturally,' fitting it effortlessly into family, friendship, work and leisure and in some respects they seemed to experience the internet as itself 'naturally Trinidadian.' . . . It provided a natural platform for enacting, on a global stage, core values and components of Trinidadian identity" (p. 2).

This revelation of nonwhite culture manifested through information technology was mind-blowing to me in the era of the digital divide, when many argued that Black Americans were technologically and computationally deficient. The lessons I learned from Miller and Slater, then, are equally applicable to African American uses of information and communication technology: Black folk have a natural affinity for the internet and digital media.

By *natural*, I am by no means arguing that internet use is an "essential" quality of Blackness. Essentialism, for nonwhites, has a long, pejorative history within Western culture; only nonwhite bodies suffer reduction to a perceived intrinsic characteristic. Instead, my claim is pragmatic; Black expressivity is rightfully lauded in literature and in art, but Black linguistic expression is denigrated in modern (i.e., technical and professional) society. Indeed, Black identity is associated with many things, but the internet—or more specifically, the expertise in information and communication technology practice—is not usually one of them.

My claim is ecological: Black folk have made the internet a "Black space" whose contours have become visible through sociality and distributed digital practice while also decentering whiteness as the default internet identity. Moreover, I am arguing that Black folks' "natural internet affinity" is as much about how they understand and employ digital artifacts and practices as it is about how Blackness is constituted within the material (and virtual) world of the internet itself. I am naming these Black digital practices as Black cyberculture.

> Black cyberculture can be understood as the protean nature of Black identity as mediated by various digital artifacts, services, and practices both individually and in concert—or Blackness as
>
> - an informational identity premised on
> - libidinal online expressions and practices of joy and catharsis about being Black
> - expressed through semiotic and material relationships between content and hardware and code performances and cultural phenomena online as Black cyberculture.

> At the intersection of the digital and Black culture, Black cyberculture offers a transformative cultural philosophy of representation, technoculture, politics, and everyday life.

Blackness Online

Black folk have been online inhabitants nearly as long as the commercial internet has existed. It is only in the last decade, however, that their digital practices can be seen as a reimagining of what information spaces can be in the West—a cultural virtual space like that of China, India, and Nigeria, to name a few. I'm not referring to the political and civic prowess of Black Lives Matter, even though many consider their online activism to be the pinnacle of Black digital practice. Instead, I am much more interested in the ways Black folk use the internet as a space to extol the joys and pains of everyday life—the hair tutorials, the dance videos, the tweetstorms, and more—using its capacity for multimedia expression and networked sociality to craft a digital practice that upends technocultural beliefs about how information, computers, and communication technologies should be used.

I should distinguish here between Black cyberculture and Black culture online. Research on Black culture online examines Black arts, literature, multimedia phenomena, artifacts, and audiences, whereas research on Black cyberculture interrogates an ontological perspective of what Blackness means for technology use and, occasionally, design. There is an inevitable overlap between the two; for example, Black artists and creatives are often hyperaware of how their art contravenes American/Western aesthetics. Keith Obadike's "Blackness for Sale" eBay page is a canonical example of Black art being deployed as a critique of technology and of whiteness. However, research on Black culture online enters the domain of Black cyberculture when it incorporates respectability politics into evaluations of Black online culture—that is, when writers, academics, and pundits find ways to criticize "inappropriate" Black technology usage. In later chapters, I will cover respectability and Black online virtue as frames of Black digital practice in greater detail.

Despite protestations about color-blindness or neutrality, the internet should be understood as an enactment of whiteness through the interpretive flexibility of whiteness as information. By this, I mean that white folks' communications, letters, and works of art are rarely understood as white; instead, they become universal and are understood as "communication," "literature," and "art." This slippage allows for a near infinite variety of signifiers for linguistic and aesthetic concepts—absent the specific racial modifier centering them in white American culture. From this perspective, Western technoculture has an inordinate role in shaping the internet experience in many online environments. "General interest" websites, apps, and social media services target unnamed, unraced, and often ungendered users but inevitably are represented through white bodies and white cultural commonplaces.

This interpretive flexibility allows whiteness to operate paradoxically as the individual and as humanity—to be "spirited" and in control of the body and other bodies (Dyer, 1997). In doing so, interpretive flexibility undergirds one of this manuscript's claims about Western technoculture: the internet's base purpose is to behave as a rational, productive information space because of its association with whiteness. Even when online whiteness becomes unruly and deadly, Western beliefs drawn from classical liberalism serve as warrants for individualist—never to be understood as cultural—white digital practices such as incivility, racism, xenophobia, misogyny, and violence in the name of "protecting" the freedom of speech and property rights.

"If You See a Fork in the Road, Take It": Double Consciousness and Black Cyberculture

This text is deeply invested in the material, technical, and social multiplicity inherent in Black cyberculture. These arguments would not be possible without Du Bois's (1903) canonical formulation of the interweaving strands of Black embodiment and American identity. In that vein, the doubleness in this text takes form in the interweaving of a methodological approach to examining culture online with a theoretical approach spanning critical race theory, libidinal economy, and science and technology studies. This book is best read as a journey, moving from my maturing work on Black digital artifacts and discourses to a more interpretive, theoretical approach to Black digital practice. It marks a way station (never an end point) for my thinking about how Black folk "make it do what it dew" on these internet streets. In doing so, I sketch out and fill in blank spots vis-à-vis Blackness online, from the infrastructural utopia of "bridging the digital divide," to the elision of Black digital practice in the BlackVoices/BlackPlanet era, to the ongoing conceptual lacunae normalizing whiteness as cultural information use in the English-speaking West. My approach is methodological and theoretical—a doubly conscious corrective to Western misconceptions of Black subjectivity and agency in online spaces.

"I Count Two Guns": Critical Technocultural Discourse Analysis and Libidinal Economy

Methodology arises from epistemology, ontology, and axiology. How we know what we know, how we know what is true, and how we know what is good provide the tools for examining the world around us. Thus CTDA is the organizing framework for my arguments throughout the rest of the book. My training as an interdisciplinary scholar—whose boundaries cross over new media studies, internet research, information studies, communication, ethnic studies, and even sociology and anthropology—makes it necessary to describe *how* I devised the explanatory power of CTDA. The ontological aspect, or the *what*, is (and isn't) the technological artifact; it's the *assemblage* of the artifact and its practices and, importantly, the technocultural beliefs about the artifact as evinced by its users. The *why*, or the critical axiological rationale for CTDA, is immediately apparent to those interested in analyzing identity, difference, and the digital.

CTDA interrogates culture-*as*-technology and culture-*of*-technology, examining information technologies alongside discourses about them. CTDA is innovative for two reasons. The first is its holistic inquiry into tech artifacts, practices, and users. Reducing technology analysis to the design and function of artifacts obscures the beliefs embedded by the designers, systems, infrastructures, and the users themselves. The second, and most important, innovation is the centering of technology use by marginalized groups within their own understandings of themselves rather than unmarked racial and socioeconomic standards of "modern" technology use. CTDA is designed to be open to any critical cultural theoretical concept—as long as the same approach is applied to the semiotics of the information and computer technology (ICT) hardware and software under examination as well as the discourses of its users. This openness features prominently in the organization of this text, as each chapter utilizes CTDA but invokes different Black cultural concepts to center its respective conceptual framework. For example, chapter 3 on Black Twitter draws on Black discursive identity in the form of "signifyin'," while chapter 5 delves into Black respectability politics as a frame for Black digital practice.

Critical Technocultural Discourse Analysis in Brief

CTDA serves as the organizing principle of this book. Many of the insights throughout would not have been possible without CTDA's conceptual frameworks and a systematic critical cultural analysis linking Black culture to disparate information technologies and digital practices. This stems in part from CTDA's cultural imperative; the conceptual framework allows for considerable latitude in selecting cultural concepts and theories designed to represent the standpoints of underrepresented users. There's also an element of analytical flexibility; CTDA was designed to evaluate a wide range of digital artifacts and practices. Each chapter is a showcase for CTDA's utility, from covering various aspects of the digital artifact under examination to integrating a discussion about that artifact as part of a holistic analysis.

CTDA was designed to counter the epistemological drawbacks of normative, instrumental, and theoretical approaches to studying information technology. To do so, it operates as a discourse-hermeneutic analysis (Wodak, 2000) of the practices and users of information and communication technologies. An essential part of any CTDA analysis is the attention paid to the material substratum underpinning the interactions of people "through, around, and with technologies" (Hutchby, 2001, p. 450). CTDA does this by operationalizing the computational object as a discourse (technology as a "text") to be read for the mediation of the discursive actions enacted as digital interfaces and associated practices. As such, a CTDA analysis "reads" graphical user interface (GUI) design, narrative, and context of use against the discourse of its users.

An equally essential component of CTDA is a critical analysis of the ways people manage technological constraints on action, agency, and being (the "technocultural" aspect). People follow the interactions and practices mapped out by the designers and engineers who code the technology, but they also find ways to create additional pathways and practices to represent themselves within that technology—an excess energy that helps make the technology part of their everyday lives. In doing so, they draw on their cultural, environmental, and social contexts to make meaning from their technological interactions. CTDA's hermeneutic approach thus interrogates ideological influences within the technological artifact, within the practices incurred through the artifact's design, and within the discourses of that technology's users.

Libidinal Economy

This chapter also includes an overview of *libidinal economy*, which I use extensively in the second half of the book. Libidinal economy offers a powerful counter to rationalistic, modernist (and postmodernist) theories used to understand both Black agency and information technology uses. These theories, when addressing information technology, are themselves often beholden to pejorative beliefs about nonwhite users, leading either to deficit models of technology use or, conversely, to glorifying nonwhite capacities for resistance. Libidinal economy makes clear the affective tensions undergirding modernity and Western technoculture and provides a path toward conceptualizing Black technology use as a space for mundanity, banality, and the celebration of making it through another day.

The libidinal is closely related to affect. Massumi (2002) argues for affect as apart from cultural context and prior to an indexed referent. Ahmed (2013), on the other hand, situates affect (as emotion) as an orientation between things (and bodies)—relations that shape the contours of social imaginaries. The libidinal is also integral to cultural contexts; it is the value-laden tension underlying the beliefs within which we operate *where* we operate. Like Ahmed, I argue that the libidinal illuminates social imaginaries while also undergirding social realities. The libidinal is neither precognition nor preintention. Instead, it can be understood as the combustion powering the engine—a visceral, powerful, and necessary component in any figuration. It is infrastructure, invisible to our perceptions just like the materials and processes we pass by or utilize every day—until a rupture occurs.

In this way, I contend that the libidinal can also be understood as *pathos*. Pathos, the most misconstrued sibling behind *logos* and *ethos*, must be interpreted as the speaker's mastery of the shared cultural commonplaces and energies that will support arguments made *to* an audience. For example, an argument about how Black poor folk don't deserve to spend money on luxuries like iPads is not an argument about money, although conservatives certainly frame it that way. Instead, it is an argument about what money signifies—whether the poor possess the capacity for pleasure—contextualized by the subjects' race and socioeconomic status and the speaker's and audience's beliefs about technology (technoculture). Moreover, the conceptualization of technology as leisure—particularly with respect to Apple products—also signifies how certain goods and practices are deemed "appropriate" for consumption by certain folk. Thus the explanatory power of libidinal economy vitalizes this text's analysis through the term *jouissance*, which represents "an excess of life," often sexual (the libido), visceral, and subconscious. Importantly, *libidinal economy* highlights the difference between discourse and praxis, especially with regard to technology's promises of progress and innovation. *Affect*, for this text, undersells the intimate power of the libidinal.

I came to libidinal economy through the works of Frank Wilderson (2010), Jared Sexton (2010), and Fred Moten (2013), prominent theorists of Afro-pessimism and the powerful concept of antiblackness. Their argument, broadly explained, is that antiblackness connotes the incommunicability/incommensurability of Blackness to the West—aesthetically and politically. Wilderson and Sexton specifically reference antiblackness as a libidinal economy powering Western arts and literature. Antiblackness and Afro-pessimism, however, are strikingly devoid of the creative and inventive capacity of Black culture. As I will explain later, this text instead turns to Afro-optimism and the standpoint epistemology of Black pathos to ground my explanations and theorization of Black digital practice.

"Do You Know the Importance of a Skypager?!": A Road Map to Studying Black Technoculture

> Gramsci understood that [epochal] concepts have to be applied to specific historical social formations, to particular societies at specific stages in the

> development of capitalism, the theorist is required to move from the level of "mode of production" to a lower, more concrete, level of application.
>
> —Stuart Hall (1986, p. 7)

As Hall notes, it is crucial as a theorist to make concepts that change how we think about the world as accessible, relevant, and concrete as possible, especially when they are applied to specific cultural moments. Chapter 1 of this book unpacks the concepts grounding CTDA and, by extension, the entire project. I am heavily influenced by introductions to translated works by European scholars, where alert translators offer prospective readers insight into the thinking behind the explanatory power of the concepts to come. While it may read a bit like a literature review, outlining my inspirations in this way is a marker of critical qualitative scholarship; I cannot assume everyone is aware of the authors and concepts here. I must admit to having been cautioned that you, dear reader, may already be aware of the concepts ahead, but I can assure you they have never been assembled in this fashion with the intent of analyzing race, the digital, and technoculture. For example, this text's definition of Blackness *qua* racial identity begins with a sociological concept of ethnic identity, where ethnicity is understood as the agreement between in-group and out-group members on what the in-group says, does, and believes. I chose this formulation to relinquish the Middle Passage epistemology (Henry, 2006; Sharpe, 2013; Wright, 2015) often used to define Blackness and also to allow Black folk—inescapably connected to the concept of race in the West—to define themselves, in their own voices, as members of a multitudinous culture without being reduced to the political or historical positions proffered by academics.

This move allows two signal contributions to the study of Black internet use, extending Du Bois's canonical concept of "double consciousness" to digital practice. The first contribution frees articulations of online identity from essentialized notions of Black identity tied to physiognomy, as markers of human deviance, or as political entities based on their resistance to white racial ideology and neoliberal capitalism. Drawing on libidinal economy (Jared Sexton, cited in Wilderson, 2010), I argue that Black digital practice is mediated through, but cannot be fully explained by, the productivity and efficiency paradigms of modernity and digital technoculture. Instead, Black digital identity draws in equal measure on expressions of joy and pain in everyday life in American racial ideology, which are articulated as cultural critiques and enacted online. As such, Black digital identity can be political, caustic, or both, and in so doing, it troubles utopian ideals of the internet as an apolitical, rational space.

This second contribution of double consciousness to this research is a discursive and informational formulation of networked online identity. Networked online identity makes internal Black communal discussions visible to an audience that is primed to receive and respond to those struggles while also making them visible to an audience of out-group members who might not be directly addressed but are always present as signifiers. Networks, bandwidth, interfaces, hardware, and environment mediate social performances of online identity, but the ways in which racial identity affects those performances are understudied.

Chapters 2 and 3 employ CTDA to establish evidence for a matrix of Black cyberculture by conducting inquiries into beliefs about Black uses of information and communication technology. Studies of cultural online performance must incorporate *both* the intended and the unintended audience's technologically and culturally mediated reception of that performance. These chapters examine intersections of race and the digital, but libidinal economies and Black technoculture do not feature prominently. Instead, they offer insight into the heterogeneity of Black online existences. Examining Black digitality mediated by the interface rather than focusing on remediated content posted online fosters an inductive, empirical approach to Black technocultural practice and the digital performance of Blackness. In chapter 2, I turn to the Blackbird browser, which is specifically targeted to Black users, to unpack how software applications and beliefs shape Black identity from a technocultural framework. Web browsers led the Web 2.0 charge into the personalization of the internet's vast content; their interfaces and practices encourage beliefs about the web as simultaneously universal and individualized. These individualized perspectives, shaped by the availability of content and popular narratives about internet use, tend to default to representations of whiteness in code and in content. I argue here that racial digital practices can and do shape information design and behaviors and introduce Black users' beliefs about their role and presence in information technology as a metric for technology analysis.

Moving from browsers to microblogs and social networking services, chapter 3 answers a question that's rarely been considered: What would a Black online network look like? Amiri Baraka (1965) presciently asked a similar question in the mid-1960s: Could information technologies possess a "spirit as emotional construct that can manifest as expression as art or technology"? My answer to both questions is Black Twitter. Black Twitter manifests style-in-space; in the raceless void of social networking services that are premised on "interests" and "friends," Black Twitter deploys Black discursive identity and intentionality to vivify the service as an emotional construct centered on catharsis and invention. This chapter argues that Twitter can be understood as an online venue for shared pathos and catharsis due, in large part, to the contributions of Black culture and cultural content. By introducing ritual catharsis as a meaning-making strategy for computer-mediated communication, I lay the groundwork for employing a libidinal economic approach to Black digital practice.

Turning to libidinal economy for the remainder of the book offers insights into broader genres of Black digital practice and discourses than simply evoking "use" or "content." In doing so, I find that Black digital practice reveals a complicated mix of technological literacy, discursive identity, and cultural critique. By making libidinal economy explicit in CTDA's conceptual framework, I illuminate the digital mediations of Black communities' political, technocultural, and historical commonplaces. These commonplaces are here articulated as three frames, or topoi, shaping Black digital practice—ratchetry, racism, and respectability.

Chapter 4 examines the first two frames of Black digital practice: ratchetry and racism. I keep them together because racism and ratchetry are inextricably interrelated tensions pulling on Black identity, and I consider these two frames to be incomplete articulations of the libidinal economic tensions within Du Bois's double consciousness. Writing about the two frames in the same chapter will, I hope, encourage a dialectic about how it feels to enact Blackness and how Blackness feels when acted upon. In the vein of public health studies, this chapter focuses on how racism affects Black folk by examining online responses to "racial battle fatigue" as well as conceptualizing how online Black enclaves can manage racists without encountering direct racism from nonwhites.

Chapter 5 argues for framing online Black respectability adherents as dogmatic digital practitioners who legislate Black behavior by promoting a specific set of moral virtues in and around digital practice. The libidinal tensions between racism and ratchetry overdetermine the libidinal frame of Black respectability. By this I mean that respectability, in its quest to be modern and thus fit into white American culture, overcorrects for ratchetry and undertheorizes racism to coerce Black folk into becoming civil subjects in a white supremacist regime. Thus it deserves its own chapter.

The final chapter is a provocation rather than a true conclusion. The preceding chapters place Black folk at the center of their own information technology use rather than at the periphery, fighting to be heard. Chapter 6 furthers this work to extend the possibility of libidinal economies of information technology to build out a matrix of Black cultural beliefs about technology and self, or a Black technocultural matrix. Afrofuturism is rightly understood as a cultural theory about Black folks' relationship to technology, but its futurist perspective lends it a utopian stance that doesn't do much to advance our understandings of what Black folk are doing now. This chapter, then, articulates my concern about Black digital practice as vitality, energy, and occasionally, joy. While these libidinal impulses may become commodified or surveilled, the embodied cognition expressed preexists the digital platforms on which they are visible, published, and deemed appropriate for consumption.

"What Does It All Mean?"

I began this introduction by referencing *The Negro Motorist Green Book*, which, upon reflection, is an appropriate metaphor for describing this book. While the internet is not nearly as physically dangerous as the roads and highways traveled by Black motorists between 1930 and 1970, it is still a largely uncharted space within which Blackness manifests for safety, leisure, and joy. These uncharted spaces of the internet, like the areas between American roads and byways of the early twentieth century, are marked by whiteness. To understand the inroads that have been made by Black digital practitioners and designers, then, it is necessary to interrogate not only the spaces they have made their own but the beliefs behind the networked materials and practices that made their efforts necessary.

Along the way, however, I realized that online Blackness wasn't always clearly defined. This book also shows my evolution in that regard; I began with Du Bois because one *should* begin discussions of Blackness by citing the father of American sociology and critical race studies. From Du Bois, I dialed into rhetorics of Black discourse-as-identity, citing the works of Geneva Smitherman, Claudia Mitchell-Kernan, and Henry Louis Gates Jr. As I continued researching, I found and incorporated philosophers of race such as George Yancy and Charles Mills to deepen my arguments about the metaphysics of Blackness; I later included arguments by Fred Moten, Frank Wilderson, and Jared Sexton to further my arguments for the libidinal, rather than political and economic, possibilities of Blackness. Without the arguments made by Black feminist scholars such as Patricia Hill Collins, Evelyn Brooks Higginbotham, Francis White, and Kimberlé Crenshaw, this book would be woefully undertheorized.

In the end, I believe I've crafted compelling arguments for beginning science and technology studies from racial and cultural grounds rather than limiting analyses to the technologies themselves. I'm not saying this as an "all cultures matter" argument; this book wouldn't have been written if I didn't love my Blackness and that of others first and foremost! Instead, I'm noting the applicability of a culturally oriented conceptual approach so other scholars—especially white researchers—will see that cultural particularity offers powerful insights into technology use and design that color-blind, instrumental, or political-economic approaches do not. Happy reading!

1

Distributing Blackness

Ayo Technology! Texts, Identities, and Blackness

This text situates Black culture within a Western—specifically American—ideological context, where Blackness operates as a cultural and social nadir in the white racial frame (Feagin, 2013). Black information technology use highlights Black technical and cultural capital while disrupting the white, male, middle-class norms of Western technoculture. Black digital practice challenges these norms through displacement, performativity, pathos, and the explicit use of Black cultural commonplaces. These practices are optimized for communicative efficiency on their respective media, drawing from a pleasure in creative linguistic expression and the historical, discursive practices and experiences of evading white racial surveillance in plain sight. An externality of Black digital practice—thanks to the codifying, broadcast, and textual qualities of networked digital media—is the uptake of Black digital content by out-group audiences. Accordingly, Black digital practice has become hypervisible to mainstream white culture and the world through positive, negative, and political performances of Black cultural aesthetics and, more recently, social media activism. This is in marked contrast to historical media portrayals of Blackness, where the white racial frame positioned Blacks as bestial, deviant spectacles or as culturally and mentally impoverished wights. It also differs from popular and academic accounts of the Information Age, which either elided Black participation in digital design and use or rendered Blacks as unable to surmount the digital divide due to their essential lack of material, technical, or cultural resources.

For the few of us researching Black folk online during the first decade of the new millennium, there were only brief, isolated examples of how Blackness could operate in online spaces.[1] BlackPlanet (est. 1999) was one of the first Black online meccas to receive sustained scholarly attention (Byrne, 2007; Banks, 2006), but by the time much of that research was published (and read!), BlackPlanet had been pushed aside—first by Myspace, then Facebook. Banks (private communication, May 13, 2017) notes that pioneering websites like NetNoir (est. 1995) and BlackVoices (est. 1997) sustained Black online communities for only a few short years before faltering. The realities of media consolidation, site maintenance, and server costs led to many of these early Black online destinations either being bought out or withering on the vine. In their place, Black entertainment and political blogs did enormous work to grow Black online communities between 2005 and 2010 (e.g., Jack and Jill Politics, Prometheus6, WhatAboutOurDaughters, AfroBella, and Racialicious), but blogs were overtaken (and subsumed by social media platforms) by the surge of attention to social networking services. In today's milieu, Black digitality is often referenced by platform or service (e.g., Black Twitter and the "Gram" [Black Instagram]).

In the aggregate, Black websites are labeled as niche online spaces in part because of the technocultural belief that Black folk lack the capacity for "appropriate" internet practices. Historically, these sites were difficult to conceptualize as fully formed Black cybercultures for a number of other reasons—namely, their ephemerality, the still vast numbers of Black folk who hadn't gotten online, and the unnoticed growth of Black online reflexivity and interiority. This is true even for my Black Twitter research. I researched Black Twitter before the murder of Trayvon Martin and before Ferguson. At the time, I was intent on fleshing out the research into Blackness and the digital, celebrating moments of Black online culture in the process. It felt imperative to examine Black culture's mediation by a service that seemed ephemeral and niche even with respect to its then burgeoning user-generated practices of second-screen shared media viewing and political activism. In that long-ago moment of the first dot-com hype, too many social networking services and other Silicon Valley darlings had crashed and burned—Path, Dodgeball, and so on—for me to think of Black Twitter as anything but a momentous yet momentary marvel.

Identity as the Tension between the Self and the Social

This warrant (and the next) emerged out of my need to explain racial and cultural identity without relying on an essential quality of Blackness or on the materiality of Black phenotypical qualities. As I began formulating arguments for this book, I realized I also needed to argue for an internet identity that was not dependent on materiality—neither the ownership of an internet-enabled device nor the virtual manifestation of the web page. I have argued across my research stream that written text is the preeminent mode of identity creation and maintenance across online and digital spaces—even with the rise of image-oriented social network services (SNS) such as Instagram and Snapchat—so I needed to develop warrants for precisely how discourse and semiosis work to fix identities in physical, political, and virtual spaces.

The internet's interactivity and archival capacities provide interesting spaces within which to articulate identity. In these areas, digital text and multimedia—information—become the meaning-making substrates from which we understand individuals and groups. Goffman's (1959) formulation of identity as conveyed through "expressions given" and "expressions given off" (p. 4) is manifest in digital practice and online media, where profiles, likes, and status posts are equated to representations of the self. Where once people relied on memory and anecdotal experience to fix individual identity in time and space, the internet provides an endless archive of identity performance—or as Black online culture calls it, "the receipts."

Cultural online identity is trickier (for me) to argue for, however. While websites and social media services construct individual identities for internet and computer users through affiliation and practice, group identity is constrained by the technological environment in which it occurs. Thus we easily group Twitter users or LinkedIn users—or alternatively, email users or short-message service (SMS) users—but these are communities of practice, which may offer a social collectivity but only a weak cultural one. This is not the place for a history of the concept of community in internet studies, but suffice it to say that Ferdinand Tonnies's ([1887] 1999) concepts of Gemeinschaft and Gesellschaft, along with Benedict Anderson's (2006) "imagined communities," have had an oversized effect on the way internet communities are argued for. Both concepts have some place in my research stream—how could they not?—but my warrant for group and cultural identity instead draws on sociological and philosophical perspectives on race and identity.

As I began collecting my thoughts about Black cultural online identity for this text, I was reminded that all identities are racial identities; the digital is a mediator of embodiment and identity, not an escape from it. For example, how exactly does one identify white online identity? Whiteness is often conflated with computer use. It's easier (and tricky) to argue for Black internet identity based on its differences from white digital practice, but as USC[2] found out, Black people are *very* concerned to not be conceptualized as a "low class, undifferentiated mass" (Du Bois, 1940) of computer users (Newitz, 2014; Callahan, 2014). As Tate (2011) writes, there is much that needs to be said about "how it is that racial objects become raced, gendered and sexualized subjects through . . . racialized imaginaries, and everyday race performativity" (p. 94).

The warrant "identity as tension between self and social" supports a cultural formulation of networked online identity. Networks, bandwidth, interfaces, hardware, and environment mediate social performances of online identity, but how racial identity affects those social performances is understudied. The effects are bidirectional; an examination of cultural online performance must incorporate both the intended and unintended audience's technologically and culturally mediated reception of that performance. This has not always been the case in internet and new media research.

This final point deserves elaboration. Internet and new media studies have historically proceeded with the presumption that disembodiment and distance render potential digital interlocutors as an imaginary audience. The Black community, as understood through Du Bois's double consciousness, has never had the luxury of pretending that their interlocutors were imaginary. The in-group interlocutor was necessary as a warrant for a communitarian human identity. Meanwhile, the community's interactions with the out-group interlocutor—if heard or seen—could and often did result in deadly consequences. Networked online identity distributes internal Black community discussions, rendering them visible to an audience who is primed to receive and respond to those struggles. Networked Black online identity also makes Black community discourses visible as a textual and multimedia archive to out-group audiences; these audiences are not always directly addressed in internal Black discourses but are always present as signifiers.

Race has always already been an informational group identity, designating class and cultural capital (or the deliberate denial thereof). In the case of Blackness, the group identity is applied indiscriminately to denigrate individual bodies, whereas whiteness operates as an individual identity and as a designation for "people" and humanity. One sees this happen in the context of internet and computer use: the default internet identity is anecdotally white, male, and middle class, but there is surprisingly little research on how internet practice enacts these normative identity markers. Jessie Daniels's (2009, 2013) groundbreaking research on white supremacist websites affixes an extreme racial and racist identity to white digital practice, but the vast majority of new media and internet research references white bodies without remarking on their whiteness as a constituent factor for their internet practice. Identity emerges in discourse through the shared communication of concepts, which are encoded and decoded through cultural and social signifiers. Even coherent displays of identity—such as those performed and visible on-screen when examining virtual spaces—rely on interaction and ideological constraints. From this perspective, I argue that whiteness's interpretive flexibility and hegemonic positioning render it as a technical identity even across the technical incoherence of multiple platforms and services.

By postulating that identity is the tension between the self and the social, I can examine the tensions between the digital as an avatar of white technical expertise and Black sociality, performativity, and agency. Because I'm arguing for Blackness in the context of American culture, arguing for identity as socially constituted allows me to contextualize the ideological apparatus through which Black identity came to be.

Black Bodies, Blackness, and Black Culture

Racial online identity, for this text, gets dematerialized and reconstituted both as a discursive-social relationship *and* as a code-content-hardware relationship—all while enacted by Black embodied existence. This is Blackness as an "informational identity," a doubly conscious figuration of Black discursive identity and digital practice. As mentioned, my definition of Blackness qua racial identity stems from Du Bois's "double consciousness." Tal (1996) cogently observes that double consciousness offers a conceptually rich approach for cyberculture researchers examining identity in virtual spaces; Du Bois's concept addresses community and alienation experienced by the same body/person. While Tal does not specifically reference cyberculture scholars of color writing about online people of color, my research incorporates her admonition.

To flesh out Tal's claim about cyberculture, double consciousness, and Blackness, I incorporated Hughes's ([1971] 1993) contention that ethnic identity is to be studied by examining the relations between groups coexisting within the society rather than assuming that a group can be studied without reference to others. That is, it "it takes more than one ethnic group to make ethnic relations" (p. 155). This observation repositions double consciousness away from observable differences between Blacks and whites, instead focusing on how individuals learn the realities and the fictions of their position as a member of an ethnic group (p. 156). It also allows for the incorporation of the digital as the relation, which has been essential to my critical technocultural discourse analysis (CTDA) of race and digital practice. That is, while internet users bring offline ideologies to bear upon their digital discourses, the digital is the mediator, the enactment, and the performance of the relationship between Blackness and whiteness. Finally, this move allows conceptions of Blackness to be freed from essentialized notions of Black identity tied to physiognomy, as markers of human deviance, or as political entities based on their resistance to white racial ideology and neoliberal capitalism. It does not, however, leave Black bodies behind.

Following Robert Gooding-Williams's (1998) admonition that there is a difference between the Black body and Blackness, this second warrant is my definition of Black culture: *Blackness as a dynamic core of narrative gravity (pace Yancy) sustained through intentional, libidinal, historical, and imaginative Black agency in the context of navigating American racial ideology.* My approach to digital identity takes on additional salience when studying Black bodies and Black culture. Previously, I mentioned whiteness's interpretive flexibility, which is premised on a pejorative fixity imposed by the materiality of Black bodies onto Black culture. Blackness anchors whiteness in the West and in American culture by serving as the nadir of white racial epistemology and ontology. Morrison (1993), in writing about the American literary imagination, argues similarly in her claim for American Africanism, where

Africanism stands for "the denotative blackness that African peoples have come to signify, as well as the entire range of views, assumptions, readings, and misreadings that accompany Eurocentric learning" (p. 7).

This quote animates my claim for (online) discourse's figuration of online identity. I am, like most Black academics writing about Black identity, still enamored of Du Bois's formulation of double consciousness. I have employed it in some form or another across my entire research stream, but not always for the same reasons. Originally, I utilized double consciousness to illustrate how Black folk, in the course of their everyday existence, were always already deeply enmeshed in the kind of virtual existence and social alienation that cyberculture theorists of the early aughts were so ready to proclaim as that new-new. I now see double consciousness slightly differently: double consciousness expresses Blackness as a discursive, informational identity, flitting back and forth in the virtual space between a Black communal context and a white supremacist categorial context. The virtuality of race offline extends my argument that Blackness "double voices" in virtual online spaces, adding a technical-technological-digital dimension to Black identity.

Thus the interpellation of Blackness in digital spaces can be understood as intentional and agentive. In contrast, Blackness in offline spaces is often hailed deliberately or inadvertently by white racial ideology to affix Black bodies at the bottom of a social and cultural order. This should be uncontroversial, but it's a necessary step for arguing about Blackness in online and digital milieus.

Let me offer an example: In my research on Black Twitter, I argued that Black Twitter hashtags brought that digital space to mainstream attention, where it became understood as a Black social public. But even then, Black Twitter practitioners continued making Twitter "do whut it dew"—using cultural commonplaces, digital affordances, and digital sociality to build out a culturally coherent digital practice. My concern was to separate out the social from the cultural and to highlight the contributions of Blackness to digital practice. Black Twitter's agency manifests through Twitter as a discursive digital social public. In this I am inspired by Ian Hacking's (2002) "dynamic nominalism," where he argues that "a kind of person comes into being at the same time as the kind itself was being invented" (p. 106). This is not a refutation of Black online existence prior to Twitter; I'd be foolish to repudiate my own research.

Instead, Twitter's status as a reputable information technology (precarious though it may be) mediates Black culture, reframing Blackness as a source of digital expertise despite Black culture's signification as the nadir of American technoculture and racial ideology.

Black cyberculture directly refutes "context collapse" (Marwick & boyd, 2011). Marwick and boyd argue that it is impossible to differentiate self-presentation strategies on a service like Twitter (or any combination of social networking services). But if anything, context collapse is better understood as a descriptor of white racial ideology and identity. What Marwick and boyd are referencing is the collapse of categorial identity, or what Rawls (2000) references as white folks' display of hierarchical identities designed to reveal labor status and individualism. Individualist identities are constrained by the informational scale necessary for the success of SNS; thus these identities could be understood as collapsing under the coercive instrumentality of self-presentation afforded by social media profiles. But individualism is a perk that white folk have long reserved for themselves and denied to others—that is, Marwick and boyd overlook another manner in which context collapse could be better understood: as stereotype.

As Du Bois writes in *Dusk of Dawn*, Blacks are considered "a low class, undifferentiated mass" by American culture, so Black folk have long had to manage cultural multiplicity (double consciousness) in a cultural context where Blackness had to manifest against the context collapse of white supremacist ideology—where overlap was criminalized or barely possible (e.g., interracial marriage, or even passing for white). Part of the pleasure of living while Black is the daily contravention of expectations and stereotypes even when we know negative expectations are levied against us anyway. In his presidential address to the Canadian Ethnic Studies Association, Isajiw (1977) argued that ethnicity has important affective dimensions. He cited Rose and Rose, who wrote that race "involves not only a recognition that because of one's ancestry one is a member of a racial or religious group, and a recognition that the majority group defines one as belonging to that racial or religious group it also involves a positive desire to identify oneself as a member of a group and a feeling of pleasure when one does so" (p. 80). This is the jouissance that informs Blackness and, by extension, Black digital practice.

Blackness—in the guise of Black digital practice—opens the "Black box" of the digital to show that all along, culture has warranted information and communication technology use. I argue that Black facility with digital artifacts and practices displays a technical-cultural identity defying technocultural beliefs of Black primitiveness. Indeed, Blackness brings a particularized coherence to digital practice that affords my claim for Blackness as a normal digital identity. My claim for Black cyberculture builds a compelling vision of Blackness as an informational identity that avoids the essentialization of Black cultural identity despite the hegemonic influence of Western racial and technocultural ideology. In the sections that follow, I discuss the concepts powering the analyses of digital artifacts throughout the text, perceived through the lens and practices of Black cyberculture.

(Information) Technology as Text

At this stage of internet and new media studies, it might seem condescending to argue for operationalizing digital technologies as texts. After all, cultural and media studies scholars regularly conduct close readings of texts enframed by media artifacts; that methodology is well represented in humanist and qualitative research on internet, new media, and digital phenomena. My CTDA approach asks that internet and new media researchers "read" the mediating artifact—the interface, client, hardware, software, and protocols—as a text. This happens in my work as a hermeneutic of the cultural and social influences on design but can also operate as a semiosis of the technology's communication of its needs and uses. This section serves as a warrant and as a reflexive moment to explain why this is important for understanding Black online cyberculture.

Here I pull from Woolgar's (1991) thesis that technologies should be read as texts, which buttresses my rationale for a cultural and media studies approach to interpreting information technologies. Woolgar notes, "Readings of technologies are accomplished both by technologist subjects *and by the analyst*" (p. 39; emphasis original). This is an epistemological standpoint; the reflexivity directly connects my technology research to my beliefs and practices as a critical race theorist. The analyses and readings I conduct are as constitutive of the technology as the readings and interpretations conducted by the technology users I study. My subject position as a Black male information technology researcher has much to do with how I study my natal community's use of technology; I have long been observant of the ways in which information technologies permeate Black communities, even (or especially) in their absence.

While the internet today is easily understood as a technologically constructed and mediated web of communication and sociality, when I first began studying the online doings of Black folk soon after September 11, 2001, those understandings were not as widespread. Computer-mediated communication researchers were still largely focused on Multi-User Dimensions (MUDs) and MUDs, object oriented (MOOs) while social informatics was driven by studies of institutions and computer use. While individual scholars (Lisa Nakamura, Judith Donath, Anna Everett, Lori Kendall, Sherry Turkle, Ananda Mitra, and Janet Murray) were penning important texts investigating internet culture and sociality (Nakamura, Everett, Kendall, Turkle, Donath, Mitra), the academy overall was only just marshaling the disciplinary resources it needed to delve into the phenomena arising from the commercial internet's introduction in 1996—a task that was complicated by the internet's recovery from the dot-com crash of 1999.

Meanwhile, the terms *Web 2.0* and *social media* had only recently been coined for the new types of sociality and digital practice emerging online in 2001 (O'Reilly, 2005). At the same time, weblogging became characterized by platform-based software rather than hand-coded websites, leading to astronomical growth. Prototypical social networks like BlackPlanet and Friendster also coalesced during this moment, while chat and SMS communication steadily grew in mindshare. I believe that lowered barriers to internet practice, coupled with the growing standardization of content platforms (less hand-coded HTML), encouraged academics to study emerging internet communities and subcultures, but most did so with only marginal attention to the meaning-making strategies of the artifacts and protocols being used by those same communities and subcultures.

Fortunately, social informatics shares a conceptual space with computer-supported collaborative work, computer-mediated communication, and later, community informatics. Collectively, scholars in these disciplines take an empirical approach to the specificities of computer use, interface design, and information behaviors, and they collect this information to assess how users in a social context utilize computers. This instrumental approach to information technology often elides cultural[3] factors such as race or gender. Escaping this instrumental conundrum requires a different understanding of technology as well as a revised epistemological and methodological stance to unpack how culture affects technology use and design. Ronald Day (2007) argues that social informatics has three strands: normative, analytic, and critical. In response to Day's argument, my research builds out an interpretive critical approach to social informatics, pulling from science and technology studies and cultural studies.

This text operates based on a triadic formulation of technology drawn from Arnold Pacey (1984) and also found in the work of Clifford Christians (1989) and Ivan Illich (1973)—namely, technologies should be understood as having three aspects: material, organizational, and cultural. Pacey's original concept located technology practice as a part of the material aspect, but I chose to instead rephrase *organization* as *practice*. That is, "a kind of person comes into being at the same time as the kind itself was invented" (Hacking, 2002, p. 106). I arrived at this formulation because of the computer's ability to re-create practices, people, and even environments through virtuality. The computer user is an informational being—she is constructed, conceptualized, enacted, and received through code. The graphical user interface (GUI) obfuscates this textual, informational reality; it does not erase it. Indeed, the GUI adds additional complexity through the semiosis of social and technical signs that contextually configures meaning and practice. Thus "technology as text" warrants that technologies are constituted within, and have an impact on, social relations and cultural meanings. This move affords my research technique: a discourse hermeneutic (cf. Wodak, 2001) "discourse-historical" mode of critical discourse analysis of technology as constructed through the influences of society, *techné*, and culture.

The Limits of Rationality and Resistance: Political Economy and Cultural Theory

How best to study what Black folk do in online spaces? The first step is to relinquish the ways in which whiteness has been centered in sociological and cultural research into information and media use. In Brock (2018), I argue that neither cultural studies nor social science offers compelling possibilities for studying nonwhite digital practice. I reserve my ire specifically for social-scientific, political-economic analyses of digital and new media—particularly the Marxist or critical theory strains.

My concern with these theories, who share some commonalities in their examinations of economic and class struggles, is their focus on domination, hegemony, and ideology—or conversely, on resistance and emancipation. The first set of positions have been the lot of Black folk in the Americas since the 1500s, while the second set has been only incompletely articulated for Blacks by the academy since the middle of the twentieth century. While the critical tendencies of political economic analyses ostensibly speak to the ideologically and culturally curtailed information experiences of an underclass, these theories neglect to account for the information experiences of the *ur*-underclass, Blackness, which Orlando Patterson (1982) accurately describes as "social death."

What becomes clear when evaluating digital practice is that political economy does not do well analyzing cultural commodities as artifacts (e.g., Vine videos as a social media service) or audience commodities as cultural collectivities (e.g., Black Twitter hashtags; Meehan, Mosco, & Wasko, 1993). Critical political economy offers possibilities for understanding Blackness online, but its focus on oppression and resistance lingers on labor, the state, and the public sphere, leaving cultural aspects behind. For example, Faltesek (2018), using a political-economic lens to investigate social media, contends, "Facebook, Twitter, Snapchat, YouTube, LinkedIn, and dozens of other services have been described as the vanguard of creative destruction across the media industries-disruptors of established business, heroes of a new economic narrative that supposes that the attention of individual users can be measured, managed, manipulated, backing methods that securitized, patented, and litigated attention in ways impossible before. Selling Social Media catalogues the key terms and discourses of the rise of social media firms with a particular emphasis on monetization, securitization, disruption, and litigation" (n.p.). Cultural studies of media shares political economy's interest in media industries; new media and internet research from this perspective examines texts, identity, and audience reception and limits its critical take on communication and media to commodification, oppression, or resistance. When directed toward representation in digital spaces, cultural studies often glosses over race as a salient category to instead argue for internet culture as a freestanding aesthetic that is separate from offline identity politics.

Afrofuturism, a term coined by Mark Dery in the late 1990s, has waxed and waned in popularity as a powerful, culturally centered analysis of Black culture and technology and is often deployed as a supplement or alternative to political-economic approaches or cultural studies. Its most potent applications have seen Afrofuturism combined with Black feminist epistemology (Womack, 2013; Weheliye, 2002; Morris, 2016) to conceptualize Black digital practice, but Afrofuturism's futurist perspective and utopian leanings often occlude the possibilities of the present digital era for Black folk. In the same vein, Black and Africana studies should be at the forefront of examining Black digital practice, production, and industry, but apart from a few isolated researchers (many of whom are not in Black studies departments), that field is only slowly beginning to systematically investigate Black digital practice and production. The final chapter in this book offers a full-throated argument for these particular claims for those who are inclined to dispute this position.

Political-economic and cultural-theoretic analyses of new media and the digital fall short for Blackness and Black digital practice. Mosco (2009) contends that political economy is the study of control and survival in social life, which leaves little room for linkages between desire and activity. Political economy elides creativity and aesthetics in its analysis of digital practice, design, and consumption. From a communications perspective, political economy interprets relationships between media institutions, structures of production, and the state. A political-economic analysis of digital media and information, then, examines the social production of digitally mediated meaning, focusing on linkages among new media, capitalist development, and state power.

This focus on control and survival leads me to argue that the aesthetics at play in a political-economic analysis of digital practice draw on technocultural and capitalistic *virtues*: beliefs about rationality, productivity, efficiency, or commoditization. Any deviation from the realization of these beliefs is read as "play," "leisure," or "deviance." Under political economy, Black digital practice is rarely understood as productive or efficient. For example, political-economic analyses of the "digital divide" tie information use and access to the "social and economic progression of nation states" or view them as opportunities to overcome social inequality (Selwyn, 2004). Researchers examining minority informational and digital practices deemed them deficient based on the minorities' lack of access to institutions (education or home ownership), to the state, or to structures of production (material and information deficits). All the while, Black musical artists of the era—in hip-hop and R&B—were discussing the mediations of social, extralegal, and cultural relationships through information technology practice. I mention these artists, but I am not excluding earlier Black sonic luminaries in other genres interrogating Blackness, modernity, and sound, such as Derrick May, George Clinton, Roger Troutman, and even Sun Ra.

Even when positively argued from a political-economic perspective, Black digital practices receive short shrift. They are limited to being rebellious and resistant, commoditized and branded, or they are seen as (futile) attempts at seeking authentic representation in a white-dominated media sphere (Smith-Shomade, 2004). Writing about Black technoculture often revolves around oppression, resistance, labor, and consumption (Fouché, 2006; Sinclair, 2004; Pursell, 2010), including research on

- Black Lives Matter and online activism,
- the digital divide, and
- Black Girls Code camps and other science, technology, engineering, and mathematics (STEM) efforts.

Even as Black Lives Matter was celebrated for its digital media use, the movement was also derided for its lack of efficacy in shepherding members to "actual" political activity that would benefit Black communities. The activists were also unfairly criticized for contributing to online incivility, lending credence to the arguments made here about the perceived rationales for Black digital practice.

The blind spot of all these approaches—quantitative social science, political economy, cultural studies, and Afrofuturism—lies within the ideology of Western technoculture. Technoculture is often sutured to political economy to justify beliefs about technology as an avatar of productivity. This leads to evaluations of technological practice through progress, efficiency, or in more recent decades, ideological capture. Even when cultural studies or Afrofuturism addresses Black technology use, the previously mentioned perspectives on Black cultural production as evidence of resistance and oppression limit the possibilities for articulating a more nuanced understanding. In response, a cornerstone of this text is that it is more productive to understand technoculture through the concept of *libidinal economy* (Lyotard, 1993; Wilderson, 2010). Libidinal economy undergirds political economies, driving political and economic processes through affect. Incorporating a libidinal economic analysis to digital practice, then, offers a release from considerations of Black digital practice as labor or commodity.

Libidinal Economy

Incorporating libidinal economy into analyses of information technology use allows us to examine how racial ideology powers digital practice. Libidinal economy, as defined by Lyotard (1993), describes the libidinal impulses powering the machinations of any political economy. Libidinal economy is in turn fueled by jouissance, which, as I have said, is a conceptually rich word describing an excess of life. Jacques Lacan, who coined the term, writes that jouissance "begins with a tickle and ends with [a] blaze of petrol" (Seminar XVII, 72).

What does the libidinal mean, and how does it power an economy? Lyotard (1993) argues that events and actions are stabilized by interpretation, but there are always excess elements outside these interpretations. For example, consider a police report detailing an encounter with a Black woman. The report will represent the encounter from the perspective of the state, especially if the woman "somehow" ends up being shot by the officer. Missing from the report is whether the police officer is racist or misogynist, whether his department is known for mistreating minorities, or whether the city itself is racially segregated. Occasionally, the encounter will be captured on video by a dashcam, a bystander, or the victim herself, and the libidinal intensities of the situation and the participants become more (but never fully) apparent. The recording itself is invested with libidinal energy; we often take the regard of the camera as a "truth" to be trusted even as we understand that the perception of the truth varies with each individual, institution, or system. Thus libidinal economy aids in understanding why police encounters with armed white men vary greatly from those with unarmed Black men.

Lyotard (1993) argues that capitalist exchange is inescapably infused with libidinal intensity; similarly, I contend that informational exchange is laden with libidinal energies. For example, online incivility, née trolling (Nakamura, 2013; Phillips, 2015), can be understood as a pleasurable, white masculinist, patriarchal digital practice, even or perhaps because of its deviance. Along these same lines, "callout culture," which is often described as the bane of white feminism and, by extension, online civility, is more properly understood as discursive, gendered Black cultural critique—a Black womanist signifyin' practice transposed to social media environs. Finally, the long-delayed "last mile" implementation of broadband service to segregated urban neighborhoods is not a technical problem; it is best understood as part of long-standing antiblack technological policies of residential planning, urban planning, and segregation. While Lyotard's libidinal concept incorporates affect, it is not limited to that. Drawing on Freud's concept of the libido, the libidinal is energy—generated by phobias and desires—that has a visible effect on the world. Affect more properly describes an emotional state, whereas Lyotard's deployment of the libidinal is meant to capture the "whole structure of psychic and emotional life" (Sexton, cited in Wilderson, 2010, p. 24).

Political-economic analyses foreclose the sensual, the erotic, or the deviant by arguing that they have no value in a rational worldview, but the denial of their "exchange value" does not negate their existence. How does one value love or anger? Political economy claims that if a thing cannot be exchanged, it has no value and does not exist on the market. This position works only for the interests (desires) of those who benefit from amoral, unemotional rationalism (e.g., capitalism). Lyotard (1993) writes, "One must realize that representing is desire, putting on stage, in a cage, in prison, into a factory, into a family, being boxed in are desired, that domination and exclusion are desired" (p. 12). He continues, "Even when the capitalist machine is humming in the apparent general boredom and when everyody [*sic*] seems to do their job without moaning, all these libidinal instantiations, these little dispositifs of the retention and flow of the influxes of desire are *never unequivocal* and cannot give rise to a sociological reading or an unequivocal politics" (p. 114; emphasis original).

In Shannon and Weaver's ([1949] 1998) canonical illustration of information transfer between entities, where sender and receiver are two points connected by information while any misunderstanding is noise, jouissance suffuses the entire rationalistic, instrumental process—whether the transmitter/receiver is machine or human. That is, jouissance is the impulse that initiates the communication in the first place, the power maintaining the connection, the various impulses distorting the message (noise), and the impulses and feedback following the transmission. The flexibility of *jouissance* does not translate well to English; it can at once reference "affect," "intensity," "pleasure," "catharsis," and "sexuality." While *jouissance* is seminal to the arguments made throughout this book, I find that the term's linkage to capitalism (especially by Lyotard) is too transactional for how I argue for Black digital practice.

Lyotard (1993) notes that "it is extraordinarily difficult to recognize the desire of capital" (p. 110), but I believe this difficulty can be reduced by examining the social and cultural contexts in which capitalistic endeavors take place. Wilderson (2010) is helpful in this regard, expanding the definition of libidinal economy to encompass racial ideology. He identifies antiblackness as a desire of American society and culture, writing that "Blackness overdetermines the embodiment of impossibility, incoherence, and incapacity" (p. 73). The devaluation and reduction of the human body to its technical and labor potential are clearest when the body is Black. Moreover, the specter of antiblackness allows whiteness to devalue the labor of non-Black bodies, encouraging nonelites to accept less economic capital in exchange for the cultural capital of not being Black. For example, Donald Trump, who won the presidential election in 2016 by appealing to xenophobia and nativism, has had his inchoate antiblackness codified into Republican legislative proposals to transfer wealth to white elites by defunding social welfare programs that are perceived as aiding minority families, eliminating environmental protections (disproportionately affecting minority and poor communities in the process), disenfranchising religious and ethnic minorities, and expanding military aggression in the name of xenophobia.

Given the ephemeral, immanent nature of desire and the protean qualities of information technologies, it seems difficult to identify the desires of new media. But if one accepts Dinerstein's (2006) figuration of whiteness as seminal to the American technocultural mythos, then the characteristics of whiteness—organization, embodiment/disembodiment, and enterprise (Dyer, 1997)—can be understood as the jouissance, or desires, of new media and information technologies as well. Dinerstein also references "religion"—in this case, Carey's technological sublime—to highlight how relating information technologies to the domain of "the spirit" locates new media and information desire in transcendence. That is, removing the limitations of embodiment from traveling through space and time—or even the identification of a disembodied, ephemeral textual practice—defaults to whiteness.

Wilderson (2010), in writing on antiblackness, offers Jared Sexton's clarification of libidinal economy: "The economy, or distribution and arrangement, of desire and identification (their condensation and displacement), and the complex relationship between sexuality and the unconscious . . . a dispensation of energies, concerns, points of attention, anxieties, pleasures" (Sexton, cited in Wilderson, 2010, p. 24). Building on this, I argue that one should understand the distribution and arrangement of Black digital practice as digital labor *and* desire, as online politics *and* desire, or as digital representation *and* desire. Removing desire from Black digital practice reduces agency—online members become "users" or, even worse, "data." Further, invoking the libidinal highlights how the removal of the erotic and the banal from "appropriate" Black digital practice renders said practices—constituted as resistance or commodification—as sterile attempts to escape "the master's house using the master's tools" (Lorde, 1984). My argument for a libidinal economy of new media and information technologies incorporates the concept of pathos to show why digital practitioners engage in "nonproductive" and "inefficient" online activities.

Pathos as a Determinant of Digital Practice

Lyotard's (1993) conceptualization of desire does not limit itself to expressions of pleasure. The translation of *libidinal economy* from French to English retained the concept of jouissance to refer to the enjoyment of use and the seeking of pleasure, play, and climax. Similarly, Wilderson (2010) notes that libidinal economy is linked not only to "forms of attraction, affection, and alliance, but also to aggression, destruction, and the violence of lethal consumption" (p. 24).

To clarify the ontological power of libidinal economy, I replace *jouissance* with the term *pathos* for this text. While modern definitions of *pathos* revolve around sympathy and empathy (both descended from the term), for Black digital practice, I evoke the Aristotelian definition. Aristotle argues that pathos encompasses the speaker's familiarity with her audience's value and belief systems, preferred presentation styles, and techniques of argumentation. It is tempting given pathos's association with style to infer that pathos's emotional appeal is illogical and shallow, but that is far from the case. Logic (logos) depends on a particular style of presentation (objectivism), a particular set of values and beliefs (rationality and positivism), and specific techniques of argumentation (e.g., the scientific method and syllogism) in order to be effective, rendering "science" as a set of emotional appeals to a specific audience. Indeed, there is an entire field of study dedicated to the rhetoric of science and technology that is intent on unpacking the persuasions underlying science and engineering research, but the inquiries only superficially address issues of race.

Pathos is also stunningly relevant as a conceptual framework for the Black experience in the Americas. The United States was founded on the cultural logos that Blackness is not an intelligible part of society. As such, ethos was denied to African Americans based on the ideological assignation of deviance and embodiment. To counter these discourses, which were presented as "logical" and juridical, Black discursive culture cultivated a warrant of pathos to ground their identity. My definition of pathos also draws from Joan Morgan's "Black Feminist Politics of Pleasure" (2015). Morgan asks how desire, agency, and Black women's engagement with pleasure can be developed into a viable theoretical paradigm. While doing so, she argues for Black female interiority as "the broad range of feelings, desires, yearning, (erotic and otherwise) that were once deemed necessarily private by the politics of silence" (p. 37).

Similarly, I argue for Black culture's interiority in an online milieu, or as Yancy (2005) describes it, "In my everydayness, I live my body from an existential *here*. Wherever I go, I go embodied . . . in my phenomenological return, however, I am *reduced* to a point that is viewed. My *here* is experienced as a *there*" (p. 221). The epistemological awareness Yancy articulates—that Blackness is consciously and experientially reduced to an object from an agentive being through ideology—can be understood as Black interiority and thus serves as a warrant for my use of pathos. Digital practice encourages us to appreciate and evaluate Black identity performances and activities in situ, contributing to my claim for online interiority. From these warrants, I argue that the reductive power of the phenomenological return is significantly decreased thanks to the affordances of digital and online spaces.

Black Pathos

Given the Black experience in America during and following the Middle Passage, I incorporate an approach that allows me to systematically situate Black philosophy and knowledge in history and technoculture. Sandra Harding's (1992) discussion of standpoint epistemology and feminist accounts of science and technology have proven especially valuable, as they encourage an evaluation of the world from the perspective of the oppressed rather than the elite. She writes, "In societies where scientific rationality and objectivity are claimed to be highly valued by dominant groups, marginalized peoples and those who listen attentively to them will point that from the perspective of marginal lives, the dominant accounts are less than maximally objective" (p. 442). Standpoint theory encourages inquiries into the material, political, or cultural aspects of social structures; more importantly, it is a structural intervention focused on the creation of group consciousness rather than shifts in the consciousness of individuals. I see standpoint epistemology as a complement to a libidinal economic analysis in that it specifies *whose* libidinal energies are important to the institutions or phenomena under examination. Crucially, standpoint epistemology is a focus on how practices—digital, material, and ideological—demonstrate human relations with each other and the natural world.

Thus I have chosen to identify Black pathos as the epistemological standpoint (Harding, 1992) of a libidinal economy of Black technoculture. This epistemic stratagem allows me to incorporate race—in this case, Black culture and Black bodies—without permitting America's antiblackness to overdetermine Blackness. This approach offers multiple beneficial outcomes, such as the disinvestment of technoculture's substrates of logic and rationality. Replacing the highly circumscribed positivist and "objective" emotional character of logos with pathos allows this inquiry to incorporate analyses of Black digital practice engendered by joy, sexuality, playfulness, anger, and politics. Another benefit is the acknowledgment and theorization of Black communal identity as a meaning-making strategy. In this way, we can understand Blackness as a discourse in conversation with, but not wholly subject to, whiteness as epistemology—a refutation of the categorial nature of capitalist identity and, most important, antiblackness. As KRS-One says, "Rap is something you do; hip-hop is something you live." This distinction also exposes a critical perspective on racial ideology by interrogating and speaking to the contradictions of practice and belief. Finally, a libidinal economic perspective on Black technoculture allows us to tease apart the reasons behind Black digital practice's distribution, performance, and aggregation across digital and material social structures. Black folk use technologies that were not designed for or about them in ways that confound traditional technology analyses, and this approach is intended to redress that shortcoming.

The claims I make about Black cyberculture throughout this text are driven by three warrants:

1. Technology as text
2. Identity as the tension between the self and the social
3. Blackness as a dynamic, protean core of narrative gravity and weightlessness

These warrants, which I will develop in the following chapters, lead to my claim for Blackness as an informational identity. Let me be clear: I am arguing for Blackness not as a *virtual* identity but as an informational one—an identity powered by discourse, technology, and the phenomenology of embodiment in a white supremacist ideology.

2

Information Inspirations

The Web Browser as Racial Technology

In the previous chapter, I claim that Blackness is a discursive, informational identity—one that brings a particularized coherence to digital practice. While Twitter is perhaps the most publicly available manifestation of online Blackness, Black digital presence existed before the dawn of the commercial internet. The traces of digital practice manifest on-screen and in code, but the means (the devices and applications) through which users conduct digital practices are typically not of interest to media researchers. This chapter asks, Can Blackness can be discerned at the level of digital infrastructure? The design and launch of the Blackbird application offers insights into how Blackness could operate as a design principle for one of the most integral pieces of informational infrastructure: the web browser. Formally, Blackbird should be understood as a conceptual attempt to revise an infrastructural application to serve a different type of user—to make Blackness intrinsic to the enactment of Black online information needs and desires. This chapter examines discourses around the release of a web browser that explicitly enacts a racial epistemology. In doing so, this examination also interrogates how technoculture—Black and Western alike—shapes our beliefs about appropriate digital practices and racial inflections of internet content.

Given the demographic composition of the tech industry, it is unsurprising how little attention has been paid to how whiteness structures application design. Reflexivity has never been a benchmark for information technology industries; instead, these institutions focus on instrumental outcomes of "improving" computers and code, burying their cultural influences behind technical protocols and limited imaginaries about users who are not themselves. How, then, does one locate Blackness, much less race, in the applications we use? McPherson (2011) offers one possibility for examining race at the code level by interrogating how whiteness and masculinity shaped Unix. Moreover, recent studies of GitHub (Romano, 2013) have also revealed racism, masculinity, and homophobia as discursive phenomena in programming code repositories. These studies' focus on operating systems and programming code, while admirable, does not account for how Black folk, much less Black epistemologies, are present in the internet's infrastructure.

To address the lack of research on racialized applications and platforms, this study begins by considering the lowly web browser. Like Xerox became a generic term for photocopies and Coke a generic term for soda (at least in the southern United States), the web browser is the sign for the internet. When people say "I was on the internet today," we visualize their use of a window through which they access the World Wide Web. Browsers organize and frame the incredible amount of content, media, and protocols we know as the World Wide Web.

Although early adopters and power users may scoff at the synecdoche (where a specific thing is used to refer to a more general class of things), it is not difficult to see why users would understand a complex assemblage of hardware and software through their use of a particular application. The browser as a medium is a cultural artifact, defining its users as technologists, as curators, and as social actors. Once considered valuable enough to trigger a government-led antitrust lawsuit (that Microsoft lost), today's web browser is remarkably deprecated in today's app and mobile economy. Social networking apps, incorporating web viewers in place of full browsers, have nearly usurped the browser's enticement to explore and experience the web. It is part of our communicative infrastructure—invisible to our information literacy practices until a rupture occurs.

A confession is necessary here: I employ a gloss to make my claim. The technical infrastructure powering the commercial internet that we know as the World Wide Web should be properly understood as networks of cables, satellites, and servers as well as the protocols, policies, and netcode that enables digital media and information to be transmitted across the globe at high speed. Billions of internet users, however, have never seen these technologies at work. (How can one tell if a cable is actually transmitting information without some mediating interface?) What they have seen, and extensively interacted with, is a client application—the browser—to access the internet.[1] This chapter argues that the browser *is* the internet for many people, given that many visits to the internet begin by opening this application.

Why is this important? In short, browsers are where our identities as digital practitioners are enacted rather than simply performed. I offer the term *enactment* to highlight the substrate of practices underlying online performance and consumption; these browser-specific activities (e.g., refreshing the page) bracket online participation. The quotidian nature of actions associated with the browser, however, is still subject to technocultural beliefs about appropriate technology use and users.[2] For example, the "browser wars" of the early aughts featured debates about the ideologies of their developers; people also argued about the construction of each browser's imagined or ideal user as signified by the browser design (including the chrome!). Firefox/Mozilla users were presumed to have different information behaviors than Safari users, whose information behaviors differed from Chrome users. Thus the libidinal economic analysis here highlights how beliefs about Black digital practice prefigure the use of an application designed specifically for Black users.

The Soft Bigotry of Low Information Expectations

Unfortunately, there is a dearth of critical research on the internet browsing beliefs—not browsing habits or digital content—of Black folk even as more Black folk are online than ever. I base this argument on the excellent data compiled by the Pew Research Center's Internet & American Life Project[3] (especially that of Aaron Smith), who deserve recognition for their ongoing series of surveys on race and social media. Their research is notable in part thanks to survey methodologies that oversample minority and underserved internet users; many disciplines attempting to survey and study Black communities don't include adequate numbers of Black respondents, fail to separate socioeconomic status from race, neglect in-group heterogeneity, or are tainted by interview bias. These problems are apparent when reviewing social science research on internet access or the digital divide, which is morbidly fascinated with promulgating "facts" about the limitations of and on Black folks' internet use. Researchers are often concerned, for example, with the structural and cultural drawbacks associated with Black folks' frequent social media use, which is operationalized as less "productive" than other forms of digital practice and thus less reliable for "rational" information gathering.

Additionally, researchers' failures to disambiguate race from socioeconomic status when measuring disparities in information access for poor and low-income (see also *urban*) families are also conceptualized as disparities for Black digital practitioners en masse. What does this mean in practical, technocultural terms? High-priced, prepaid mobile broadband data plans paired with low-budget, moderately powered feature phones and smartphones are primarily marketed to poor and minority communities, whose members are often unable to secure postpaid mobile service. As mobile service has been found to be the primary means by which Black folk access the internet (Smith, 2010b, 2015), these phones and plans are seen as limiting factors to accessing the commodified, data-intensive internet of today. For Black folk to use them to primarily access social media—and then to view and post content revolving around racial identity—is often understood as "inappropriate," as Black digital practice should revolve around economic, educational, or productive information concerns instead.

This chapter evaluates Black digital practice and practitioners from a Black technocultural perspective rather than from the standpoint of the hegemonic and coercive standards of Western technocultural beliefs, which position Blackness uncritically as the nadir of humanity. A critical approach should reformulate how productivity and, more important, creativity can be hallmarks of engaging with and fulfilling Black digital practice. Grounding research into Black digital practice from a Black cultural perspective does not separate those practices from beliefs about respectability, economic progress, or social propriety. However, the technocultural perspective employed here encourages perceptions of Black desires for and the pleasures of having a universe of information and media production at one's fingertips. In doing so, it serves as an additional warrant for Blackness as an informational identity premised on culturally competent semiotic and material relationships among content, code, hardware, and culture.

Introducing Blackbird

The Blackbird browser was designed to abet and promote the discovery of African American internet content. Blackbird can be understood as part of a genre of web browser client apps known as niche browsers. These browsers were intended to serve specific internet user types (not communities per se): Songbird for music lovers, Flock for social networking, or the now discontinued Gloss for women. More specifically, these browsers were built on the open-source Mozilla browser, then popular for its astonishing number of customization options for users. Niche browsers feature targeted content, services, and advertising all integrated with thematic interface elements designed to appeal to their prospective audience. Blackbird's targeting of the Black community as preferred users occasioned a startling response for the introduction of an information technology product. Whereas most tech products are evaluated in terms of their ease of use or feature set, Blackbird's reception as an information and computer technology (ICT) artifact was "colored" by the racial frames of the pundits, bloggers, and commenters who discussed it.

To return to the organizing metaphor of this text, the browser's ubiquitous distribution—packed in as essential software for every operating system (OS) and the primary interface from which to interact with the World Wide Web—introduced information without limitations (e.g., as a set of dictionaries or a thesaurus) in a private, domestic space for the first time. Absent the physical and geographic limitations of the library and the segregationist constraints of educational institutions, Black households, workers, and students were able to experience and interact with information on their own terms. To unpack the cultural and technocultural implications of a software artifact like Blackbird, I analyze the following:

- histories, practices, and beliefs about Blackbird/browser use
- hardware and protocols necessary to use Blackbird
- Blackbird interface (client)
- practices and conventions—social, technical, and cultural—necessary to use Blackbird
- out-group beliefs about race and technology
- in-group beliefs about race and technology

The interface analysis of the browser and the discourse analysis of a select few blog posts and their associated comments are laid out against a critical race framework integrating theories of technoculture and the libidinal energies powering them to understand how the browser is constructed through practice, experience, and identity.

Critical Frameworks: Technoculture and Racial Formation Theory

To fully understand how digital technologies are cultural, one must analyze the ways in which they manifest cultural meaning alongside their meaning-making capacities as functional and instrumental artifacts. Thus to analyze Blackbird, my conceptual framework for this chapter incorporates concepts from racial formation theory, critical race theory, and theories of technoculture. Each instance of critical technocultural discourse analysis (CTDA) research—my preferred methodology—requires assembly; this is in part because the object of inquiry changes and also because the inquiry itself may differ. The central conceit of CTDA is the application of a critical discourse analytic to the interface and to the discourses about the interface.

My first step in assembling a conceptual framework, then, is to turn to Omi and Winant (1994), who contend that race is a matter of social structure and cultural representation, or racial formation. Blackbird's design and reception make it possible for one to infer that all browsers are racialized social structures. Before you scoff at this seemingly facile observation, consider this: The browser is typically understood as a neutral conduit for information. If there are any cultural implications to browser use, the association of these practices with navigational metaphors (e.g., surfing, exploring) is nearly completely dissociated from the imperial and colonial histories of Western seafaring. Instead (and similarly), the web is popularly understood as a limitless resource—like the ocean—belonging to no one and accessible to everyone. The explosion of information—commercial, artistic, banal, quirky, or journalistic—that quickly populated the web browser from the mid-1990s on was considered universal even as it became apparent that the typical internet user was white, male, and middle class.

Thus an unavoidable first step for examining the browser is *excavation*: evacuating the browser from its infrastructural home to unearth a better understanding of its meaning-making practices and beliefs. Infrastructure most frequently becomes visible when it ruptures, causing interruptions in the everyday use of otherwise invisible resources and capacities. By front-loading the racial identity of its users and designers, Blackbird is not an infrastructural rupture in the traditional sense. Instead, its existence and capacity rupture beliefs about who and what should be the focus of a computational and informational artifact, particularly one that accesses the "neutral" World Wide Web. From this perspective, the browser is an odd duck. While nominally it is a social structure—indeed, a social infrastructure given the number of platforms, protocols, and practices enacted within as well as the invisibility of the browser window to our internet usage—it should be given serious consideration as cultural representation (at least from the perspective of the Blackbird developers).

If one accepts the synecdoche that a browser is the internet, then the browser as a social structure represents and maintains Western culture through the dissemination of content while embodying Western racial ideology through its information practices. The browser indiscernibly frames the racial ideologies that users, content providers, and designers deploy to encode and decode their internet experiences. But, you may exclaim, so does the graphical user interface (GUI) or the computer monitor—the browser is just a window through which we observe the goings-on online! In response, I must reiterate that all technologies—and to an even greater extent, all information technologies—are socially and culturally shaped. Information technologies are more complicit because of their capacity (though limited) to re-create entire institutions, practices, and worlds. The application known as the web browser is the result of countless semiotic decisions about practice, visual interface elements, and display. These stipulations, which are normative and seemingly implacable, become clearer when race is brought to the forefront as a design imperative.

The flip side of using racial formation to discuss the meaning-making capacity of the web browser leads to a discussion of cultural representation: How does the browser perform racial ideology? Later in this chapter, I will delve into how elements of browser interfaces and practices promote racialized practices. For now, it is important to consider how race and racial ideology contribute to patterns and practices of browsing itself.

Internet usage, from a critical race and technocultural perspective, can be understood as the evincing of racial dynamics for information seeking and information behaviors—partially mediated by the user's cultural milieu and racial ideology—in a digital medium. This takes place while the user simultaneously redistributes cultural resources (e.g., attention, audience, cultural capital, and political capital) along racial lines. This has become increasingly clear during our social media era; Anderson and Hitlin (2016) of the Pew Internet & American Life Project report that Black social media users are significantly more likely to post or encounter racial content across their online travels, whereas few white users report seeing race at all in the spaces they visit. The browser offers a starting point from which to view and interact with online content and spaces, but the content-neutral perspective it offers prioritizes mainstream websites that present information from a technophilic white, middle-class, male viewpoint. This perspective works to re-create social dynamics online that mirror offline patterns of racial interaction by marginalizing women and people of color.

Consider the default set of bookmarks shipped with any browser; the developers offer a limited variety of websites to prime the internet experience. Many of the sites are simply the home pages for technology and lifestyle brands while others represent destinations for various interest genres such as technology, travel, or food. If there is a set of bookmarks for culture, the gesture is toward a vaguely defined "internet culture," where the peculiarities of internet ephemera are on display.

Race plays an integral role in technoculture, although it is rarely acknowledged for digital media or practice unless nonwhite practitioners are under scrutiny. Blackbird was designed to satisfy the information needs of Black internet users, so racial formation theory and elements of the Black technocultural matrix will be used to understand the meanings Black and white users assigned to Blackbird's practices, features, and discourse. However, Blackness in the American cultural context is juxtaposed against white racial ideology, which offers the opportunity to interrogate the absence of Blackness in technocultural belief through critical whiteness studies. Dyer's (1997) concept of whiteness as paradoxical identity and Harris's (1993) arguments for whiteness as property are also used to understand users' meaning-making strategies. This is not a comparative analysis of Black and white users; instead, it properly grounds Blackness as an American cultural identity—for good or for ill.

American identity (in particular, whiteness) is bounded and extended by negative stereotypes of Black identity (Morrison, 1993). Giroux (1996) adds that "whiteness represents itself as a universal marker for being civilized and in doing so posits the Other within the language of pathology, fear, madness, and degeneration" (p. 75). Civilization here should be understood as the technologies for managing and controlling natural, social, and cultural resources; from there, it's not a huge leap to include communicative technologies as markers of civilization. Harris (1993), while arguing that whiteness is an ideological proposition imposed through subordination (p. 1730), also contends that "whiteness serves as reputation in the interstices between internal and external identity and as property in the extrinsic, public, and legal realms" (p. 1725). This latter assertion leads to my own claim that "unmarked" digital content, services, and artifacts are commonly understood as white, as belonging to whiteness, and as "civilized" *until* a nonwhite actor or group is seen utilizing them. Thus whiteness is infrastructural; this can be understood through the realization that science-fiction stories populate entire universes with fantastic aliens *and* white folk.

Finally, Dyer (1997) contends that white identity is founded on a paradox: whiteness entails being a "sort of" race *and* the human race—an individual subject *and* a representation of the universal subject. This claim neatly supplements Harris's (1993) concept of interstitial whiteness, lending whiteness a universalist individualism that is still socially constructed. Dyer returns to the idea of control—over the self, over the spirit, over others, and as the engine of enterprise—as a hallmark of white identity. Dyer's observations tie neatly into Western histories of political and economic expansion, where trade and communication networks were deployed as national policies to extend cultural hegemony over "undeveloped" countries with abundant natural resources. In particular, the ideals of technological progress and technology as means to reach the future foreground whites' use of technology to control the natural and man-made world.

Without closing off possibilities for understanding race as a relational construct, my conceptual framework encourages a view of race as an infrastructural quality. By *closing off*, I mean that Blackness is not defined solely by being subordinated, nor is whiteness only understood as a subordinating identity. The browser affords an implicitly "unmarked" technological commons even as each internet surfer personalizes his installation to conform to his personal browsing habits through bookmarks, cookies, add-ons, and user scripts. The seeming openness of the platform, coupled with libertarian (and neoliberal) rhetoric about the internet as a culture-neutral space, obscures the reality that most online content available through the browser and its technological implements still constructs and maintains Western and modern notions of race, gender, and class. Without examining content specifically, the next section begins the analysis of Blackbird by briefly outlining the browser's representation as an informational, racial, and cultural artifact.

The Web Browser

Browsers are general-purpose applications designed to retrieve and display a variety of multimedia resources (print, image, audio, video, code) linked to a specific User Resource Identifier/Locator (URI or URL) on a remote server. In many ways, they are similar to word processors, which also allow users to compose digital texts with images. Browser design has not drastically evolved since the introduction of Mosaic in 1993 even as seminal technologies such as Adobe (once Macromedia) Flash have largely disappeared from browser spaces. They feature now commonplace design elements such as a home button, a refresh button, and a back button in a bar across the top of the window while the remainder of the space is dedicated to displaying content. As Jakob Nielsen (1993) writes, "UI is the barrier through which [users] reach for the content they want" (p. 66).

The browser's utility in delivering multiple types of networked information—including but not limited to advertising—has led to plenty of invective against manufacturers and software developers. Browsers can be intimately wired into an operating system (e.g., mobile Safari and iOS or Internet Explorer and Windows), guiding the user to employ programs created by first-party developers while limiting access to, if not outright excluding, browsers by third-party developers. The legal furor over predetermined browser integration is tied to the belief that the browser is the manifestation of the open, democratic nature of the internet. In *United States v. Microsoft Corporation* (2001), the US Department of Justice argues successfully that the browser's integration into the operating system inescapably frames the user's access to the type, amount, and quality of information available online even while allowing for a near-infinite personalization of the internet experience.

Thanks to the dictates of capitalism, even the lauded capacity to personalize and individualize one's browser experience has been exploited through the browser's susceptibility to invasive digital advertisements. Advertising tactics—ranging from pop-under windows to click-jacking to following users away from commerce sites—are often framed as part of the debate on how to monetize the internet, both to rescue legacy industries such as newspapers and also to support the immense amount of technological investment necessary for start-ups to reach scale. I argue, however, that this is as an inevitable consequence of the browser's commitment to interstitial whiteness. That is, the browser's designed enactment of a "color-blind" technological, implicitly white reputation allows for the imposition of a class-based, implicitly white identity ripe for the exploits of advertisers looking to market to this lucrative group of consumers. These enactments do not transfer to my Black online experiences; I can certainly tell you that advertisements for Black cultural products never follow me around during my online travels.

The browser's institutional/individual identity, as it is understood and articulated by users in the blogs analyzed here, maps closely to Dyer's (1997) definition of white identity. As mentioned earlier, Dyer argues that whiteness operates as a marker for both individual humanity and universal humanity. The browser's computational position (prominently displayed on default installations of virtual desktops) and capacities (framing networked digital content through a patina of personalization) render it as a communication device for "humanity" while obscuring its underpinnings as a legacy artifact of communication networks in its continued bolstering of economic and sociocultural imperialism. Meanwhile, the overwhelming amount of content designed by and for mainstream audiences who are familiar with older forms of broadcast media extends the perception of universal (access to) information. From an individual perspective (particularly since the rise of Web 2.0), the browser has been designed to encourage customization of web use based on personal preferences. Thus while many people use the same browsing software, few will experience the web in the same way. The dual experience of universal application and individual preferences, then, prejudices users to assume that the "universal" web, configured to their liking, is similarly configured for every other user. This is borne out by the posts and comments analyzed later in the chapter, but this universalist rhetoric echoes today's rhetoric of color-blind identity that serves to protect the interests of whiteness in popular and political arenas.

Blackbird

The whiteness of the World Wide Web was documented as early as 1998 in Hoffman and Novak's canonical report on the digital divide. They argue that one of the more likely factors in the digital divide's perpetuation was a lack of content—and the mechanism to discover it—addressing the information needs of Black users. I would be remiss if I did not point out that Hoffman and Novak's findings unknowingly echoed those of the 1968 Kerner Commission (United States National Advisory Commission on Civil Disorders, 1968), which concludes that Black unrest and protests have some impetus in the lack of positive Black content available across the mass media of the time. Nevertheless, these calls for the development and dissemination of culturally competent content have only been sporadically addressed across any media. For example, a recent report noted that less than 5 percent of all television writers are Black (Hunt, 2017). While comparing the tech industry to the entertainment industry doesn't offer a fair comparison, it's telling that Blacks represent less than 5 percent of that industry as well.

40A Inc., a company founded by three Black entrepreneurs,[4] is Blackbird's developer of record, but there's very little information online about the company. Blackbird was designed to address the difficulties of finding content oriented toward the information needs and interests of African Americans. Constructed from the open source codebase of Mozilla Firefox, it is structurally and thematically similar to the Flock (social networking), Gloss (women-centric), and Mozilla-variant browsers. Each variant features custom interface tweaks (chrome) designed to visually identify the browser as well as plug-ins, custom searches, and other tweaks designed to enhance the targeted user's experience. From the features available, it is clear that the Blackbird creators intended to leverage social networks and web services already in use by African Americans by integrating them into an application-based social network offering cultural content. The browser was initially released for Windows[5] in February 2009, with a release for OS X (Mac) users in October of the same year. The Windows release can be understood as pragmatic yet identitarian through its technical standardization of Black digital identity as users of the OS with the largest install base. This OS-level homogenization was an early indicator of the compromises 40A had to make to accommodate Black users.

Visually, the browser used a black theme with red accents and white-on-black buttons to frame the content. A small circular logo featuring a raven's wing with orange tips can be found in the upper right-hand corner of the application window. By default, two customized toolbars (a ticker and a set of large buttons) were enabled and visible. The layout resembled a standard Firefox browser, with the search and address bars sharing space on the top toolbar, while yet another toolbar offered a selection of bookmarks. The interface could get busy; the ticker toolbar streamed Really Simple Syndication (RSS) feed items across the top of the content window (like a chyron) while a notification pop-up occasionally surfaced in the lower right-hand corner.

Feature-wise, Blackbird could be customized with Mozilla extensions and add-ons that were specifically tailored for the browser, but few, if any, were ever released. The Blackbird install automatically imported preexisting Firefox passwords, bookmarks, and plugins but asked whether to import Internet Explorer settings. It seems the designers intended to leverage the growing popularity of Mozilla's browser while taking advantage of Firefox's customization features. For example, a popular power user JavaScript extension called Greasemonkey,[6] which enabled an augmented browsing experience by modifying web content while the page was loading, seems to have been available to Blackbird users. There was an indication that Greasemonkey user scripts could be invoked (a "user scripts" button in the email services tab of the service preferences), but there is no documentation about the feature.

With respect to built-in features, Blackbird tailored the browsing experience by offering custom features designed around African American content:

- Blackbird News Ticker: a preloaded (but customizable) RSS ticker toolbar
- Black Bookmarks: preselected bookmarks featuring African American websites
- Black Search: a customized Google search prioritizing African American content
- Blackbird TV: a customized YouTube video channel available only to Blackbird users featuring Black content
- Blackbird Community: a browser-centered social network allowing users to share content through the in-browser Grapevine (a Digg clone)
- Give Back: a feature linking users to designated charities serving African American communities

Blackbird also offered web service–centered features. On the services toolbar, users would find a button that could be configured to run Yahoo! Mail, Windows Live (Hotmail), or Gmail. The button offered a badge displaying unread notifications and another power user accommodation: the ability to switch between email accounts without resorting to a bookmark or the address bar.

Users could also take advantage of a social network feature allowing them to access either Facebook or Myspace with one click. For both buttons, the active service was represented by the appropriate logo on the button, or favicon. Blackbird also featured an active sidebar where Facebook could be viewed without leaving the main browser panel to encourage multitasking and increase immersion without leaving Blackbird. When signed into Facebook, this sidebar showed the user's profile picture, status, links to the inbox, and invites. It also showed a friends list that was sortable by last update time, status update time, profile update time, or name. Logging into Facebook also enabled the aforementioned browser-oriented notification system to inform users of friend activity.

Blackbird, like Firefox, featured a search box next to the address bar to reflect the growing dominance of search as a means to discover content.

While it could be configured with the user's choice of several search engines, the default engine was a customized Google search intended to prioritize results that may be of interest to African American users. It appears that Blackbird's developers paid for Google's "siteSearch" variation of the custom search feature site:search function, as the free custom search engine (CSE) version would have populated results with AdWords advertisements before, between, and after results on each returned page. In a highly unscientific comparison, I entered "Barack Obama" into the Blackbird home page, which features a Google search bar and a button for "Black Search" and "Google Search." My results suggested that the Blackbird search properly gave greater weight to information coming from Black cultural sites such as BlackAmericaWeb (the internet home of the *Tom Joyner Morning Show*), BlackVoices (AOL's portal for Black news and lifestyle information), Black Entertainment Television, and *Black Enterprise* magazine's web home. When attempting to replicate these results in a vanilla Google search (without being signed in), the Black cultural results didn't show up at all in the first fifty pages—five hundred results without reference to information curated by authoritative Black online entities. To be fair, a page from Bossip (a popular Black celebrity gossip blog) was listed, but there was also a result marking Conservaepedia's derogatory web page on Obama. The Blackbird developers' contention that Black content can be difficult to find using regular searches seems to be valid given the results of these searches.[7]

In a regrettable move, Blackbird tried to capture users with browser-only features. For example, the browser asked users to create a Blackbird profile, which was meant to populate a browser-based social network. This network was intended to power social features such as the Blackbird-only Grapevine, where members could share items and vote on items of interest. In format, Grapevine resembled Digg.[8] Items were sorted by the date they were submitted to the site, and users could up-vote or down-vote them. Items could also be arranged by categories or tagged and sorted by popularity in a tag cloud. When comparing Digg and Grapevine, however, it's possible to see that 40A's aim to encourage cultural content sharing could have borne fruit. Every article on the Grapevine page back in 2009 mentioned race or racial issues, compared with only two of the twenty most popular articles featured on the Digg home page. At the time, I speculated that the cultural orientation of Blackbird's user base (plus the preloaded content served up by Blackbird's content features) helped promote content that validated Black cultural epistemologies of race and racism that would otherwise be of no interest to mainstream audiences.

Another browser-locked Blackbird component of note was the "Give Back" feature. Part of Blackbird's promotional strategy for the browser's introduction touted the developers' intention to fundraise for charitable and educational organizations that positively impact the African American community. Their primary philanthropic tactic was to donate 10 percent of 40A's 2009 revenue to their nonprofit partners. To encourage a similar charitable spirit among its user base, Blackbird offered a "Give Back" button in the services toolbar. This button led users to the "Do Good Channel" page, where they could enter their location and find charitable organizations in their area. The organizations could be sorted by cause or ways to participate. The Blackbird Do Good Channel was a branded version of the nonprofit endeavor of the same name run by good2gether, a website that offers nonprofits a way to advertise their services and content on the web for free and generate revenue by adding sponsors.

The Give Back initiative was impressive because internet browsers rarely offer users possibilities for interacting with the outside world in a manner that isn't commercial, much less offering users dedicated channels within the application for charitable donations. Blackbird was one of the first general-purpose applications to encourage users to engage with nonprofit community-based and national organizations. Blackbird's version of the Do Good Channel, like its other content, focused on African American–oriented charities and nonprofits (when compared to good2gether's version), but it did not limit its users to selecting those organizations. Since Blackbird's introduction, sites such as GoFundMe have arisen to provide individuals and nonprofits an electronic space to solicit donations for philanthropic purposes. While there are social websites and services that work to bring together people with like interests, their emphasis is on helping isolated members find others who are like them. Alternatively, web surfers can donate processor cycles to distributed computing projects like Folding@home or unused bandwidth to peer-to-peer applications like BitTorrent. Few of these spaces, however, focus specifically on philanthropic enterprises dedicated to aiding the Black community.

The features that differentiate Blackbird from Firefox speak strongly to 40A's concept of embedded social networking as an electronic definition of community. The browser encouraged its users to integrate their existing social networks and web services in the application. It sweetened the pot by offering customizable presence and status notifications that allowed users to monitor their social networks while surfing other websites. However, the implementation was not as refined as Flock, Mozilla's variant social networking browser. Flock featured a broader set of social media features, including Facebook Chat, Twitter, Delicious bookmarking, Picasa photo streams, Digg, Bebo, and Xanga access as well as YouTube and Truveo video subscription feeds. Flock even included drag-and-drop capability between the social media pane and the main browser window.

The inclusion of content specifically targeting African Americans layers a cultural definition of community on top of the software / internet instantiation and offers a compelling visualization of the explicit integration of ethnic and technocultural practices. 40A's implementation of the browser is a criticism of the structural inequities of "mainstream" internet content, which privileges the information needs of middle-class white male users. Moreover, Blackbird's incorporation of links to charities and nonprofits also speaks to a communal support model that addresses the implicit affluence of web users (those with time to surf and the wherewithal to afford the equipment) and asks them to aid their identified cultural communities. This was a paradigm shift, first popularized by MoveOn.org and other nonprofit sites, where the internet's pan-location is used to leverage the power of local connections for civic gain. By tying together nonprofits and Black online visitors, Blackbird's Give Back initiative was a powerful attempt to close the digital divide by asking a community to support its own using information technology resources.

Technology as Belief: Online Reactions to Blackbird's Ethos

In the introduction to this text, I discussed Pacey's theory of technology as a triadic entity composed of an artifact, practice, and belief. Popular conceptions of technology center on the first two pieces, often obscuring the beliefs that power the dissemination and use of the technology. The internet provides a unique vantage point for observing the beliefs that people associate with their use of a particular technology artifact. As the web has matured as a communications platform, weblogs have become a popular feature for articulating viewpoints on any number of personal, societal, civic, social, or arcane matters. They are embedded within an information ecosphere that implicitly and explicitly demands interactivity among software, authors, audiences, and the world. When examining a web event around a cultural object, then, the interactive nature of the web encourages discussions across multiple digital and online spaces. These conversations construct or reconfigure the properties, practices, and beliefs that people bring to their understanding of that object (Nakamura, 2006). As such, we can gain additional understandings about any cultural object that finds an interested web audience.

Social networking services—particularly in their mobile incarnations—are the most visible representations of an internetworked cultural identity bounded by a digital frame. Prior to the meteoric growth of smartphone use (and broadband internet), however, distributed Blackness manifested unevenly across blogging platforms and websites. This was because blogging platforms were conceived of as publishing spaces for individuals who *might* want to connect; accordingly, their search features prioritized topical content over community building. In the early days of blogging, practitioners worked around the individualist nature of these platforms by creating webrings and bloglists,[9] but as blogging went mainstream, these folksonomic features proved difficult to update and maintain. Still, Black blogger–led endeavors to build out Black blogging communities like the AfroSpear and others should be understood as the first attempts to seed a distributed Blackness spread across hundreds of Black-authored blogs and within the comments of thousands of enthusiast and general-interest mainstream blogs.

While Blackbird did not highlight blog content as a primary information source for Black community content, the blogs analyzed here can be understood as paratexts: the reactions offered by expert users, by expert Black users, and by Black users contextualize the various information needs that the browser serves and provides as a cultural infrastructure for Blacks and mainstream users. Blackbird's launch received a fair amount of press from technology blogs as well as blogs that featured dialogue on racial issues. To understand Blackbird's reception, I gathered a small set of blogs publishing reviews and reactions to the browser from a variety of perspectives.

The selected blogs are examples of how ideological and cultural factors influence users' technology analyses. They were selected through a purposive sampling of twenty-six blogs retrieved from a Google search using the keywords "Blackbird browser."[10] I created three categories from the results: high-profile (mainstream) technology blogs, Black technology blogs, and general-interest Black cultural blogs. All the blogs published a Blackbird review and include threaded comments featuring responses from the blog's community. To support my claim for a Black informational identity, this inquiry required data evincing conversations that (1) were about Blackness and the digital; (2) were not simply focused on the instrumental aspects of Blackbird's use; (3) involved multiple participants, none of whom were the original poster; and (4) contained multiple threads.

The Blogs

I feel compelled to write a historical note: when I first conducted this research, blogging was at or near its zenith as a Web 2.0 long-form mode of information publishing, consumption, and sharing. Since that time, social networking services have almost completely subsumed blogging content and practices. For example, Facebook (181 million US visitors) is eclipsed only by Google (206 million US visitors) as a space where users routinely visit to learn about the world's goings-on (Amazon, YouTube, Wikipedia, and Yahoo! round out the top six). In terms of longer-form information and news, only the *New York Times* and BuzzFeed crack the top twenty websites visited monthly (as of March 2017; Desjardins, 2017). Updating this inquiry to reflect changes in online information behaviors was never an option, however; Blackbird was an ephemeral creation of its time, and the analysis of the blogs presented here work well as a hermeneutic for understanding not just Blackbird but the World Wide Web, Black technoculture, and digital practice at a specific moment.

Gizmodo, formerly of the Gawker Media Group and now owned by Univision, is one of the most highly trafficked websites—not just technology blogs but all websites—in the United States on desktop and mobile (Alexa.com, n.d.). The financial success of its mission—providing breaking news on information technology, gadget and hardware reviews, and insight into tech industry culture—reveals much about Americans' fascination with computers and the internet. For this research, however, I chose two smaller technology websites. The first, TechCrunch—which at the initiation of this inquiry was still owned by its founder, venture capitalist and journalist Michael Harrington—was once one of the most popular destinations for Silicon Valley technology news and views (it has since lost many followers and now is *merely* in the top six hundred most-visited sites in the United States). The second technology website selected is Ars Technica. Ars was chosen because it, like many blogs of the time with journalistic aspirations,[11] features news and other stories written in an engaging, semiformal style while encouraging participation and feedback from a highly engaged, enthusiast community. Many of Ars's contributors hold postgraduate degrees, lending a certain measure of intellectual expertise and authority to the perspectives they bring to their technology coverage.

In terms of viewership, there has never been a Black technology website equivalent to Gizmodo. The closest current comparison is Marcus (MKBHD) Brownlee's extremely popular YouTube channel of technology reviews, but Brownlee does not feature breaking tech news or cultural takes on technology design and use. The Black tech blogs examined here, Roney Smith's site and BlackWeb 2.0, represent a less visible (and sadly, even less visible today) strain of technology blogging emphasizing coverage of technology products impacting African Americans. This is not to say that these two websites only focus on African American–oriented tech; rather, they were conceived to address the perceived lack of coverage of technology by, for, and about African Americans. Smith's blog features a banner image with text (originally in all caps) proclaiming the site's mission: "Readers of my blog will benefit from my technological experiences, exploits, misadventures, and learn from my mistakes. The topics discussed will not be limited to technology issues alone but since most blog entries are created through my cell phone, sharing opinions about technology will be at the forefront."

Angela Benton and Markus Robinson founded BlackWeb 2.0 in 2007. Their mission is to redress Benton's difficulty in finding information on

Black technology entrepreneurial and industry efforts. The site discusses key topics at the intersection of Black culture and technology, including Black media products and digital strategies. Thanks to Benton's acclaim as a digital influencer, BlackWeb 2.0 content is occasionally cross-posted to TechCrunch.

April Davis of AroundHarlem.com achieved fame in the late 2000s for her coverage of New York City's Black community events. Davis's archived "About Us" page mentions that Around Harlem was a national lifestyle magazine—primarily online—focusing on African Americans and people of color. The Angry Black Woman (TABW) blog, whose tagline is "Playing the Race Card since 2005," was founded by K. Tempest Bradford, a speculative fiction author of some renown. Bradford was a notable presence at LiveJournal, where she authored posts on science fiction, fantasy, race, and gender. TABW was a leading online voice among African American websites for its pungent critiques of racism, sexism, and stereotypes in various forms of media.

The chosen blogs are critical of Blackbird's feature set for many practical reasons, thanks to shared beliefs about what information technology in the age of Web 2.0 should do. In this, they highlight constructions of Western technocultural identity, which is shaped by ICT practices and technological determinism. Racial frames, however, also shape these technocultural identities. Of particular interest for this chapter is how, due to the racialized design intention of the browser, the respondents—regardless of racial affiliation—mediate their explanations of racial identity through articulations of information technology. By examining how web users understand technology through their proclaimed cultural affiliations, we can better comprehend how belief and ideology shape information technology use, implementation, and design.

Analysis: Features

I found that the Blackbird feature set triggered discourse about the racial implications of a cultural browser. These discussions were rarely complimentary of either the design or the implementation, regardless of the cultural orientation of the critiquing website and community. Reviewers tended to focus on an "ideal" browser as a culturally neutral information space for internet consumption—configurable for individual browsing preferences but initially set up to be as generic as possible in order to serve the greatest number of people. By fixating on a browser's capacity for individualization and personalization, the reviewers' instrumental approach elides the cultural and ideological nature of the content the browser allows access to.

For example, in his review of Blackbird on TechCrunch, Robin Wauters notes the browser's capacity to reach culturally relevant content but does not assay whether that should be an incentive for use. This is significant because Wauters also mentions the browser-specific features (e.g., the ticker) and writes that their addition does not seem like a compelling incentive for Black people to download yet another browser; however, he does not go as far as to speculate what features would entice Black browser users.[12] TechCrunch's commenters, however, pile on to Wauters's instrumental and ostensibly neutral review by adding racial considerations to their discussion of the feature set.

A commenter called Que notes the lack of in-depth Black cultural content:

> One good thing I can see it has a bookmarks [*sic*] to most Historic African American Colleges everything else looks like this was put together by a focus group which was asked a bunch of question and they built it from the results and that way you would never gets things right.

Dentalchicken writes,

> Does the browser know the difference in content? Facial recognition for the imagery, looking for definitive slang terms in the textual content?

Jason Jobbs, concerned about the elision of Black-run online communities, asks,

> Also, whats [*sic*] with Facebook and Myspace? Where the true Black communities, Blackplanet.com, Nuplay.tv, if they actually had brothers making this software it would reference true Black communities.

Max, writing about perceptions of the lack of Black digital expertise, says,

> It's one thing to build CONTENT targeted at [a] particular target audience. . . . It's another thing to build a TOOL that essentially implies that the standard tool (regular Mozilla) is somehow "too smart" "too white" or otherwise not good enough for blacks. That's just insulting.

Concerns about digital segregation also arose in the TechCrunch comments. Around Harlem's April Davis writes,

> I don't like filtered browsers because I see it [as] a step backwards in technology. . . . Once you control content through a browser you control access to information.

An anonymous commenter emphatically chimes in from a color-blind perspective:

> This is hilarious. HEY GUYS, LETS [*sic*] MAKE A BROWSER THAT HAS A COMPLETELY SUPERFLUOUS FUNCTION! ALSO I REALLY LIKE THE IDEA OF A BROWSER MEANT TO CREATE NEW SOCIAL BARRIERS IN AN AGE WHEN INTERNET ANONYMITY MIGHT ACTUALLY BREAK THOSE BARRIERS DOWN!

Jdb, expanding on the cultural neutrality of color-blind technology use, writes,

> No one is going to convince me that Google is white by default unless you want to argue that being simple, quick and useful is "white." LOL. The thing is that from an ideal perspective when a user logs onto the Internet they are starting from a "unified" and "unfiltered" position and choose to navigate toward targeted content. The difference here is that someone has developed a "tool" that controls and filters the "experience" right from the start. They've found a way to create a segregated experience.

Finally, Pat Long writes in support of Blackbird's mission by comparing it to Apple's control of the user experience with Safari:

> I am an African American male, have been in technology for over 10 years, and don't see anything wrong with the idea of a browser that serves content that may interest me and my demographic.
>
> When I buy a new Mac, by Safari browser sort of does the same thing. It has a start page and preset bookmarks that appeal to me as a Mac user.
>
> With the popularity of African American culture, I am sure a lot of people will be checking it out. Anyone is free to use it, it doesn't care who you are.
>
> Advertising partners and content relationships seem to be the next natural progression for this browser. Except for not running on a Mac, the initial concept seems fine by me.

Over on Ars Technica, David Chartier (2008) begins his Blackbird review by claiming that the internet created "a largely color-blind World Wide Web." He comments that Blackbird's only notable changes from a standard Firefox install are the ticker and a toolbar that incorporates cultural content–oriented features. Chartier also mentions the Blackbird custom search, as it returns results for African American users that would not be returned from a standard Google search. Overall, however, Chartier argues that Blackbird's feature set is "nothing new" in the vein of targeted browsers. To contextualize this claim, Chartier compares Blackbird to the Flock browser, which he argues for as something "altogether different" from a default browser and a "great all-in-one-tool."

Chartier's review deserves praise for his interview of Ed Young, the Black CEO of 40A. He asks Young why 40A did not simply produce Firefox add-ons (at the time, Firefox enjoyed a 21 percent share of the browser market) and appears to question whether Blackbird could be considered exclusionary to whites. Young fields these questions deftly, relating Blackbird's audience to another highly engaged tech community (Warcraft gamers) and arguing that Blackbird was intended to bring "those people" closer to the sites they are interested in.

In the Ars Technica comments following the article, the audience apes the behavior of the TechCrunch commenters, racializing their responses regarding Blackbird's feature set.[13] For example, Murph182 worries that the custom search will be biased against white folk, asking,

> If Obama starts doing all kinds of nutty stuff, will a standard search return news articles and criticism and the Blackbird search censor such things?

Davidd adds insult to injury, suggesting that Blacks primarily search online for help with criminal behavior:

> So it comes pre-loaded with links to Public Defenders, and tips on how to beat weapons charges. . . . Great.

Rpgspree argues that the browser will prioritize Black culture over "authoritative" information, writing,

> If the browser, as the article states, skews results away from potentially more informative and authoritative sources of information in favor of those that are more culture centric, then it really is doing it's [*sic*] users a disservice.

Some Ars Technica commenters fight back against the tone of these comments. Oluseyi writes that the browser's intent is inclusion rather than segregation:

> You could argue that the browser is not an "African American browser," but rather an "African American Interest browser." Nothing precludes non-Black Americans from using it, and it's very likely that a large number of its eventual users will be non-blacks.

Stagoleee adds that Blackbird's intent is to provide specific information to an underserved audience:

> The browser developer is saying "if you would like a browser that helps to narrow down content to what our team has identified as having an African American focus, then download/install/use Blackbird."

Anechoic writes that the long-term sustainability of the product might be questionable, but its ethos is not antiwhite:

> Blackbird isn't about "walled gardens" or "separatism"—it doesn't take you to some blacks-only internet, it doesn't wipe your harddrive [*sic*] if a white person tries to use it, it's a product designed to appeal to the needs and wants of blacks. You can disagree with the viability of this model (which I do) but there's nothing wrong with the motivation.

On Black tech blogs, analysis of Blackbird's feature set was seated within a positive communitarian framework even as the observers took an instrumental approach to the technology itself. That is, while mainstream blogs featured many comments slamming the feature set and Black culture, Black tech blogs and their audiences evaluated Blackbird's features from a Black communitarian perspective. For example, blogger Roney Smith has a complimentary yet critical review of the browser. He compliments the RSS ticker but points out that allowing users to access social services they subscribe to within the browser itself yields "no newly created value." Smith adds that because many African Americans access the internet at work or school, Blackbird's browser-centric orientation limits them to access only on their home machines. This criticism is valid given the nature of corporate and institutional IT policies, which seek to prohibit their users from installing unapproved software on company machines in order to prevent viruses or software malfunctions. Smith's other feature criticism is directed toward Blackbird's video channel, which is also limited to in-browser viewing. While noting that the feature represents Blackbird's greatest opportunity for user adoption and growth, Smith contends that if a user found a video of interest but wanted to share it with a non-Blackbird user, that friend would be unable to view the content. While these comments stem from a Black cultural perspective, they are embedded in a pungent critique of TechCrunch's review and of mainstream tech pundits' reactions to Blackbird. Smith's commenters do not directly respond to his analysis point by point; however, one commenter, TGrundy, praises the review by calling it "sensible, rational, technical."

BlackWeb 2.0's initial appraisal of Blackbird's feature set, written by frequent contributor Markus Robinson, is positive. Robinson briefly mentions the ticker, video channels, and Blackbird's search engine under the premise that they provide a tailored experience for Blacks that was previously hard to find. He enthuses about the possibility of Blackbird allowing developers to customize add-ons through the import of Firefox plug-ins from preexisting Mozilla configuration files. A follow-up Black-Web 2.0 post on Blackbird written by a less prominent contributor named Rahsheen delves more deeply into the browser's unique features. He compares Blackbird's Grapevine feature to Digg while knocking it for being accessible only through the browser. Rasheed also remarks on a feature other reviewers missed: the Blackbird Local business directory. This feature was designed to address the enormous difficulty Black information seekers encounter when searching for Black-owned businesses online. Neither print directories, search engines, nor review sites highlight "culture" as a prominent search criterion; thus Black consumers must rely on word-of-mouth to find businesses catering to their needs. On a follow-up post published to his personal blog, Rahsheen positively reviews Blackbird's video channel and is encouraged by the browser's stance on philanthropy. However, he argues that Blackbird is not innovative because it uses preexisting features that power users can install on their own as plug-ins, themes, and custom Google searches. Rahsheen also brings up the idea of the "browser as information portal," which was a point of contention for both of the Black general-interest blogs. He contends that a browser oriented toward information of interest to Black people limits access to the wider, mainstream internet while potentially stifling Black innovation and interest in creating online content for audiences outside the Black community.

Blackbird's feature coverage by BlackWeb 2.0's writers consisted of mostly instrumental analyses of features or interface elements. However, their appraisals of Blackbird's utility as a digital artifact also incorporated perspectives on mainstream technology website responses to Black technology efforts. This leads to my arguments for Black technology blogs employing a communitarian frame to understand the browser. For example, Robinson closes his review by arguing that Blackbird's identity affiliation is not a separatist or segregationist approach; it only differs from Flock (and Gloss) in that it places Black information needs and Black culture at the forefront. Similarly, Rahsheen asks, "Do we gain anything by gathering all of this useful and relevant African American information only to lock it inside of a walled-garden, only accessible via a single niche browser?" These perspectives signal an awareness of the diminished visibility of Black digital content and the concomitant antiblack dismissal and perception of the value of Black information to Black online users.

Over on the Black general-interest blogs, K. Tempest Bradford of TABW criticized Blackbird's hijacking of the "default application" status for internet access. In her review, she argues against the browser as a targeted marketing application intended to serve a demographic to advertisers:

> If someone wants to de-marginalize news relevant to Black people, videos relevant to Black people, and social networking/bookmarks relevant to Black people, that's great. I am all for it. But I think doing it through a "Black" browser isn't terribly affective. Or, I should say, it's effective from a marketing standpoint, but from a user standpoint, not so much. What if I like my current browser?

In TABW's comments on the analysis, however, the audience members offer a different take. Jermyn asks, "When will Black innovation avoid criticism and get the respect it so much deserves?" Ben notes that culture can predetermine online behavior:

> Perhaps Mozilla will hire some Black developers (these 3 gentlemen?) in the future and bring more culture-based (not necessarily race) ideas into the way we use the internet. . . . Take a look at the way the Japanese use the internet. They do not use URIs, only "search" to get to websites. That has greatly influenced the way we are using Firefox and other browsers over the last year.

Balabusta adds that mainstream search engines obscure Black search results through noise:

> It is true that if one is very interested in African-American perspectives on news and social issues, one has to be savvy in the use of search engines, which do not cough up those results without good Google-fu. . . . As a white person with an anti-racist ideology who is interested in reading from [a] Black perspective, I would have downloaded and used the browser just out of curiosity.

April Davis of Around Harlem included her commentary on the browser on TechCrunch as part of her perspective on Blackbird's feature set. She remarks that customized searches and developer-implemented filters are counter to the internet's inherent properties of open information access and could be considered segregationist:

> As a website publisher, Blog-AroundHarlem.com, I totally believe in, support, and understand connecting with African Americans online.
>
> However, I have a problem with using and suggesting that a technology product is superior because it's geared towards African Americans.
>
> Surely, with the filtering process, my content is being limited.
>
> There are several reasons for websites geared towards African Americans, and other niche populations, but I feel that this must be done in a manner that engages and supports without making products/services subpar because of limitations and tech sacrifices that are made for revenue generating purposes.

On her blog, Davis begins by unequivocally stating, "I don't need anyone helping me find Black content." She also argues that Blackbird's implementation reveals a lack of innovation: "(Skinned = same technology with custom user interface.) Bad idea. Very bad." Davis then gets to the heart of her instrumental critique of Blackbird: "Technology can't be African American. Or, any other ethnic/racial group." She continues by asking,

> How is my web experience enhanced by letting Blackbird filter information through their browser? By visiting African American sites "they" select? Who are "they"? What qualifies them to select African American content? Any Black Studies PhDs or "African American experts" affiliated with the site to determine "the best content"? What is their criteria for acceptable content? Is there any?

Davis's query proffers an individualist and color-blind argument for Black heterogeneity set against a backdrop of American racial ideology's perception of the Black community as an undifferentiated, low-class mass. Moreover, this query also sharply criticizes information technology's cultural competence for defining Black digital practitioners and "acceptable content." Her structural criticism about the culture-neutral orientation of technology belies her earlier statement about being able to find cultural content using the same technology, given her status as a power user. Davis's view possesses validity from experiential, material, and instrumental perspectives—a browser *is* ostensibly designed to agnostically display content—while glossing over the ideological nature of Western communicative artifacts and the content they disseminate.

Around Harlem's commenters picked up on Davis's argument and added some additional considerations and caveats. Allison writes about the possibilities of online segregation:

> Instead of pushing for major browsers or websites to feature AA interest [*sic*], separate browsers and websites are built.

Tiffany adds,

> Blackbird is basically catering to a niche. . . . It's certainly not taking America back by offering a web browser that caters to a particular group of people.

DryerBuzz counters with appreciation for 40A's attempt to provide a curated Black online experience:

> If there are two products and one is provided with me distinctly in the demographic, its conducive to my uniqueness (being that I'm so unique), then I'm gonna go for it. . . . In my browsing experience I don't want to see watered down diversity with a few curly heads pictured and peppered here and there. While my brilliance will allow me to conform anything to my uniqueness, I appreciate those who at least attempt to make me a priority.

Some Black tech bloggers and enthusiasts dropped into the comments to support Davis's perspective on Blackbird limiting the internet. Rahsheen (BlackWeb 2.0) compares Blackbird to a content-limited version of Twitter, arguing,

> How useful would Twitter be if you could only see tweets that have #blck in them? You could only follow people who use the #blck tag. Everyone else disappears. That sound cool? Ok, now do the same thing with the entire Internet. Does that work for you?

Karsh, of BlackGayBlogger.com, said Blackbird was commercially unsustainable, writing that the browser was "as inane and untenable a concept to bring to market as any other web product or SaaS [*sic*] which tries to commodify African-Americans."

The Around Harlem debate over the feature set reveals an urgent concern over how a racial identity frame could limit an ICT's usefulness. This concern is remarkable precisely because of the linkage between Blackness and limitation, where the internet's value is somehow lessened because users seek Black content. Note that the critics of Blackbird's feature sets—regardless of venue—deride the browser because they assume it will *only* allow access to Black content, which is contrary to the browser's intent and design. Blackbird allows users to specify multiple search engine plug-ins and websites, just like Firefox. Thus while the objections are ostensibly directed against the browser's limitations, the limitations discussed are primarily ideological. That is, the objections derive energy from a white racial framework, where Blackness signifies a lesser state of being; an all-Black internet is argued as being less valuable than an internet where Blackness is (at best) an insignificant presence in a universe of content supporting a white ideological frame. Blackbird's highlighting of African American content is seen as an imposition on the universal appeal and beliefs of the internet's informational "neutrality."

Analysis: Browsers and Beliefs

Up to this point, my inquiry into Blackbird as an information technology artifact has focused on discourses about the instrumental and material aspects of the browser: the chrome, the interface, and the various functions. These discussions evaluated the efficacy and design shortcomings of the browser's features as measures of whether they addressed an ideal Black information user. This is largely in line with my theory of Western technocultural belief, where progress and modernity are thematic concerns informing technology design and use.

I have long argued that information technologies have a racial aspect—moreover, that racialization only clearly manifests when one takes seriously Pacey's (1984) argument that all technologies have a belief aspect. In other words, the default belief of many is that technologies are value-neutral. This claim is extraordinarily well supported when examining the responses to Blackbird as a racial apparatus and belief structure on the mainstream technology sites. Given the majority-white demographics of the tech communities at TechCrunch and Ars Technica, it was surprising to find so many commenters denigrating or defending the internet as a social structure based on the perceived limitations of a Black informational identity.

While both mainstream online communities are considered information technology interest sites, Ars can be characterized as more of a professional community, whereas TechCrunch is an enthusiast and tech industry site. These characterizations help determine each site's discursive ethos. Because Ars is professionally oriented, moderators can (and do) openly intervene in conversations by closing threads and banning commenters for conduct that is unbecoming the site. TechCrunch has tried a number of comment-moderation platforms to manage their community; at the time of this research, they were using Facebook (and its "real name" feature) in an attempt to rein in their commenting audience.

On Ars, JChops goes directly to racist stereotypes to contextualize Black internet user behavior:

> Blackbird browser? Next thing you know, they'll have their own computer company. Instead of Apple, it'll be Watermelon. And the CEO will be Steve Jobless. And it'll run OS X BLACK PANTHER.[14] Hell, the browser can send its user agent string as "Blackbird" and you could tailor your site to shovel KFC ads and overpriced futon furniture at them. Can you see the 404 pages for this thing? Instead of "404," you'll get "Nigga, you isn't makin' no sense!" I'll be here all week.[15]

I Palindrome I, an Ars Technica managing editor with more than seventeen thousand posts, apparently does not see the humor. They quote JChops's post and add, "Actually, you won't." Since I Palindrome I has the power to remove offensive commenters, it is entirely possible that they banned JChops for this unnecessary insight.

I have characterized Ars's and TechCrunch's commenting communities as largely white, which gives short shrift to the nonwhite commenters who frequent these spaces. For example, another commenter on Ars, stagolee (a reference to a mythical Black hero), writes about the consequences of acknowledging race online:

> As an African American my senses get prickly when posts like this pop up on race-neutral sites. I can be confident that there will be a rash of the following: "If white people did this the world would end!!!" "But we're nice to Black people now, why do they insist on still being blackity Black black?" "Are the dialog boxes in jive talk?" Some of you are thoughtful, but some others here are right and proper assholes who are not worthy of an intelligent response.

Of the sites collected for this research, TechCrunch had the largest number of comments. The site's technoenthusiast and business-friendly ethos attracts a narrow range of highly engaged, technically proficient internet commenters. In many cases, their activity consists of complaining about the shortcomings of TechCrunch's technological expertise or the perceived biases toward certain manufacturers. There is some measure of the complaining ethos apparent in the comments about Blackbird, but the discourse on display at times pushes the limits of civility thanks to the rupture provided by Blackness. One comment by a thoughtful contributor named Nigger is simply the word *NIGGER* repeated 1,681 times, which coincidentally happens to occupy two and a half screens of text. This tactic is as old as chatrooms, where trolls would seek to disrupt discourse by not allowing anyone else to participate.

If I were to characterize TechCrunch's discourse regarding the Blackbird browser, I would say that many argued for the internet as an artifact promoting a color-blind ideology (from Blacks and from whites). The user Ben W offers a thorough example of color-blindness in tech, deprecating race-as-culture in the process:

> Silly? Yes. Racist? No.
>
> People self-assign to the groups, and there is no advantage gained by neither its use nor disuse. It may just be a bit segregationist, but Marcus Garvey would approve.

> People choosing to identify on the comments that their comment is from a Black person just shows how little race matters on the internet, and how it only becomes an issue when someone pushes it. Anonymous exists in a sphere beyond race. It does show a scary trend that now people need to share their race with strangers to be considered relevant.
>
> The mere existence of this browser has much less effect on racist tensions than making people feel guilty for trying to identify with their culture. That being said, race isn't really a good indicator of culture, especially for the tech crowd (early adopters or people willing to try new web browsers). It just suffers from poor naming a few lame features that use "black" instead of "urban" or some other equally lame non-racial identifier.

Other TechCrunch commenters have no problem displaying their racial animus. Their arguments draw on a technocultural frame promoting (racial) progress, modernity, and a social status quo that implicitly continues white domination. For example, L. applies a "reverse racism" fallacy, writing,

> I agree with many people here. To be honest, I think this is the most racist thing I've seen. If this was whitebird, it would be hit with thousands talking about racism, but because it's for african americans it's not racist at all? This isn't a biased opinion considering I'm latin american, just in case you were wondering.

Loris directly links Blackness, crime, and information seeking:

> Um. . . . What news does a Black person want to hear and what makes that any different than the news the rest of America hears? Let me guess, they're going to bring up articles on local gang shootings and the newest rap cd's? Give me a break. What makes ANY demographic so different that they'd need their own web browser. Corporate America is getting out of hand with this.

Commenter lola applies stereotypes of Black laziness to the browser:

> I guess since it's "black" it will never work ☺

Whereas yeswecan, arguing from a Black-oriented color-blind perspective, rails against the implied segregation from mainstream information sources:

> Its like the perfect tool to help reinforce modern day Black boundaries and limitations. Brilliant. Its the kind of condescension only the kkk could consider backing. Fortunately it will fail. Anyone with an ounce of dignity would shrug this off. I am not a target market for your bullshit. I am a people. And my color is not your business. Build a website for this kind of content is fine. But i arrive there and depart anonymous. The advertisers can bite it.

This is not to say that incivility characterizes TechCrunch's discourse community; there are some excellent comments excoriating the racist attitudes on display. For example, NO ID demurs from using Blackbird, drawing on an individualist Black perspective, but still supports the browser:

> Naaah, I won't use this browser. The same way I won't go to a Black hair salon (since I wear locs) the same way I won't go to a Black club, listen to Black radio, watch Black cable channels, go to Black bookstores or join a Black sorority or fraternity.
>
> Can't see why any of the above would be necessary . . . yet they all exist.
>
> I downloaded the browser and love it. The news ticker alone is worth it. Instead of having to go through zillions of content aggregators or RSS feesds [*sic*], I can have content at my fingertips which helps me in my job.
>
> People on this board remind me why even in the midst of an economic recession and with jobs hard to find, I'd almost rather go back to working for Black media than having to work with folks whose attitudes (and I'm sure anonymity helps) reflect the folks on this board. I'm going to check out this sister's Black2.0 website so thanks for that info, as I'd rather be there with people that I likely don't have to explain the 400 odd years of racism in this country nor defend the fact that actually I love and revel in Black culture. I don't want to be "mainstream," I want to be myself. And that is why despite the naysayers here, amongst non-tech heads, the browser is likely to be successful.

On both Ars and TechCrunch, counterdiscourses featuring social justice themes are deployed by a number of commenters. They are remarkable in the amount of thought and detail put into them; some are nearly a full page in length. These remarks, however, are far outnumbered by comments featuring color-blind ideology and others that use the internet as a racist framework. For example, Sick of Ignorant Racists debunks color-blind ideology while noting its implicit racism:

> Equality does not mean that anyone of any race need[s] to leave interests unique to their culture at the door. Ironically, it's only the worst type of racists who try to sell the idea that this is necessary for eliminating racism. Those who truly celebrate equality celebrate the right of every group to express the uniqueness of their culture—without being so threatened that they have to resort to petty namecalling and thinly (VERY THINLY) veiled racism.

Amber is not sold on the idea but joins in to contextualize the furor over the tech within the longer arc of civil rights struggles in America:

> While I personally think this is a stupid idea (though the news ticker is genius) the comments here have made me sad. I sit here and say wow you know just 40 years ago my grandmother was getting spat on and getting rocks thrown at her for being Black but today look how far we have have come . . . and then I see really not that far when I see this kind of stuff.

A Black Avatar of Digital Civil Rights

Finally, at the time, TechCrunch was home to one of the most peculiar examples of the internet as a racial apparatus I have ever come across in my research. Several commenters invoke President Barack Hussein Obama to contextualize their responses to the features and intent of the Blackbird browser. OoOo writes,

> Obama, Blackbird . . . are whites a minority now? Btw not racist in the least bit but theres [*sic*] too much African American pride going around nowadays.

Jdb comments,

> To me filtering the experience from the start is antithetical to this dream. I don't get it and don't see how anyone would want this in this day and age especially right after we've elected a Black president which demonstrates how far we've come to achieve this [MLK's] dream.

Obama is conjured here to demonstrate the ongoing degeneracy of an American society that caters to the needs of African Americans. Moreover, Obama's name is also invoked to show that America has become postracial and that our browsers should reflect this supposed state of racial comity. Blogger Roney Smith links Black respectability, Black radicalism, and cultural technology design:

> Currently Blackbird has a Civil Rights mindset when a Barack Obama approach is preferred and welcomed.

Obama can be understood across these examples as an avatar for the Black digital in the American tradition both as a sign of technological progress and as a component of Blackness and deviance.

Laying the Body to Rest: Analysis Summary

In retrospect, the Black bloggers' and commenters' noncommittal responses to Blackbird outline several possibilities for Black cyberculture. Several describe their blogs and websites as interventions—as acts of resistance against mainstream technology sites that rarely cover material of interest to Black technology and computer enthusiasts. In this vein, TABW and Around Harlem's reviews of Blackbird promote positive Black cultural values even as they strongly criticize the technological and cultural limitations of the browser. Their reactions to the guided nature of Blackbird's interactions with the web conflate the libertarian, individualistic rhetoric of internet use with a Black cultural resistance to white racial ideology's assignation of Black identity to the nadir of modern society.

On the Black blogs—both tech-oriented and general-interest sites—reviewers draw heavily from a Black communitarian perspective to contextualize their findings. Indeed, I was impelled to create a Black technocultural matrix in part because these Black websites articulate nascent rationales for Black technology use predicated on Blackness as a norm for information use and behavior. The Black technocultural matrix is responsive (and often resistant) to Western technoculture given that Blackness is a syncretic creation of Western imperialism and thus inseparable from Western conceptualizations of white identity. Blackness, from the perspective of the Western technocultural matrix, can be understood as the antiblack libidinal economy of Western whiteness and technology.

TABW's and Around Harlem's interpretations of Blackbird's potential, however, give weight to my arguments about racial identity—that is, their elucidations are Black respectability–based versions of Western technoculture's antiblackness formulations of Black behavior and culture. Both groups view Blackbird's approach as segregationist. The mainstream tech blog commenters conjure up images of Black pathology (e.g., weed locators, twenty-four-inch rims) while arguing that culturally oriented approaches are divisive and racist. Similarly, the Black cultural bloggers (and their audiences) worry about the technocultural consequences of being "left behind" or segregated from the wider economic and technological possibilities of online information through Blackbird's selective focus on Black cultural websites and media.

Discussion

Given the increasing levels of complexity in our information and communication devices and the interpenetration of internet-hosted content into our everyday lives, we often have little time or energy to reflect on how ICTs will improve our lives. Upon its introduction, Blackbird made an astonishing claim: it would curate a heretofore unconsidered experience—an informational online Blackness for personal improvement and empowerment. New technologies—and browsers are no exception—claim to be faster, shinier, and more customizable; as a "niche" browser with new features designed specifically for Black users, Blackbird claimed to be "all that and then some." However, Blackbird's reception marks a rupture in American communicative infrastructure, achieving a level of scrutiny and critique that other browsers have never had to undergo—namely, the open articulation of libidinal energies and beliefs about appropriate technology use and appropriate technology users. For example, this inquiry marks one of the few times in my personal recollection that a sitting president was used to exemplify the power *and* the failure of a computational artifact and its constituent networks.

In the examination of a technological artifact and the practices associated with it, beliefs about American technoculture invoked in the blogs examined are made apparent. The niche community targeted by Blackbird—the 13 percent of Americans collectively labeled "African Americans"—occupies a disproportionately large mindshare in American culture, much of it pejorative and discriminatory. Some comments reveal the libidinal energies of anger and despair over the perceived erosion of white hegemony and American culture. They show that technocultural beliefs about the web as a color-blind space are, in truth, markers of whiteness and its control of the future. Indeed, several commenters are outspokenly racist at a time when *postracial* had become the watchword of the day. Many others reveal confusion at Blackbird's temerity in imposing a Black cultural framework on ostensibly neutral information and communication technologies. These comments, made in online spaces dedicated to technorationality and its adherents, significantly outnumber reasoned responses to the browser made by other commenters.

My analysis emphasizes the role of paratexts in articulating beliefs about technology use. Blogs, where audience members become coauthors in the contestation or maintenance of arguments presented by online content, illustrate the influence of sociocultural factors on the publication of and participation in web content. These websites can be configured to provide minorities and women the opportunity to populate and maintain discursive spaces that may differ from (or support) mainstream attitudes and beliefs. Blogs' public nature and ease of access have expanded the scope of personal participation and expression and, not incidentally, contributed to the construction of online identities.

I find that the blog-based expositions of criticism, reflection, and analysis of everyday objects (like internet browsers) reveal how technology users employ tech to help process their internal identity formations. Their articulations of identity in a public networked space make apparent the importance of exteriority to the formation of the self and to conceptions of race. The internal formation takes place in the blog's intimate reveal of the author's feelings about a particular worldview. The external formation—that is, the role of the "not-I" in defining identity—becomes visible through the social interactions between the blog's author and commenters and the electronic interactions embodied in hyperlinks to social networks, externally hosted media, and other content.

Conclusions

Langlois (2014) argues that technological culture depends on the value placed on access to and use of the products of technology. Blackbird's formulation, however, demurs from technocultural values of impersonality and pragmatic rationality to instead proffer information as a communitarian, cultural endeavor. Blackbird's feature set and community orientation argue for Blackness as a collective identity—one that troubled some of the Black tech bloggers—and also for the vanilla browser's aggregation and presentation of information as a formulation of white communal identity even with the attendant personalization possibilities available to users.

Given these possibilities, I contend that the Blackbird browser can be understood as a digital manifestation of double consciousness. Rawls (2000) contends, "Double consciousness has to do with differences in the experience of being an individual in [the] two communities, and not with marginalized social roles within a single community" (p. 244). Blackbird's execution of internet access and information provision illuminate content that is reflective and responsive to concerns of Black everyday life even while it mediates that content through an artifact that "take[s] the role of the white 'other' towards the [white] self" embodied within information "without any fundamental contradiction" (p. 244) or reflection.

April Davis's powerful question regarding the validity and authenticity of African American online content is the basis of my claim for Blackness as an *informational identity*. This term is meant to reconfigure Black discursive identity inclusive of Black digital practice—that is, the enactment of Blackness through the mediation of computational and digital technologies. These computational and digital aspects are not traits of Blackness per se; they are culturally inflected curatorial, archival, data, and metadata practices needed to build out and maintain Black digital spaces and communities. Informational identity differs from discursive identity in that it places the medium on a near-equal footing with the content of the discourse; in many ways, informational identity allows one to capture the nonverbal components of Black digitality (a la signifyin' discourse) necessary to evoke online Blackness.

Blackbird's design and reception offer potent demonstrations of the intersubjectivities between technological capacity and racial identity. The browser—a banal technology if ever there was one given its invisibility as a mediator of information—structures the internet as an individual endeavor. That this individuality maps onto the accessibility of and access to content that is amenable to the informational pleasures and needs of whiteness is not accidental. The internet's command and separation of space, time, and communication is the latest iteration of modernity's imputation of the *transcendence* of white racial identity, particularly with respect to enterprise, rationality, and command of the earth itself (Dyer, 1997).

Blackbird ruptured Western technocultural belief in its formulation of Blackness as a normal internet identity even as its reception revealed the connections between white identity and technical capacity. Blackbird's efforts to make Black internet *content* visible to Black *users* revealed beliefs about whiteness as the default racial identity associated with internet use and design, as demonstrated by proficient white users on enthusiast blogs like Ars Technica. Blackbird's release also showed that technorational values represent a racialized libidinal economic perspective on information access and use even as it proved that these values are not the only available perspectives.

3

"The Black Purposes of Space Travel"

Black Twitter as Black Technoculture

> He can read my writing but he sho can't read my mind.
>
> —Zora Neale Hurston

Forty-five years ago, long before the commercial internet spaces we know as the World Wide Web timorously considered the possibility of Black folk online, the poet Amiri Baraka turned his considerable intellect toward contemplating the possibilities of Black culture and information technology. Citing Norbert Wiener's contention that machines are an extension of their creators, Baraka (1965) argues for an informational Blackness, writing,

> If I invented a word placing machine, an "expression-scriber," if you will, then I would have a kind of instrument into which I could step & sit or sprawl or hang & use not only my fingers to make words express feelings but elbows, feet, head, behind, and all the sounds I wanted, screams, grunts, taps, itches, I'd have magnetically recorded, at the same time, & translated into word—or perhaps even the final xpressed thought/feeling wd not be merely word or sheet, but itself, the xpression, three dimensional—able to be touched, or tasted or felt, or entered, or heard or carried like a speaking singing constantly communicating charm. (p. 154)

Baraka's "informational Blackness" has three components. The first is cultural. By arguing for Blackness as embodied cultural cognition, Baraka's premise drives my arguments for Black pathos as an epistemological standpoint, where one's body is the interface between the world and sociocultural phenomena and cognition. The second is technological. Baraka fantasizes about inventing a modern communications device, firmly situating Black creativity as *techné*, or practice grounded in theoretical understanding.[1] The final premise is technocultural. Baraka transforms Black cultural practice into informational Blackness by linking cultural communication practices to then extant music-recording technologies or even future iterations of information and communication technologies.

Baraka's words could easily apply to today's digital and social media practices and technologies. Specifically, his description of the "final xpressed thought/feeling" as three dimensional or "heard or carried like a speaking singing constantly communicating charm" neatly maps onto the ways in which our smartphones have become part of our embodied cognition; it also speaks to Black Twitter's demonstration of how culture crafts digital practice.

Baraka asks an important question, one that Western technoculture and algorithmic computation rarely ask—namely, Could an informational technology possess a "spirit as emotional construct that can manifest as expression as art or technology" (p. 154)? Baraka's "expression" involves kinesthetics, linguistic discourse, visual aesthetics, and affect overlaid upon (and perhaps even supplanting) the rationalist, neoliberal practices envisioned by Western information technology creators and policy makers. I extend his definition of *expression* by linking spirit to Black interiority and reflexivity, or as Moten (2013) would say, the "dispossessive force of Black speech" (p. 770). Interiority and reflexivity demand a full engagement with a world structured to displace Blackness. Black speech, from this position, signifies upon and through discourses to communicate and socialize within a reality where we can recover subjectivity and agency. That Black discursive styles are rhythmic, stylish, striking, and visceral is an inevitable facet of engagement with a world that demands rationality, hierarchy, and control.

Finally, Baraka closes by asking, "What are the Black purposes of space travel?" My answer to this question is Black Twitter. What is Black Twitter? The answer to this second question has evolved since I first wrote about Black folk on Twitter in 2012. The brief answer: Black Twitter is Twitter's mediation of Black cultural identity, expressed through digital practices and informed by cultural discourses about Black everyday life. One cultural-digital practice, the hashtag, works to bring Black Twitter to the surface of mainstream visibility.

The longer answer: Black Twitter is an online gathering (not quite a community) of Twitter users who identify as Black *and* employ Twitter features to perform Black discourses, share Black cultural commonplaces, and build social affinities. While there are a number of non-Black and people of color Twitter users who have been "invited to the cookout," so to speak, participating in Black Twitter requires a deep knowledge of Black culture, commonplaces, and digital practices. As I briefly noted in the introduction, being Black in the American racial context requires intentionality; representation and recognition are only part of the equation. Thus Black Twitter users intentionally signal their cultural affiliations to a like-minded audience in a space where, until recently, racial identity was considered a niche endeavor. While their use of Twitter accrues to them a technological identity that intersects with their racial and gendered selves, Black Twitter users are as heterogeneous as the community they hail from. The combination of social affinities, network participation, and content enables Black Twitter hashtags to "trend," or gain visibility through Twitter's trending topic algorithm.

More specifically, the digital + virtual practices and affordances of Black Twitter map onto the ritual, formalized performance of embodied, libidinal Black identity discourses, distributing Black discursive identity across the service and into the wider information sphere. Libidinal discourses drive the joys of Black Twitter musings on #DemThrones[2] and other manifestations of Black everyday life. Libidinal energies also power Black Twitter catharsis: the political engagement and righteous anger of Black Lives Matter and articulations of racial fatigue syndrome characterized by #SayHerName.[3]

This longer definition acknowledges but does not overly emphasize the contribution of the Black Twitter hashtag to either the formulation or the composition of the community. The hashtag offers participants and viewers topical and cultural coherence and in the process renders Twitter slightly less chaotic. However, its primary utility for Black Twitter is the visibility of a Black informational identity to the mainstream afforded by its uptake in Twitter's trending topic feature. The hashtag and trending topic work together to make Black Twitter visible to users of the service and to the wider information sphere, allowing non-Black outsiders to see an informational culture that is strikingly similar, yet significantly different, from their own.

Analyze This

As with other chapters, I analyze Black Twitter as a three-part phenomenon:

1. As a technical artifact
   - hardware and protocols necessary to use Black Twitter
   - Twitter interface (client)
2. As a practice
   - technical and digital literacy conventions
   - discourse conventions
   - Black discourse conventions
3. As a set of beliefs
   - in-group beliefs about race and technology
   - in-group beliefs about race
   - out-group beliefs about race and technology
   - out-group beliefs about race

This chapter focuses primarily on the Twitter interface. As was made clear by Blackbird, digital technologies hail their users, primarily defining and capturing them through interactions with the interface. It is tempting to reduce Twitter to the tweet, but doing so reduces the possibilities for understanding digital practice as expertise, which allows one to examine the material and functional rationales behind Twitter use. Thus I also survey selected Twitter antecedents—mobile phone adoption, short-message service (SMS), and the messaging application TXTmob—to highlight how a number of elements contribute to Twitter's capacity to mediate Black discursive practice. From the interface, I move on to the technical practices that are necessary to participate in Twitter, with an eye on how those practices build discourse communities.

Next, after a brief overview of signifyin' discourse, I analyze how varying signifyin' practices—including style, format, and audience—map onto Twitter practice. This analysis explores why Black Twitter hashtags and the tweets powering them are able to influence Twitter's trending topics. I argue here for Black Twitter as an example of Blackness-as-discursive-identity by exploring the affordances of a specific information and communication technology (ICT) as a mediator for articulations of Black online identity. By using *affordance*, I build on Hutchby's (2001) definition, where artifacts have functional and relational aspects that frame the possibilities for agency in relation to those artifacts (p. 445). For Twitter, I argue that format and device (among other things) frame the ways that Twitter users converse but do not wholly determine them. Similarly, for Black Twitter, discursive rituals, culture, and performativity frame Twitter participation but do not wholly determine them.

While analyzing functions and discourses brings light to how Black users enjoy Twitter, technology use doesn't occur in a cultural vacuum. Cultures build and reinforce beliefs about appropriate users and technologies; Twitter is not exempt from judgments about either. Indeed, Twitter has been repeatedly called out for its diminution of the gravitas and civility of online discourse as well as for its role in promoting "identity politics." Trending topics and hashtags brought Black Twitter to the attention of other Twitter users, to online and mainstream media, and eventually, to the wider world. The reveal encouraged both in-group and out-group members to articulate cultural beliefs about race and information technology, which is valuable in understanding how beliefs power technology use. I analyze selected online responses to Black Twitter from out-group and in-group media and online figures during the early days of Black Twitter's emergence in 2010.

Finally, after examining online responses to Black Twitter, the chapter closes by discussing how racial and technocultural ideologies shape mainstream perceptions of minority tech use. There I speculate about how to understand technology as a cultural rather than simply social endeavor. After all, the activities of whites on Twitter are never assumed to have political goals—with the unpleasant exception of racist Twitter trolls. Non-Black Twitter, despite its multimillion-dollar valuation, instead struggles against the dictates of neoliberalism and capitalism, whose constituents question its use-value daily. Unpacking #SayHerName and #DemThrones gives rise to one of the more compelling questions about Blackness's engagement with Twitter: What are the "ends" of Black

Twitter? Black Twitter engagement has certainly served as catharsis and a call to action, but asking Black Twitter to do "more" is clearly a question about the leisure and technical capacities of the Black body rather than a coherent inquiry about Twitter's productive capacity.

Research Background

To situate this chapter in research and conversations about social network services (SNS) in general and about Twitter in particular, I offer a brief review. Hoffman and Novak (1998), in their canonical work on the digital divide, noted that a lack of Black-oriented online content should be considered a serious impediment to Black participation. As Byrne (2007) pointed out, BlackPlanet.com's sixteen million users serve as evidence that sites promoting Black cultural interactivity can become enormously popular. Similarly, Banks (2006) writes, "Black participation on [BlackPlanet] also begins to show the ways cyberspace can serve as a cultural underground that counters the surveillance and censorship that always seem to accompany the presence of African American speaking, writing, and designing in more public spaces" (p. 69). Accordingly, Black Twitter can be understood as a user-generated source of culturally relevant online content, combining social network elements and broadcast principles to share information.

In their canonical research article, boyd and Ellison (2007) defined SNS as web-based services that feature profiles, lists of social connections, and the capability to view and navigate profiles, connections, and user-generated content. Many SNS allow comments, which operate as threaded posts by network members about user-generated content (UGC). Twitter differs from other SNS in that the "comment," or tweet—not profiles or networks—is the site's focal point of interaction as opposed to an ancillary part of the intended content.

Some researchers take an instrumental approach to Twitter, which enables them to perceive and measure social interaction quantitatively, but this method assumes that Twitter is culturally neutral. Although Twitter has been examined as a social microblog (Java et al., 2007), as a social network (Huberman, Romero, & Wu, 2008), and as a messaging application (Krishnamurthy, Gill, & Arlitt, 2008), there are cultural affordances that are missed by each of these approaches.

Turning to communications research on Twitter, Marwick and boyd (2011) argue that Twitter users imagine their audience, citing Scheidt's (2006) statement that online audiences exist only as written into the text through stylistic and linguistic choices. However, in examining uses of Twitter's "@" function, Honeycutt and Herring (2009) found that it enabled direct conversations by reinforcing addressivity. Tweets including @ were "more likely to provide information for others and more likely to exhort others to do something" (p. 6). Zhao and Rosson (2009) found that Twitter's "follow" mechanism serves to curate content, allowing users to build personal information environments centered on topics and people of interest. Frequent, brief updates reduced the time necessary for interaction with others, paradoxically allowing users to feel stronger connections to their Twitter contacts. Twitter's capability for real-time updates on current events or social activities increased engagement as well.

To recap, Twitter's temporal, electronic, and structural discourse mediation encourages weak-tie (Granovetter, 1973) relationships between groups through informal communication practices. Analyzing Twitter as an information source captures data about social use and information types but elides cultural communicative practices. Communication studies research offers greater insight into sociocultural rationales for Twitter usage, but such research rarely examines the influence of race on online discourse. Examining paratextual reactions to Black Twitter's online articulations of Black discursive culture illustrates how culture shapes online social interactions. These paratexts also show how Twitter's interface and discourse conventions helped frame external perceptions of Black Twitter as a social public.

Public Sphere? Black Twitter as "Mature" Digital Practice

Writing about Black Twitter as a public sphere after the presidential election of 2016 is bittersweet even as it also seems superfluous. It is bittersweet because Donald Trump, the forty-fifth president of the United States, is increasingly seen as a Twitter power user, although the source of his social media expertise has yet to be understood as drawing on white Twitter / American culture (Brock, 2017)—even as he built on long-standing themes of xenophobia, nativism, and racism to power his campaign. Instead, pundits and academics view his Twitter savvy as an appeal to class, unreason, or nationalist rhetoric. Arguments for Black Twitter as a public sphere are slightly superfluous because the Democratic Party's failure to retain the White House has had the unanticipated effect of turning down the volume of organized Black online activism; the widespread attention that activists were able to marshal for Black political causes has been subsumed as a palliative for wider-scale, more frantic white liberal and progressive reactions (e.g., white fragility) to the Trump administration. Nevertheless, Trump's Department of Justice and the FBI's designation of Black Lives Matter as a "Black identity extremist" terrorist organization (prompted by alt-right and white supremacist media) render it necessary to address the political possibilities of Black Twitter at this point in the chapter.

As Black Twitter has become more widely known, many have sought to ratify the phenomenon by locating the political valences of Black Twitter within the concept of a counterpublic. Squires (2002) contends that *counterpublics* occupy and reclaim dominant and state-controlled public spaces while strategically using enclaved spaces. Utilizing public and private spaces in this fashion increases interpublic communication as well as interaction with the state. Moreover, counterpublics employ protest rhetoric and reveal "hidden transcripts" of Black discourse to argue against stereotypes and describe group interests. In an earlier version of this chapter, I argued for Black Twitter as an *enclaved counterpublic*, but upon further reflection, I am here arguing for Black Twitter as a *satellite* counterpublic sphere. Squires's differentiation of Black counterpublics hinges on defining the spaces and discourses in which these publics operate. Enclaved counterpublics hide themselves from oppression in private spaces (often in plain sight, like churches, salons, or the stoop or corner) while internally producing lively debates about Black life.

Squires defines *satellite publics* as occupying independent—not private—spaces that are open to group members. While these spaces are not completely detached from other publics or the state, their separation reflects the lack of a need to regularly engage with nonmembers rather than the result of oppression. Squires defines these satellite spheres as publics that seek "separation from other publics for reasons other than oppressive relations but [are] involved in wider public discourses from time to time" (2002, p. 448). Think of, for example, the Bechdel test, an informal assessment of gender equality in televisual media that measures whether at least two women talk to each other about something other than a man. Similarly, Black Twitter often engages in conversations about Blackness that have nothing to do with whiteness or white folk. Most importantly for this chapter, members of satellite publics do not feel compelled to hide or change their cultural particularities. Black Twitter, whose everyday interactions between members only occasionally rise to a level of visibility for mainstream Twitter users, fits this definition perfectly.

Twitter—the service—has messily, exuberantly become the public sphere we deserve even as it does not neatly fulfill technocultural expectations of productive, rational informational exchange. Similarly, Black Twitter was (and in many cases still is) often framed as "immature" and "ineffective" because its creative and discursive practices, in their viscerality and sensuality, do not directly lead to Black political or economic empowerment. This technocultural framing of Black digital practice is in line with long-standing Euro-American material conceptions of the Black body as labor/chattel, where Black energies must be directed toward the enrichment of their owner/institution. Moreover, Black Twitter fails under the disapproving scrutiny of Black respectability politics, where Black activities are "mature" if they are seen as leading to the political enrichment or advancement of the Black community. From this perspective, I'm sure you are nodding and saying, "Yes, that's *exactly* Black Twitter," and with respect to specific moments and instances, I would agree. However, protests and demands for state recognition of Black humanity are not the only, or even the primary, discourses of Black Twitter. Insisting that they are the only ways in which Twitter can be understood as a legible artifact of Black culture diminishes the ingenuity and pathos displayed every moment on the service by Black Twitter users.

While Black Twitter *can* be understood as a public sphere, Squires (2002) cautions that we need to distinguish the *discursive actions* of a public sphere from the *political actions* of a public sphere. Thus this chapter argues for Black Twitter as a heterogeneous Black discourse collective, bound by certain cultural and digital commonplaces in pursuit of similar and sometimes competing goals, which may include political action. This argument respects the banal contributions of everyday Black

Twitter users, who use hashtags like #ThanksgivingforBlackFamilies to celebrate and reflect on Black culture. It also allows for the possibility of international or even non-Black Twitter users—whose cultural competence aids in decoding Black Twitter's cultural commonplaces or political concerns—to be considered part of Black Twitter discourse.

Naming Black Twitter practice as an activity of a satellite counterpublic allows for the formulation of Black Twitter as a digital/virtual space where Blackness frames the politics of the everyday, occasionally breaking free of internal discourses to confront or simply inform wider publics about their concerns. Twitter is the means through which certain Black users separate themselves from mainstream, offline, and online publics, while Black Twitter hashtag use reintegrates discussants in wider discourses across the platform. Twitter makes this satellite public sphere possible in ways that other social networking services or even predecessor communication technologies have not by promoting the *public* discursive *actions* of a public sphere. These possibilities are afforded by Twitter's format, sociality, network, and material capabilities, which I will detail later in this chapter.

Finding Black Twitter

Even before surveys revealed the extent of Black folks' involvement with Twitter, it was a space where Black cultural practices helped users gain an appreciation of the service's discursive fluidity and sociality. In 2008, Anil Dash—vice president of the early blog platform SixApart, D'Angelo fan, and Prince stan—was one of the most prominent nonwhite Twitter users in the early days of the service. Dash's early adopter experiences offer a glimpse into the ways that Black expressivity can enrich information technologies. He and several other early adapters decided to use Twitter to comment about the impending McCain/Obama presidential race by "throw[ing] out some . . . snaps."

Snaps is slang for playing the dozens, one of the more prominently known (read "understood by the mainstream") signifyin' discourses. Dash, his followers, and other contributors compose their tweets using the well-worn insult trope about "yo' mama." For yo' mama snaps to be rhetorically effective, they must connect the sacred feminine body with a surreal, embodied, often ridiculous and arcane condition, phenomenon, or artifact. In doing so, they express a libidinal, sensual joy and critique in pithy, often humorous terms. Dash himself notes this, writing that one of the best snaps to arise from this event was "Absurd, obscure, specific—perfect!" However, many of the tweets he cited were not the best examples of this discursive art form.

For instance, Dash himself pens a pedestrian one:

> Yo moms such a ho they set up robocalls for all her booty calls.[4]

Wired writer Lore Sjoberg fares a little better:

> Yo mama so fat, she got an endorsement from General Mills.[5]

And Dash's previously mentioned "best" tweet is by Guillermo Esteves:

> yo momma's so fat, John McCain looked into her eyes and saw three letters: KFC.[6]

To contextualize these tweets and others in the same vein, Dash writes,

> Playing the dozens is a uniquely and explicitly African American tradition . . . it seems to me like the playfulness of the language and the absurdity of the medium may have masked something timely and fitting. This obviously and intrinsically Black tradition has been adopted by a community like Twitter that is, frankly, disproportionately not black. You could see it as the deracination of the tradition, or even worse as a deliberate omission of cultural context in its appropriation. But I actually see it as something positive.

Dash's speculation on Twitter's demographics was unsourced but later proven correct. Moreover, his designation of Twitter as an "absurd" medium speaks to a technocultural belief about Twitter as an unproductive and inappropriate technology. His argument for Twitter's potential for deracination through appropriation, however, frames Twitter as a "culture-neutral" service. From this perspective, it is remarkable that Black discourse practices can be employed to effect topical coherence over a medium ostensibly designed for a technorationalist, technologically proficient, mostly white user base. Promoting the technosocial mediation of Black culture by non-Blacks as a "positive," however, only accrues social and technical capital to non-Blacks. While Dash is in many ways exempt from this critique, several of his collaborators in this signifyin' moment were not.

When Black Twitter users employ Black discourses to interact on the service, significantly different opinions about race and information technology use emerge. Craig Wilson, on the Black interest website The Root, was one of the first in the Black press to write analytically about Black folk using Twitter. Observing the vitality of #uknowurblack,[7] Wilson (2009) speculates that the presence and popularity of trending hashtags featuring Black culture "suggest a strong, connected Black community on the site." His article suggests that Black Twitter users can be identified as deploying the following Twitter practices:

- a culturally relevant hashtag (cultural specificity)
- network participation (either a comment or a retweet) by tightly linked affiliates (homophily and intentionality)
- viral spread to reach visibility on Twitter's home page (propagation)[8]

Wilson does not specifically label these digital practices as "Black Twitter," but his informal analysis of Twitter practices of Black users provides the beginnings of a technocultural explanation of the phenomenon. He also deserves credit for being one of the first to connect Twitter usage by Black folk with Black folks' mobile and smartphone usage. Indeed, Wilson's analysis has utility not only for understanding how Black Twitter operates and thrives but for evaluating how white culture propagates across the service. For example, even with the known presence of Russian bot accounts on Twitter who artificially inflate his tweets, President Trump's early morning posts to the service still accrue vitality through his appeals to antiblackness and xenophobia.

The Great Reveal

Arguably, Black Twitter would have remained undiscovered by outsiders—or curious academics—without the hashtag and trending topic feature. Trending topics "found" Black Twitter in large part thanks to the 2009 Black Entertainment Television (BET) Awards. This event, which recognizes Black achievements in the arts, culture, and sport, can be understood as the catalyzing event bringing Black Twitter to mainstream recognition. The telecast, which aired soon after the untimely death of Michael Jackson, featured tributes to the iconic performer and received the largest audience share ever for the network at the time. During the program, Black folk on Twitter immediately cheered or jeered their favorite entertainers, which in turn powered tweets and hashtags mentioning the BET Awards, Ne-Yo, and Jamie Foxx to reach national trending topic status. The appearance of these Black cultural topics as informational trends was met with confusion—if not outright revulsion—by non-Black Twitter users. From these Twitter reactions, it is possible to see the hitherto unexplored role of antiblackness in Twitter practice, Western technoculture, and cyberculture.

Soon after Twitter's introduction of the trending topic, the *initial* mainstream recognition of Black Twitter can be attributed to Choire Sicha in his 2009 article on The Awl, "What Were Black People Talking about on Twitter Last Night?" (Manjoo, 2010; Brock, 2012). Sicha, cofounder of cultural interest site The Awl and former Gizmodo writer, named the phenomenon "Late Night Black People Twitter" while referencing the tweets curated by the blog "OMG! Black People!" In this important article, Sicha perceptively notes that Twitter allows for the bridging of online worlds. Also, in a prescient foretelling of Black Twitter's capacity for marshaling ratchet response en masse, Sicha begins his post with "At the risk of getting randomly harshed [*sic*] on by the Internet."

To provide a counterpoint, Sicha quotes a blog post by Nick Douglas,[9] former editor and writer of Valleywag (a Gawker Media tech industry gossip blog) and another early Black Twitter observer. Douglas writes that Twitter "shattered our insulated perception of how everyone uses this thing" (Sicha, 2009, para. 3). Douglas here is referring to Twitter's trending topics algorithm, which was introduced by the company after the user-generated hashtags were added to the service in 2008. Sicha's rationale for why Black folks' Twitter use dominated the late-night trends during the BET Awards is interesting. He notes that Black Twitter traffic occurred on the service all day but might have been obscured during daytime periods by the traffic from media sources and mainstream users. As that traffic waned, Black Twitter content became visible to those following the public timeline, or firehose. In closing, Sicha notes that Twitter's trending topics feature surfaces a reality that few people in tech, media, or the academy had previously considered or cared about: Black People Twitter was, two years after Twitter's debut at South by Southwest (SxSW), the enactment of Black digital identity and practice in a form that was visible to the mainstream.

These inquiries into Black Twitter before it was Black Twitter are valuable historical documents even if they're not academic research—or perhaps because they're *not* academic research. Reflective, culturally sensitive analyses into information technology are rare—in part due to deeply held beliefs and stereotypes about minorities' use of technology. These articles are powerful because while the authors are excavating digital practice, they are doing so from a cultural *and* technological perspective.

Stirrings of Black Cyberculture: Manjoo's Black Twitter Explainer

Over the last few years, a type of online news genre has grown in popularity: the "explainer." It is not the newest form of journalism; Rosen (2008) describes the explainer as a filter for those who are increasingly overwhelmed by the exploding information/media sphere, "where until I grasp the *whole* I am unable to make sense of *any* part." When they are published by mainstream media outlets, explainer articles often become *the* definitive take on complex phenomena that are frequently mentioned but rarely contextualized (e.g., Ramsey's [2015] Black Twitter explainer in The Atlantic). They typically become highly prominent in search engine results.

You should not be surprised, then, by my suggestion that Black culture is often the subject of online explainer articles, especially when the practices, politics, and aesthetics of Black culture become noticed or appropriated by the mainstream. Unfortunately, mainstream explainers tend to obfuscate Black cultural origins by attributing the phenomenon to white folk.[10] They would get away with it too, if it wasn't for those meddling kids—that is, Black Twitter's heterogeneous and wide-ranging net of media sources that are on alert for *any* mention of American Black culture.

Black Twitter received its first—but far from its last—significant mainstream explainer from the online news site Slate. Farhad Manjoo, then the lead technology writer at the site (now with the *New York Times*), penned an article that is worthy of regard thanks to his use of a technocultural (rather than ethnocentric) rationale for Black Twitter usage. This explainer is also notable because it does not attribute Black Twitter practice to a deficit model of technical or computational literacy. Manjoo's (2010) article marks the "tipping point" for Black Twitter's perception by the wider world. Although other online writers—and Pew Internet research—had discussed Black trending topics, participation, and cultural contributions to Twitter, Manjoo's "How Black People Use Twitter" authoritatively presents itself as "the latest research on race and microblogging." Despite Manjoo's balanced racial and technocultural approach, the column introduced itself as an expert on racial online activity, a claim bolstered by its publication in a mainstream news site and the subsequent uptake across the web.

Unfortunately, the article begins with a poor editorial choice of artwork to represent Black technology users, which is illustrative of my argument that technocultural beliefs about appropriate technology use and users define what technology *is* and *does*. The lead illustration is a brown bird wearing a jauntily askew baseball cap (with a hashtag as a logo) and holding a smartphone. I speculate, but cannot confirm, that the image was meant to represent race, racial aesthetics, and computational and technocultural identity. Refashioning the Twitter logo—a blue silhouette of a bird in midsong absent any technological or cultural signifiers—to imagery that is more commonly associated with "urban" masculinist fashion "plucked a nerve" for Black Twitter. As will be discussed later, Black folk are extremely sensitive about being locked into a fixed racial or cultural representation. Du Bois (1940) argues that Blacks are acutely aware of the opinions whites hold about them as well as how these opinions often negatively influence Black life.

Manjoo suggests that Black Twitter networks tend to be densely homophilic and more reciprocal than other nodes. On Twitter, reciprocity measures the ratio of followers to followed—most Twitter users tend to have fewer followers and follow people who don't reciprocate. Manjoo finds that most Black Twitter participants have a reciprocity ratio of nearly 1:1, suggesting that Blacks use Twitter as a "public instant messenger" to connect with friends.

Manjoo uses nuanced racial rationales to explain Black Twitter content as well. Noting a relationship between "the Dozens" (signifyin') and Black Twitter discourse, he writes:

> The Dozens theory is compelling but not airtight . . . a lot of these tags don't really fit the format of the Dozens—they don't feature people one-upping one another with witty insults. Instead, the ones that seem to hit big are those that comment on race, love, sex, and stereotypes about Black culture . . . the bigger reason why the Dozens theory isn't a silver bullet is that . . . people of all races insult one another online in general, and on Twitter specifically. We don't usually see those trends hit the top spot.

This reasoning has merit. Manjoo correctly identifies Black Twitter discourse as a cultural perspective on everyday Black culture. Moreover, he buttresses his argument on homophily by noting that the density of Black Twitter networks leads to their domination of trending topics, not their tendency to insult one another. Manjoo closes on another positive note, claiming that Black Twitter comprises the actions of a specific set of highly engaged Twitter users, rather than typical of all Blacks on Twitter.

These ruminations on Black Twitter can be contextualized in a number of ways. First and foremost, mainstream media has long sought to explain the significance of the Negro and his culture in ways that elevate whiteness while exoticizing Black practices. However, Sicha's and Manjoo's takes on Black Twitter do not clearly fit this paradigm; they both note the significance and the unexpectedness of Black digital practitioners without capitulating to the technocultural norms of antiblackness. Second, there is a strand across all these takes that respectfully considers the Black technical and cultural expertise of otherwise banal digital practitioners. That is, where typically Black expertise—usually in the field of entertainment or culture—is understood by evoking the trope of the "Black exception," here everyday Black discourses are understood as sophisticated, technical, expert work. This is where Craig Wilson's take on Black Twitter stands out:

he evaluates Black Twitter practice from a communitarian perspective without prejudice or antiblackness.

Finally, these perspectives can be seen as reshaping beliefs about who digital technologies are "for." That is, they open digital technoculture to a new awareness about appropriate users of digital technologies in general, of social networking services in general, and of Twitter specifically. In doing so, they also point to the capacity of Black discourse to provide topical coherence to technical, as well as cultural, artifacts and practices. The next section provides a brief summary of the conceptual framework employed in this analysis, which allows me to make this claim.

Conceptual Frameworks

As with other chapters in this text, this chapter utilizes critical technocultural discourse analysis (CTDA) to analyze a networked, computational digital artifact. By operationalizing technology as a "text" (Pinch & Bijker, 1984; Brock, 2016), I conduct a critical discourse analysis of the artifact, the practices powering that artifact, and the beliefs powering the use of that artifact. Beliefs are the most powerful yet least examined aspect of digital technology use, circulating as "common sense" understandings of why people use digital technologies that are unavoidably inflected with cultural biases. CTDA is careful to ground its discourse analyses of technocultural beliefs through explicit connections to the empirical analyses of interface and function. CTDA's conceptual framework incorporates critical cultural theory originating from the group under examination to understand how culture and technologies mutually constitute one another. In the previous chapter on Blackbird, the analysis employed racial formation theory and critical whiteness theory to unpack the browser's ideological presentation of information. In this chapter, I switch from Blackbird's CTDA framework of critical race and Black culture to drill down into a specific enactment of Blackness—that is, a focus on signifyin' discourses and Black discursive identity. This chapter's CTDA framework draws heavily on Du Bois's (1940) concept of double consciousness as well as research on signifyin' published by Geneva Smitherman, Claudia Mitchell-Kernan, Ronald Walcott, and Henry Louis Gates Jr.

Racial Identity, On- and Offline

The conceptual framework powering this inquiry turns to racial identity—specifically, the production of racial identity through discourse. Discourse and discourse analysis are natural fits for online research given the prominence of textual interaction in online spaces, but the production of racial identities online necessitates some investigation into how those identities were always-already extant in the offline spaces hosting online interactions. If race is a social construct, then how does racial identity manifest online, particularly in the absence of offline signifiers like embodiment?

In the early days of cyberculture research, online identity was assumed to be fluid and playful, leading to charges that racial identity couldn't credibly be assumed to be authentic (Donath, 2002; Nakamura, 2002). As I presented research on Blackness and online, I would invariably be asked how did I *know* whether the communities I studied were *actually* populated by Black people without personally interviewing each and every one of them. Then as now, I argue that online practice—specifically (but not limited to) information exchanged between users and services—can be understood as performing *racial* identity. There is no human identity performed online that is not articulated by a racialized body. The key for online researchers interested in race is identifying the signifiers that mark ethnic or racial identity in digital practice; these signs and signifiers can be found through analysis of the written textual discourses that are the backbone of online practice.

Again, my arguments here closely follow Banks's argument for the linguistic and rhetorical capacities of Black online discourse. Banks (2005) writes that Black online spaces "mean three things: first . . . a repudiation of much early cyberspace theory that insisted race is and should be irrelevant online, that it would be made irrelevant by online subjectivities. Second, it would confirm the importance of discursive and rhetorical features that Smitherman links to African oral traditions for the written discourse of African Americans. . . . Third, it would show Black people taking ownership of digital spaces and technologies and point to the importance of taking Black users into account in technology user studies" (p. 71). My operationalization of racial identity draws on Everett Hughes's ([1971] 1993) argument for ethnic identity: "An ethnic group is not one because of the degree of measurable or observable difference from other groups. It is an ethnic group, on the contrary, because the people in it and the people out of it know that it is one; because both the *ins* and *outs* talk, feel and act as if it were a separate group (p. 153; emphasis original)." This definition maps precisely onto the ways in which online identity is constructed, contested, and deconstructed through online discourses—mainly, but not limited to, text and other user-generated content. More important, this dialogic formulation of the discursive, affective, and performative aspects of ethnic identity is also a powerful conceptualization of racial identity. It is powerful precisely because Hughes has identified and operationalized the pervasiveness of racial ideology's effect on both in-group and out-group members. Thus this definition accounts for beliefs that are evoked in everyday life in ways that are occasionally outrageous (but always problematic) for both in-group and out-group members. Finally, Hughes's explanation of how both in- and out-group members "talk, feel, and act" complements the triadic formulation of technology as artifact (talk), practice (act), and belief (feel) used across this manuscript to conceptualize information, communication, and new media technologies.

Finally, in the same way that Pacey (1984) cautions technology researchers not to limit their inquiries to just the material artifact or even the practices surrounding that artifact, Hughes warns that it is an error to consider that individual cultural traits are the measure of belonging to an ethnic group—or even a measure of the solidarity of the group itself (p. 155). An ethnic group is *not* a synthesis of its cultural traits; instead, traits are attributes of the group (p. 154). This warning is significant for digital and new media researchers excavating racial identity online. While the signs-given-off (e.g., profile pictures), or the signs (e.g., the number of self-identified Black users in a given online space), offer clues to help determine racial affiliation, it is important to not solely depend on these visual signs to ascertain race.

Racial Formation: Whiteness

As mentioned earlier, whiteness is premised on its delineation against and disavowal of "the Other." Dyer (1997) contends that white identity is founded on a paradox: whiteness entails being a "sort of" race and the human race as well as an individual subject and a representation of the universal subject. This gives whiteness interpretive flexibility even as it depends on the specificity of embodiment and practice. Giroux (1996) adds that "whiteness represents itself as a universal marker for being civilized and in doing so posits the Other within the language of pathology, fear, madness, and degeneration" (p. 75). From a discursive perspective, the white American takes the role of the white "other" toward the self without any fundamental contradiction—essentially without being aware of doing so unless prompted (Rawls, 2000, p. 244).

American identity is enframed and extended by negative stereotypes of Black culture, or African Americanness (Morrison, 1998). Indeed, for many nonwhites groups, antiblackness became a mode of achieving social parity with white citizenry. Whiteness does not limit itself to civil and political dominance, however. More specifically, whiteness is strongly associated with the instruments of civilization and modernity: technology, industry, and technical capital. Du Bois (1940), in an allegorical discourse with a white American interlocutor, writes,

> Van Dieman: Go out upon the street; choose ten white men and ten colored men. Which can carry on and preserve American civilization?
> Du Bois: The whites.
> Van Dieman: Well, then.
> Du Bois: You evidently consider that a compliment. Let it pass. (p. 146)

The recent film *Hidden Figures* (Melfi et al., 2017) excellently depicts the practices and beliefs of white male technologists in its unflinching dramatization of the difficulties, discrimination, and erasure Black women technologists faced as information professionals during the 1960s (see also Green, 2001). Curiously, the twenty-first century may have witnessed the obscuring of racial animosity through discourses of multiculturalism and diversity, but information technology and new media institutions are still predominantly white and male. While advertisements for computer and social media might feature light-skinned or mixed-race actors and actresses, the demographic numbers for minority employment in the field are grim (Myers, 2018). White monoculture in information technology reinforces beliefs about the inability of (primitive) nonwhites to participate in information cultures (Brock, 2011a).

Dinerstein (2006) calls this out specifically, arguing that technology as an abstract concept functions as a white mythology and that technology is the unacknowledged source of European and Euro-American superiority within modernity (p. 569).

Racial Formation: Blackness

Through his formulation of "double consciousness," Du Bois (1903) sets the stage for an argument that Blackness should be understood as a conflicted identity shaped by the need to participate in parallel yet discontinuous discourses. For Du Bois, personal (not individual) Black identity is the intersection between Black communal solidarity and a national white supremacist ideology. His formulation acknowledges the hegemony of whiteness without privileging it over the agency and spiritual energy found within the Black community. It is worth repeating: double consciousness, as a formulation of identity, has to do with differences in the *experience* of being an individual in the two communities and not with the marginalized social roles within a single community (Rawls, 2000). This approach highlights the protean nature of Black identity mediated through different digital artifacts, services, and practices. The digital provides an indexical location where experiences and perceptions, promoted through the acts of individuals, occur (see Alcoff, 2000). From this position, Pacey's (1984) triadic formulation for technology can be repurposed to illustrate Alcoff's contention—that is, Black identity as an "artifact" with "practices" (here argued for as Twitter practice and signifyin') and "beliefs" (double consciousness).

Robert Gooding-Williams (1998) offers an alternative take on Black racial identity as a *consequence* of white American racial classification schema rather than solely "the beliefs and practices which are shared by or distinctive to the people whom that practice designates as black" (p. 21). Gooding-Williams's definition allows racial identity to be understood as a shared, socially constructed identity that is not hard coded into an essentialized "common culture." This move sheds the need for analyses of Black online identity to rely solely on the identification of phenotypical or visual signifiers. It also avoids the epistemic closure of how digital textual practice is often conceptualized, as Gooding-Williams (1998) notes that becoming Black requires one to "make choices, to formulate plans, to express concerns, etc., in light of one's identification of oneself as black" (p. 23). Articulating Blackness in digital media then becomes the beginning of the analysis rather than the end.

Signifyin' as Black Discursive Identity

To understand racial identity as constructed through discourse, this analysis is grounded in research on the Black discursive practice of "signifyin'," which is argued here as a marker of Black cultural identity (Gates, 1983; Smitherman, 1977; Mitchell-Kernan, [1972] 1999). Signifyin' draws on Ferdinand de Saussure's ([1916] 1974, p. 67) sign/signifier/signified but purposefully reformulates that definition. Beginning with the contention that "the culture of a nation exerts an influence on its language, and the language . . . is largely responsible for the nation" (p. 20), this analysis relies on de Saussure's argument that the relationship between sign and sign-concept and sign-signifier is at once arbitrary and fixed by the cultural milieu in which the sign exists.

Signifyin' practice draws attention to the signifier. In addition to uttering the "sound-object," speech practice *publicizes* the signifier as a playfully multivalent interlocutor to a community of speakers. In doing so, the signified, or "concept," is freed from its role in creating a fixed meaning, generating possibilities (*inventio*) for chains of signifiers. Signifyin' can thus be understood as a practice where the interlocutor inventively redefines an object using Black cultural commonplaces and philosophy. For example, Gates defines signifyin' as "a rhetorical practice unengaged in information giving. Signifying turns on the play and chain of signifiers . . . the 'signifier as such' in Julia Kristeva's phrase, [is] a 'presence that precedes the signification of object or emotion'" (1983, pp. 688–689).

Smitherman adds call and response to Gates's definition, highlighting audience participation and reinforcing de Saussure's assertion that language has a social component that requires a community of listeners and speakers. Call and response refers to the speaker's reference to, inclusion of, and responses from the audience in discourse as opposed to a monologic, lecturing style of address. Smitherman and Gates each carefully point out that limiting signifyin' to insult or misdirection is reductive; it is the articulation of a shared worldview, where recognition of the forms plus participation in the wordplay signals membership in the Black community. From this perspective, Black discourse moves from a bland information transfer to a communal commentary on political and personal realities.

Finally, Hughes ([1971] 1993) declares that cultural traits are group attributes: the group is not the synthesis of its traits. In the same way, I argue that Black Twitter does not represent the entirety of Black online presence. As Freelon, McIlwain, and Clark (2016) find, Black Twitter itself is composed of heterogeneous clusters of Black digital practitioners. Similarly, the multitude of racist responses to Black Twitter and its practices do not compose the entirety of the technocultural matrix within which Black culture is understood. While antiblackness is an enduring and powerful context within which Black identity exists, instrumental and functional aspects of technology also determine Black online identity. Thus I analyze the Twitter application and the interface's mediation of Blackness and responses to that mediation, drawing on technocultural and racial ideologies in keeping with my goal of understanding how racial beliefs shape technology use.

To recap, racial and technocultural ideologies play a part in understanding how online discourse "works." White participation in online activities is rarely understood as constitutive of white identity; instead, we are trained to understand white online activity as "stuff people do." Black Twitter confounded this ingrained understanding while using the same functions and apparatus by making it more apparent through external observation and internal interaction how culture shapes online discourses. Given these warrants, let us turn to Twitter and its interface to see how culture shapes code, interface design, and ultimately, information practices.

Twitter Affordances: Minimalism and Malleability

I conducted a close reading of the affordances (Norman, 1988; Hutchby, 2001) and discourse conventions of Twitter-as-a-service as part of my argument that these interface elements contribute to the Black Twitter phenomenon. Norman defines affordances—or more precisely, "perceived affordances"—as design that relies on "what actions the user perceives to be possible" (p. 9) rather than what is true. Twitter's discursive minimalism and subsequent malleability, then, are perceived affordances that shape cultural uses of the service. The social and mechanical discourse conventions—message length, hashtags, and trending topics—map onto Black culture's performativity, signifyin', and publicness in ways that add an unexpected sociocultural dimension to the service.

I will not repeat the apocryphal story of Twitter's design by Jack Dorsey and former Odeo developers here. Instead, in the spirit of history of technology and science and technology studies, I'd like to briefly discuss an often overlooked design influence on Twitter's functionality and interface. Some influences can be traced to early attempts to diversify Web 2.0 services, such as direct microblogging competitors like Dodgeball, Jaiku, and Pownce, but there was one application in particular whose features can be understood as forming the foundation of what we know as Twitter today.

TXTmob, an open-source software app, allowed political activists and protestors to the 2004 Democratic and Republican National Conventions to organize via a text message broadcast system developed by Tad Hirsch and John Henry (2005).[11] They developed TXTmob in conjunction with a number of activist organizers seeking to incorporate communication and tactics while coordinating dozens (if not hundreds) of members during protests. Hirsch (2013) describes TXTmob as "essentially bulletin board software optimized for mobile phones and the web" (p. 1). Deploying text messaging (hereafter referred to as short-message service, or SMS) to support and enact political resistance resulted in a decentralized communicative structure that was of great benefit for organizers, demonstrators, and those wishing to lend support. Notably, upon its release, TXTmob immediately fell under the scrutiny of various police surveillance teams. For example, the Giuliani-era authoritarian NYPD was increasingly invested in monitoring (and silencing) all political and civil unrest following the events of September 11, 2001.

Twitter and TXTmob share feature DNA in part because engineers from Odeo were involved in TXTmob's development. Evan Henshaw-Plath was one such engineer; he helped Hirsch improve the code and even presented TXTmob to the Odeo staff a few days before Dorsey's infamous design brainstorming session that resulted in Twitter (Hirsch,

2013, p. 2). Hirsch carefully notes that Twitter made a number of innovations and improvements to the concept of text-based messaging that TXTmob had never considered. Comparing Twitter to TXTmob here helps clarify something about Twitter that capitalists, investors, and the media still find confusing: Who is Twitter for? Retelling the story of TXTmob's encoding activist practice sheds light on why Twitter became a valuable organizing tool for Occupy, for the Arab Spring, and for Black Twitter. It also highlights SMS as an embodied information technology—the mobile phones we use for these services are made to be in our hands, always in close proximity to our bodies. This relationship among embodiment, information, and utterance presages my arguments for libidinal information technology use as an expression of self and culture.

The interfaces of most SNS tend to follow a browser-determined pattern of information display—namely, there is content in the middle bracketed on either side by widgets, photo galleries, applications, and advertising. Twitter stands apart from these browser-based SNS in its simplicity; the feed is the focal point of the web version (Safari/iOS) and its first-party client (iOS 11 / iPhone X). Again, this feature resembles classic SMS client interfaces, where the messages between interlocutors are the primary rationale for visiting the application. While posts published to Twitter's feed often contain images, image macros, GIFs, videos, and other multimedia, the service prioritizes the visual representation of discourses happening in near real time. Twitter's message format is a primary determinant of this affordance; it was originally designed as an SMS application to connect people in small groups. SMS messages are 160 characters long; Twitter messages were originally 140 characters (including attribution), allowing tweets to traverse SMS networks without truncation. Sagolla (2009) writes that Jack Dorsey's Twitter design principle was to make it "dead simple for anyone to just type something and send it to multiple other phones, and to the Web" (p. xviii).

Twitter's initial configuration on top of the SMS protocol allowed for the integration of offline and online Black worlds in ways that simply adding contact names to a social network did not. For example, every entity in your phone's contacts list may have a phone number or even an email address, but everyone on your contact list does *not* have a Facebook, Snapchat, or Tumblr account. Thus all mobile phone users are simultaneously hailed as SMS users, capable of receiving and replying to text messages even if they never use the service. Accordingly, Twitter's use of the SMS protocol meant that new users were already configured to interface with the newborn service.

Dorsey's *bon mot* "Just type something and send it" (Sagolla, 2009) as a design principle demands that the client become as transparent to the process as possible. For SMS users, the Twitter short code remains "40404,"[12] and the interface is a series of threaded messages organized by time received. Limiting messages to 140 characters while using the SMS protocol enabled Twitter to be used on millions of "feature phones" and smartphones—regardless of operating system or manufacturer—as well as instant-messaging services using SMS (e.g., MSN Messenger, Yahoo! Chat, and AOL Instant Messenger). One could also send tweets using Twitter's website or third-party clients on Windows, Mac OS X, Unix, and Linux.

For web users, Twitter's interface is a two-column page prominently featuring the user's Twitter feed;[13] a floating header (for navigation and a user profile) is minimally present at the top of the page. A plethora of third-party clients and services are available, thanks to an early release of its application programming interface (API) and subsequent uptake by developers. While these clients add features such as multiple log-ins and organizational features, the focal point of all these interfaces and clients is the message and the message stream.

Unlike other social networks, Twitter was multiplatform from the beginning; was not restricted to certain types of internet access, client access, or protocol; and even encouraged a robust third-party developer ecology. For example, Facebook's early attempts at mobile were severely hampered by then extant web protocols (e.g., the Wireless Application Protocol [WAP] browser introduced in 1999). Facebook was designed for the web browser in 2004, prior to the introduction of the modern smartphone, and was criticized for its poor mobile offerings even as burgeoning mobile access threatened to destabilize its advertising revenue. In contrast, Instagram was released as a mobile-only application (actually, iOS only until 2011). Twitter's multiplatform strategy invited and encouraged users to enjoy the service without demanding a lot of screen space, while its minimalist SMS interface allowed mobile access from the beginning. This strategy enabled users to integrate Twitter into already existing SMS practices as part of their everyday communication patterns. Moreover, the web interface encouraged users to stay engaged in environments where phone usage was awkward or inappropriate. Twitter's website was the primary source of access,[14] but Foursquare, Google, Facebook, and Flickr all allowed their users to share information on Twitter. The material affordances necessary to use Twitter—an internet-connected computer, screen, and input device—are thus reduced (or nerfed, in gaming terms) to the widest possible number of information and computer technology (ICT) configurations by design. This analysis suggests that Twitter's minimalist aesthetic and ease of material access played a role in Black adoption of the service.

Black Twitter Practice: Signifyin' as Identity, Performance, and Public

Black Twitter's use of the practices and rhetorical strategies of signifyin' (Gates, 1983) discourse signals Black online identity to in-group participants and out-group viewers. Earlier, I mentioned that digital technologies interpellate, or hail, people as "users." For the digital, this can be accomplished through the interface and through the practices and symbols that help redefine user identity. Twitter's social mechanism—the hail—is enacted through discourse and interaction; it hails its users through three metrics listed at the top of every profile:

- number of tweets written
- number of followers
- number of people one follows

These metrics identify social and digital interactions, yet they do not tell us much about why users communicate. Twitter users publish information and media to a network of followers and in turn read and respond to information and media from a network of people they follow. Twitter's information stream includes, but is not limited to or even overly influenced by, hashtags. These textual and discursive practices provide a social, service-dependent context for decoding the information received while also offering an essential and understudied cultural context from which information is encoded. While hashtags organize conversations and social interaction, they are often additional visual obfuscations that hinder the readability of a tweet, further complicating comprehension. Centering a Black Twitter (or Twitter) analysis on hashtags is reductive; it flattens the richness and complexity of the conversations held by individual Twitter users.

One way to understand conversational coherence on Twitter is by analyzing follower and followed networks. Bollen et al. (2011) find that Twitter users either prefer the company of users with similar values or converge on their friends' values. They speculate, "This may confirm the notion that distinct socio-cultural factors affect the expression of emotion and mood on Twitter, and cause users to cluster according to their degree of expressiveness" (p. 248). In a Pew Internet Research (2015) survey of Black social media users, nearly two-thirds said that most of the posts they see on social media are about race or race relations, while nearly a third said that most of what they post online is about race or race relations. For white social media users, two-thirds said that none of their social media posts or shares pertained to race.[15] In discursive identity construction, such as that found on Twitter, homophilic user affiliations gain coherence and become reinforced by the use of cultural commonplaces. For Black Twitter users, posts about racial identity are the valence around which their digital practice is constructed; for many, signifyin' is the style in which their discourse is expressed.

The rhetorical and discourse conventions of signifyin' map well onto Twitter's discourse conventions and practices. Signifyin' is a Black discursive activity—nay, performance—that depends on style (wit), a knowing audience, and kairos. The term is an intentional nod to de Saussure's formulation of sign, signifier, and signified to describe meaning making in discourse. In linguistics, a *sign* refers to anything that stands for something other than itself. De Saussure ([1916] 1974) argues that signs are composed of a *form* the sign takes (the signifier) and the *concept* the sign represents (the signified). For example, the word *love* is not the actual emotion we experience or our practice of that emotion, but we (kind of) understand what is meant when someone deploys the term.

Gates (1983) contends that signifyin' is a discursive constitution of Black identity that turns on the play and chain of signifiers rather than the straightforward transmission of information. When signifyin' happens, the interlocutor is inventively redefining an object or phenomenon using Black cultural commonplaces and philosophy. In doing so, the interlocutor defines the form of the sign while *becoming* the signifier in a playfully multivalent fashion. Moreover, the signified—the concept itself—evolves in this formulation to oscillate among form, object, and metadata referencing the signified concept. Finally, the audience is hailed through their knowledge of the practice and their capacity for participation.

In offline spaces, signifyin' discourse that isn't witty or timely is considered a failure; similarly, signifyin' that goes unheard is not signifyin' at all. On Twitter, signifyin' works in similar fashion: Black Twitter tweets trade heavily in stylistic performance by a knowledgeable performer to a knowledgeable (digitally and culturally literate) audience situated in time and in digital space. The Black Twitter user is the signifier who exploits the format and conventions of the tweet to invent and invite a new way to perceive a familiar sign.

Twitter practice (indeed, much of social media practice) and signifyin' discourse rely heavily on *kairos*. I'm drawing here on a set of scholarly definitions that understand kairos as

- a situational context,
- a qualitative time, or
- most relevant for this inquiry, "a dynamism and a value dimension to temporality" (Moutsopoulos, cited in Kinneavy & Eskin, 1994).

This last definition clearly marks the temporal aspect of Twitter's publishing and display of user-generated content. "If you snooze, you lose" perfectly describes Twitter practice, as much of the context necessary to decode tweets depends on *when* you read them. To correctly and profitably engage in Twitter discourse, a tweet must be composed and published quickly enough to be considered part of a specific conversation. Hashtags have diminished, but not removed entirely, the need to be timely for Twitter participation. Indeed, hashtags have introduced another temporal consideration—virality—in Twitter's kairotic practice. "If you snooze, you lose" is even more relevant for Black Twitter signifyin', as a slow response to the signifyin' hail results in invalidity and the inability to perform to an appreciative audience.

Miller (1994) brings forth another consideration for the possibilities of kairos, Twitter, and signifyin' discourse. She argues for kairos's relationship to decorum—that is, whether discourse is fitting for a particular moment. Twitter is particularly susceptible to instrumental violations of conversational decorum, as its content-feed mechanism constantly interrupts conversations of interest to the user by publishing newer, oft-unrelated conversational moments. In other online spaces, violations of discursive decorum can be signaled as "OT," or off topic, to let participants know that the following content isn't necessarily pertinent to the ongoing conversation but still relevant to the participants. This isn't possible for Twitter use; at best, one can manually refresh the feed to load new content pertinent to the conversation, but a refresh will also load new content that is often topically incoherent.

Signifyin' discourse (and Black folk) had a complicated relationship with decorum even before Black Twitter. Decorum, in a Black communal context, can be understood as being influenced to participate in or disseminate uplift and respectability rhetorics designed to enact a modern, civilized Black body. As such, much of the embodied, sensual nature of signifyin' is a rebuke to notions of Black respectability even when the practitioners themselves are proponents. This becomes immediately clear when examining the invocation of "Black Twitter" as an instrument of critique and retribution; expectations of Black Twitter critique in these cases is that it will be savage rather than polite.

Signifyin' has its own decorum, of course, although it draws on a complex relationship between content and signification. Despite the play and chain of signifiers, signifyin' discourse *must* be discernible as relating to the signified. Going off topic—or worse, not being clever—are grounds for violation of signifyin' decorum and kairos. Returning to kairos, tweets that are time-stamped long after the bulk of signifyin' discourse about a topic are not timely. Moreover, trying to participate in a conversation that the participants have since moved on from can also be understood as a violation of Black Twitter and signifyin' decorum.

The tweet-as-signifyin', then, can be understood as a timely, discursive, public performance of Black identity. In Saussurean terms, the signifier is "the psychological impression of a sound" ([1916] 1974, p. 66). Gates (1983) defines signifyin' in multiple dimensions: the person doing the signifyin' performs a message that only represents part of the intended communication. He adds, "One does not signify something; one signifies in *some way*" (p. 689). The tweet-as-signifier thus represents the following digital and signifyin' communicative conventions:

- social affiliation (audience)
- message (presence)
- invention and subject knowledge (semiotics)

All these are tightly constrained by brevity, concision, and temporality.

Twitter, as a networked digital medium, complicates and expands signifyin' practice. The complication derives in part from its ostensible communicative purpose and networked features, which draw on technocultural expectations of efficiency and productivity. While Twitter is efficient, the spatial limitations of an individual's 140 character (and even the expanded 280 character format) tweet can render messaging incoherent, especially as the individual continues to produce tweets in response to messages that are often unrelated to the previous message. From this perspective, Twitter can easily become unintelligible to users who are not immersed in its practices and content—a charge that can be laid at the service's feet nearly ten years after its introduction.

Twitter expands signifyin' practice through its social mechanism and through its networked capacity, embodying cultural communication within individual participation and community reception. Signifyin' discourse privileges the interaction between an individual and her community. The communal audience is an essential element for Black identity formation through reception, affect, and response. Walcott (1972) writes about the influence of individual and communal style in Black discourse in *Black World*: "On the public level, the individual as stylist operates on a plane, or more accurately, out of a sphere of interest *usually defined from the white point of view as entertainment* and, more profitably, *from the Black or theoretical point as ritual drama or dialectical catharsis*" (p. 9; emphasis mine). From this perspective, Twitter-the-service can be understood as a space for rhetorical invention (*inventio*) rather than simply a service for rote information transmission. Signifyin' benefits from this affordance while providing Twitter with an alternative raison d'être: the performance of drama and catharsis, ritualized in a rigid format as a discursive style that demands attention.

Walcott (1972) defines ritual as "a highly stylized structure perceived and laid out in space" (p. 9). This clearly fits Twitter's communicative convention: 140 characters in which to proclaim something of interest, where interactants are addressed by name and context is delivered in shorthand (the hashtag). The 140-character constraint affords a ritualistic discursive presentation, similar to the haiku or the limerick, while Twitter's profile and sociality (follower/followee) offer additional scaffolding for semiosis. Black Twitter as ritual drama, then, highlights the structure, engagement, invention, and performance of these Twitter users employing cultural touch points of humor, spectacle, or crisis to construct discursive racial identity.

Performativity is a crucial element of signifyin' and is immediately obvious in the case of Black Twitter. Walcott (1972) has more to say about space and Black discourse: "Accustomed to, and perhaps most at home participating in ritual, the stylist is a performer, a man who moves in space, who *attracts attention and employs it in defining himself*" (p. 9; emphasis mine). Marwick and boyd (2011) argue that Twitter, like other social networking services, collapses social context to enforce a univocal identity presentation. I offer instead that Twitter's strict 140-character limit encourages discursive performativity and creativity (both hallmarks of signifyin') within boundaries of time and space while *expanding* offline social context to dissolve digital dualist conceptions of social presence.

The expanded yet minimal identity display differs from other SNS, where social capital accrues from the public display of connections or carefully managed self-presentation through multimedia (boyd & Ellison, 2007). In longer-form online or multimedia digital practice (e.g., blogs, news articles, essays), authors have time and space to construct nuanced arguments that may also include citations for support. Long-form virtual spaces privilege monologic speech forms, which only become dialectical through additional digital features, such as comments or hyperlink embeds. Twitter "ain't got no time for that"[16] and clearly benefits from this imposed limitation. Even as the service has expanded its discursive mechanism to 280 characters plus native tweet threading, Twitter's signifyin' capacity has remained intact.

My final argument for the tweet-as-signifier draws on Tal's (1996) observation that the construction of online identity is in many ways analogous to "double consciousness" (Du Bois, 1903). Our online personas are uneasy reconciliations of offline multiplicity and online fixity. "Context collapse" (Marwick & boyd, 2011) is one way to understand how the textual primacy of social media "fixes" identity. I argue here that *online fixity* is the assumption that online visitors occupy a "normal" online identity—white, male, middle-class, and hetero—or are so diverse that their cultural origins cannot (or should not) be ascertained. Black users' employment of Twitter's rigid format to articulate Black discursive styles and cultural iconography subverts mainstream expectations of Twitter demographics, discourses, and utility. These technocultural displays of Black identity would have gone unnoticed by the wider world except for the visibility offered by another signifier, the hashtag.

The Twitter Hashtag: Instrumental Analysis

Black Twitter's public element revolves around the hashtag. For Black Twitter practice, the hashtag serves as signifier, sign, and signified, marking the concept to be signified, the cultural context within which the tweet should be understood, and the "call" awaiting a response. From a functional perspective, hashtags digitally organize conversations for coherence and archival purposes. Hashtags operate as hyperlinked search terms encoded for human memory retrieval, retrieving up to one thousand publicly available tweets containing a formatted text string that makes sense to people sharing a cultural worldview. But this functional analysis does not offer insight into why Black Twitter hashtags are so effective at marshaling attention and participation.

The hashtag is a user-created metadiscourse convention (# + keyword, often a phrase absent any spaces between words) that was coined to coordinate Twitter conversations by providing topical coherence (Messina, 2007). Although Messina recounts that he pitched the concept to Twitter, the company chose to filter topics computationally, a process that became known as the trending topic algorithm. The hashtag (# + topic) was initially deployed to filter and organize multiple tweets on a particular topic (Messina, 2008). Initially intended as a curational feature, the hashtag quickly evolved into an expressive modifier to contextualize the brusque, brief tweet. As I mentioned earlier in the chapter, the hashtag's evolution led to the "discovery" of Black Twitter. Black Twitter hashtag domination of the trending topics algorithmic feed allowed outsiders to view Black discourse that was (and still is) unconcerned with the mainstream gaze. While hashtags predate trending topics, both played a role in exposing Black Twitter to a mainstream audience that was unconcerned with its prior existence. Twitter's enormous volume of tweets effectively obscures the activities of groups of users; third-party solutions provide some means to filter the stream but are of limited use to the general user. Hashtags and trending topics filtered Twitter in a way that identified not only topics of interest but who was generating those topics.

A brief moment of clarification: trending topics are not the same as hashtags, although they both serve to organize Twitter conversations. Hashtags are folksonomic (Mathes, 2004), and as Huang, Thornton, and Efthimidias (2010) point out, they are situated a priori for users to situate their message within a wider real-time conversation rather than a posteriori to facilitate retrieval. Trending topics, on the other hand, are intended to capture topics enjoying a surge in popularity (Gillespie, 2011). To do so, the algorithm looks at the number of tweets on a common topic and the rate of propagation across disparate clusters of Twitter users. Thus the algorithm identifies breaking topics rather than the enormous stream of tweets generated daily deeply invested fan communities (e.g., Justin Bieber fans [Beliebers] and Beyoncé fans [the Beyhive]) or through generically invoked hashtags (e.g., #Love and #Hate) that don't provoke unique content. Trending topics, therefore, provide insight into the influence of Black Twitter practice while also shedding light on topics that Twitter-the-service considers important.

Semiotic Analysis

Earlier in this chapter, I claimed that hashtags serve as sign, signifier, and signified in Black Twitter discourse:

- *Sign* refers to something other than itself as well as the call to participate awaiting a response.
- *Signifier* marks both the concept to be discussed (or signified upon) and the wit of the originator.
- *Signified* represents the relational (cultural) context within which the accompanying tweet can be decoded (and encoded).

The first bullet requires clarification: *hashtag-as-sign* refers to the hashtag's presence *and* its function as a hyperlink. The hyperlink was a sign before the hashtag's arrival; it refers to other information located elsewhere (on the same page, on the same site, or on a different site) and initiates travel to that information's location. The hyperlink often does this while presenting as text, but it can also present as an image or other multimedia object. Properly speaking, the tweet is *not* a sign, as it includes a hyperlink to the original post, which is usually encoded as the publication date stamp. In its phrase-absent-spaces virtuosity, the hashtag is not the entirety of the message encoded (thus my earlier contention that hashtags are part, but not all, of the Black Twitter phenomenon), but it serves as a visual, textual, discursive, *and* informational marker of the discourse at hand.

Mitchell-Kernan's description of signifyin' practice can thus be seen as describing hashtag use as well: "The hearer is thus constrained to attend to all potential—carrying symbolic systems in speech events . . . the context embeddedness of meaning is attested to by both our reliance on the given context and, most important, by our inclination to construct additional context from our background knowledge of the world" (as cited in Gates, 1983, p. 691). The hashtag, originally intended to collate conversations around an external topic, thus becomes a call for Black Twitter participants to recognize performance and respond in kind. In doing so—clicking a hashtag moves you away from your feed to a separate search window or tab—it also isolates you from attending to other conversations. Even so, the hashtag invites a wider audience for a signifyin' moment than can be generated using @username alone. This expanded audience—the communal one created by the hashtag's curatorial function as well as the algorithmic one created by trending topics—can then attribute Black Twitter practice to the coherent practice of a digital public instead of just noise picked up on the trending topic algorithm. Moreover, the hashtag's signifyin' and broadcast elements have significantly expanded Black identity to include a digital component even as Twitter-the-service continues to suffer from accusations of incivility and incoherence thanks to the ministrations of the forty-fifth president.

Absent the context of the signifyin' Twitter user and text, it is not always clear from a linguistic-aesthetic perspective which hashtags are Black Twitter hashtags (e.g., #ThanksgivingWithBlackFamilies or

#NiggerNavy). I argue this for several reasons. The first is functional: hashtags have become so popular and ubiquitous that many people use them for banal affective (but not libidinal) expressions. For example, #Love is one of the most popular and generic Twitter hashtags, yet it doesn't provide topical coherence because so many users deploy it indiscriminately. Thus generic hashtags are not libidinal, as they only perform an emotional response rather than signify an emotion.

Black Twitter expressions are occasionally difficult to identify because one cannot rely on the performance of African American Vernacular English (AAVE) to recognize Black Twitter content. Many Black folk don't employ AAVE as everyday speech, and many more don't employ it in public-facing spaces (e.g., code switching; Spears, 2001). Thus hashtags from Black Twitter users often trend for technical reasons—because of Black Twitter user participation *and* cultural meanings encoded within tweets (e.g., #TVOneShows)—rather than for cultural rationales, such as the signaling of and response to AAVE. Furthermore, research uniformly suggests that AAVE speakers might be familiar with the linguistic patterns of AAVE and are conversant in the meanings *even without speaking in that particular dialect* (Spears, 1999; Rickford, 1999; Labov, 1998; Wolfram, 1994). From this perspective, I argue that Black Twitter participation draws from Black technical and digital expertise, operationalized as social network practice, nearly as much as it does on being able to encode and recode Twitter content in Black cultural commonplaces.

A tertiary consideration for the expertise behind the Black Twitter hashtag is that crafting hashtags that generate attention and participation is not easy. Walcott (1972) argues that command of form is paramount for Black discourse: "One's personal victory, then, is achieved through the fashioning of an individual style that will enable one to operate in space . . . indeed to come to *invigorate the space in which one finds oneself with a sense of oneself, one's vision, values, limitations, resources, aims*" (p. 9; emphasis mine). The user's identity, her followers (and followed), and the crafting of a signifyin' chain all play a role in signaling participation in Black Twitter signifyin'. The Black Twitter hashtag invites an audience—even more so than the publication of a tweet to one's followers—by setting the parameters of the discourse to follow. It is also a signal that the Twitter user is part of a larger cultural community and displays her knowledge of that community's practices, discourses, and worldview.

The hashtag's audience invitation maps onto the signifyin' practice of call and response, which Smitherman (1977) defines as a practice where the speaker either requests a specific response from the audience or elicits extemporaneous audience responses by appealing to cultural commonplaces. Call-and-response interactions build consensus either by completion of the original statement or through affirmation of the speaker's intent. Figure 3.1 is an example of how a hashtag's deployment illustrates call and response: FreedomReeves sounds the call with the hashtag #NewTVOneShows, which refers to the Black-owned cable channel TV One. RenishaRenewed acknowledges the call and expands on it. In this thread of hashtagged responses, these Twitter users are humorously proposing culturally relevant shows for the then fledgling network. Note that FreedomReeves does not address her tweet to TV One's Twitter account (@tvonetv). Rather, TV One is the sign on which she is signifyin'. Hashtags enable Twitter to mediate communal identity in near real time, allowing participants to act individually yet en masse while still being heard.

Figure 3.1. Tweets using the #NewTVOneShows hashtag

Black Twitter's utilization of hashtags also enables the signifyin' practice of tonal semantics, or "voice rhythm and vocal inflection to convey meaning in Black communication" (Smitherman, 1977, p. 134). You may be more familiar with tonal semantics in digital form as emoticons, emoji, and stickers (Sweeney, 2016). Before smartphones and messaging apps became ubiquitous, however, Banks (2005) observed tonal semantics on BlackPlanet.com chat discourse in the early 2000s. He noted that BlackPlanet users were already familiar with deploying typographic features (e.g., parentheses and other punctuation) to denote affection, dislike, or respect between members. I offer this data point to warrant my claim that hashtags serve a similar tonal function for Black Twitter. In addition to operating as relational signals between individuals, they signal a shift from rote information exchange to a critical yet playful discourse style. They differentiate individual tweets as part of a communal wordplay and identity construction rather than as insults or banalities.

To recap, Twitter's publication mechanism makes it difficult to keep track of conversations. All public tweets are posted simultaneously to the account @publictimeline (once featured on the home page, but no longer); to the Twitter main stream, or "firehose"; and to a user's followers. The public timeline is nearly incomprehensible thanks to the volume of tweets and the lack of context, while conversations between subscribers draw context from their shared interests. Black Twitter digital practice affords Twitter-the-service a measure of conversational coherence through networks of tightly linked users engaging in Black digital practice; discursive practices, including signifyin'; and multimedia cultural commonplaces. Hashtags, in addition to their curatorial function, indicate affective, libidinal, and group-level discourses. Black Twitter hashtag use often brings Black discourse to the attention of the trending topic algorithm. The trending topic mechanism attempts to improve the service's information utility and coherence by highlighting Twitter's conversational nature. It does so by publicizing and tracking topics of interest across groups, cities, regions, and nations, but unless the topics are published in languages other than English, they are not read as "cultural" content.

Black Twitter's visibility via the trending topic algorithm—which is how the mainstream became aware of the phenomenon—led to a technocultural othering of Black digital practice as an intervention on "white public space" (Hill, 1998). Hill defines white public space as "a morally significant set of contexts in which Whites are invisibly normal, and in which racialized populations are visibly marginal" (p. 62). This space is constructed by the intense monitoring of nonwhite speakers along with the invisibility of almost identical signs in white discourse. In the previous sections, I examined how Twitter's design principles indirectly encouraged Black digital participation in the service as well as how tweets and hashtags (artifacts) can mediate Black cultural discourse (practice). The following section examines racial and technocultural beliefs about Black Twitter as a technocultural practice.

Critical Discourse Analysis: Reactions to Black Twitter

Manjoo's (2010) Black Twitter explainer can be argued for as representing a mainstream view of race and information technology use—more specifically, as a mainstream perspective on Black technoculture and digital practice. In keeping with my conceptual framework and definition of ethnic identity as generated by internal and external perception, this chapter also examined two racialized websites discussing Black Twitter: a white-authored personal blog and the personal blog of a Black journalist. To be clear, these sites are *not* definitive examples of their respective ethnic groups. Omi and Winant's (1994) racial formation theory, however, argues that individual acts of racial representation draw on social structure. As discussed earlier, Hughes ([1971] 1993) defines ethnic identity as practices and beliefs that the in-group and out-group *agree* can be attributed to the in-group. Therefore, while these websites are not wholly representative, each author recognizes Black Twitter based on their relationship to Black identity and online culture. While hyperlinks offer the possibility of online interaction, they do not necessarily confer the probability that interactants will encounter each other online. Thus the recognition of Black culture on display here depends not on whether the interactants know one another but on whether they are conversant in what American culture believes about Black culture.

An additional rationale for counterposing racial website discourses about Black Twitter can be found in the writings of Ann Rawls (2000), who studies white and Black conversational interactions. She argues,

"While Black and white appear to occupy the same world geographically, they rarely occupy the same interactional space . . . even when they do more often jointly occupy interactional space . . . *the display of moral behavior by members of one group may well look like deviant behavior to members of the other*" (p. 247; emphasis mine). Spoiler alert: the ethnic affiliation of the authors discussed in the following sections colors their perception of Black Twitter activity.

White Perspective: Too Much Nick

One of the original contributors to the "Blacks on Twitter" conversation was Nick Douglas on his personal Tumblr Too Much Nick. I chose this particular blog and post because it was one of the earliest commentaries to be found on Black Twitter, because of Sicha's reference to Douglas in his "Late Night Black Twitter" post, and because I found it through Alice Marwick's Tumblr. Marwick is a noted internet researcher on identity and social media, so her participation in this conversation signaled that it might be of interest for this inquiry.

In Douglas's 2009 post "Micah's 'Black people on Twitter' theory," Douglas mentions a friend's comment on nongeek Twitter activity: "These people don't have real Twitter friends. So they all respond to trending topics. And that's the game, that's how they use Twitter" (p. 1). Douglas's mention of his friend's commentary is an implicit endorsement of the sentiment that Twitter is for geeks; he later defines it as "white guys with collars and spelling." In contrast, nongeeky people "use text-speak" and are "minorities, women, and teens." The post also contains rebuttals from two other Tumblr users—mariadiaz, a tech blogger and coder from San Francisco, and alicetiara, the nom de plume of Alice Marwick. Diaz notes that Douglas's friend hasn't been paying attention to the Twitter communities in which those conversations happen, writing, "I follow a lot of 'those people' for my work blog and trust me, they know how to use Twitter." Marwick adds, "The hipster tech crowd is . . . a VERY small minority [of users] and so they need to stop assuming that their use of Twitter is the 'right,' 'normal,' 'correct,' or 'usual' use. It is no longer" (Douglas, 2009, p. 1).

For Douglas's friend Micah, only certain folk tweet correctly: standard English-speaking white professional male technologists, or "geeks."

From this racial and technocultural context, Twitter becomes an informational space and social network for white tech elites. Douglas clarifies in response to mariadiaz and alicetiara that neither Micah nor he thinks anyone's using Twitter "wrong," but the damage has already been done. Here race and technology are framed by the context in which they appear: Twitter as a rational discursive space. Rawls (2000), writing about white identity, says, "White Americans takes the role of the white other towards the self without any fundamental contradiction and thus essentially without being aware of doing so" (p. 244). In translation, whites assume that the rest of the world sees them as white people wish to be seen. For Douglas, geeks—a community of interest that skews heavily white and male—are the experts in arcane technologies and are thus entitled to exclusive access to Twitter. While he acknowledges that geeks are not "ideal" whites, they are entitled to use Twitter in ways that nongeeks, women, children, and nonwhites are not.

Black Perspective: PostBourgie

Shani Hilton (2010), writing as shani-o, responds to Manjoo's Black Twitter explainer on the group-authored blog PostBourgie (PB; http://postbourgie.com). While Douglas's Tumblr can be understood as a personal blog, PB was one of the more prominent Black cultural blogs in the Black blog era (ca. 2004–10). Its remit was news, politics, tech, and culture, and many of the original PB contributors were journalists interested in complicating media conversations about race and American culture. Several are now senior journalists at mainstream publications. When this blog post was published, Hilton was a contributor at *Colorlines* magazine and the *Washington City Paper*. Gene Demby (GD) now leads NPR's Code Switch division on race and American culture, and Jamelle Bouie (Jamelle) is a senior political correspondent at the *New York Times*. PostBourgie's genealogy is important for this inquiry, as it was one of the few bastions during the rise of Web 2.0 (and blogging) of experienced, tech-savvy, culturally competent journalists who happened to be Black. Thus their expertise contributes an important Black digital perspective on Black Twitter use.

Hilton's post, "You can tweet like this or you can tweet like that or you can tweet like us," takes an analytical racial approach to Black Twitter.

Her response criticizes Manjoo's authoritative stance on Black Twitter activity, suggesting that he serves as a tour guide for "befuddled and bemused Whites" because "the ways of Black folk are so mysterious." She acknowledges using Twitter and that Black Twitter hashtags—"some very tempting to join in on"—had crept into her timeline. Hilton defines Black Twitter discourse: "Black people on Twitter, just as they do in real life, maintain tight-knit communities where they trade jokes, bicker, and play with each other. The same could be said about any other community using the site." She also provides a technocultural analysis of Black online access: "To address the question about the 'dominance' of Black Twitterers, I believe the answer lies somewhere in this combination of pretty mundane facts: Poor and working class people are more likely to access the internet through mobile devices. . . . Young Black people on Twitter are right on trend. That is, when a large percentage of a racial group is young and doesn't have a lot of money, they're going to dominate a free service that ties in perfectly with their most common mode of communication."

Hilton accepts Black Twitter as normal rather than as a game perhaps because of her own identification as Black as well as her participation in and history with Black digital practice. Her commentary on Black youth and working-class folk accessing the internet through mobile devices is a welcome validation of my claims for Black internet and digital literacies being augmented and shaped by smartphone access. Similarly, she marks Black Twitter discourse as common to all Twitter users. To close her post, she asks for mainstream understanding of Black heterogeneity, online and offline, reinforcing Manjoo's point that Black Twitter is a subgroup of all Black Twitter users rather than the entirety.

Rawls (2000), writing on Black discursive identity, notes that "while Whites . . . are accountable to only one community and one set of values, there are two separate peoples to whom the African American self is accountable. If actions fulfill the ideals of the one group, without fulfilling the ideals of the other at the same time, this is a problem that 'belongs' to the African American self, but not to the white self" (p. 245). This quote supports Hilton's analysis. Hilton claims and acknowledges the actions of poor young Blacks, marking their digital practice as culturally American and technoculturally normal. Her articulation of Black technological prowess—reading Black Twitter users as agentive in their adoption and command of a nascent social network and digital service—was warranted through statistical findings. In doing so, she counters the deficit-laden moral and functional narrative of racial technology use proffered by Douglas. Moreover, despite her critiques of Manjoo's Slate article, Hilton's analysis adds much-needed nuance to Manjoo's piece by presenting activities from an *emic* perspective. This is only possible because of Hilton's critical, affiliative take on Black identity and Black digital practice.

Discussion: Interfaces, Practices, and Beliefs

Returning to my organizing principle of technology as artifact, practice, and belief, I examined Twitter's interface and features to analyze how this technology mediates Black culture. I also scrutinized online discourses about Black Twitter to understand how culture frames technology practice. I found that a tweet's content coupled with a topical hashtag, when leavened with cultural commonplaces, could enrich communal bonds between networked Twitter users. This happens regardless of cultural affiliation. Black Twitter exemplifies this phenomenon, but racial and technocultural ideologies brought cultural influences on digital practice to mainstream attention thanks to the pejorative perceptions of Black technology use.

Black discursive culture—specifically signifyin' discourse's focus on invention, delivery, ritual, and audience participation—maps well onto Twitter's focus on rapid discussion among groups of connected users. Twitter's ubiquity and ambiguity—stemming from design decisions made to encourage the adoption of the service—enabled material access with minimal loss of functionality. This is an important point to note when considering that Blacks access the internet (and Twitter) primarily through mobile devices. Black Twitter illuminates the service's role as a cultural communication medium, transcending the size limitations and conversational incoherence of chat rooms while allowing users to participate in open-ended community-building discourses in near real time.

Equally illuminating is the role that technocultural and racial ideologies play in shaping reactions to Black Twitter. While my discourse analysis was performed on a very small scale, I conducted it in this manner to triangulate beliefs about race and technology use framed by

Black Twitter perceptions. Where whiteness and tech expertise were ascendant, Black Twitter was viewed as a game and a waste of resources. Where Blackness and tech expertise were ascendant, Black Twitter was understood as the mediated articulation of a Black subculture.

As such, I have exposed myself to claims of selectivity in order to make a political statement about online racial ideology. I submit, however, that the internet does not exist in a vacuum; offline beliefs about race and technology shape online discourses about the same. In chapter 5, which examines Black online respectability politics, the critical discourse analysis is expanded to focus on internet uplift ideology as expressed by Black bloggers, pundits, and audiences discussing Black digital practice.

Conclusions

I drew heavily on Baraka's poem "Technology and Ethos" to begin this chapter, so it's fitting to return to it before moving on to the ruminative remainder of this text. Baraka's informational Blackness could not have anticipated the internetwork's capacity for *distributed* information even as he prophesied the rhythmic and expressive articulations of Blackness made possible by Black pathos and information technologies. His inventive creation of the "speaking singing constantly communicating charm"—to be worn on the person—is a prescient reference to the smartphone. More specifically, he casually references the auditory as an informational and social affordance. Our smartphones carry entire music libraries, signal sociality through ringtones, and garner attention through notification tones. These are all ways in which the auditory captures and unites audiences in a way that the domination and discrimination of our visual senses cannot hope to achieve. Our phones create a virtual space that often serves to brighten or survive the physical spaces that Black folk must navigate daily. To describe our actions in that space as *efficient* or *modern* misses the point: bridging the reaches of space and time while grounded by Black cultural discourses is the Black version of space travel.

Black Twitter came to online prominence through creative use of Twitter's hashtag function and the subsequent domination of Twitter's trending topics. I tread carefully here; Black folk have been Twitter users from the jump. Drawing on Hughes's ([1971] 1993) definition of ethnic groups, however, I argue that Black Twitter coalesced through the recognition of the unique practices of the group by in-group and out-group observers alike. To this I add Hughes's observation that cultural behaviors are attributes of an ethnic group; the group is not defined by those attributes.

Twitter's design principles allow users to access and engage with the service with little loss of functionality across a wide number of device, client, and protocol configurations, including mobile telephones. In turn, this wide reach and access enabled minority internet users to adapt an online service that appears to fit neatly into the offline practices they use in everyday life. The informal communication evidenced in Black Twitter is not idle play; it works as an affirmation of the humanity and sensuality of the Black community in an online space that is unused to this type of spectacle.

Black Twitter is best understood as a public group of intentional Black Twitter users rather than a Black online public. That being said, Black Twitter use has coalesced around the activities of critical feminist and queer activists (specifically Black Lives Matter), allowing for the interpretation of Black Twitter as a public—albeit a terribly understudied one. Like other Black online activities, Black Twitter would have been considered niche without the intervention of the hashtag or the trending topic. As it is, these two features brought the activities of tech-literate Blacks to mainstream attention, contravening the popular conception of Black capitulation to the digital divide. Hilton's recognition and Douglas's disparagement highlight the formation of the group, while Manjoo's column signaled Black Twitter's arrival.

Typically, social networks gain popularity and public notice as users encourage their networks to adopt them. Viral spread across multiple online venues (e.g., email, instant messaging [IM], YouTube) then leads to the recognition of a "social public" by academics, pundits, and the mainstream. Black Twitter did neither of those things: Black Twitter discourse works best on Twitter, although similar cultural commonplaces are employed wherever Blacks congregate. It is also unclear how many Black Twitter users engage in Black Twitter discourse practices. In fact, as more Blacks adopt Twitter and their hashtags no longer dominate trending topics, the "publicness" of Black Twitter will return to the audience that is most involved: Black folk.

This research was simultaneously made easier and more difficult by race, as a focus on "social publics" encourages analyses of easily defined online communities. If my intent was to mark white discursive styles and practices based on Twitter usage as a social public, where would I begin? Based on the inquiry above, I could have argued for "white Twitter" as banal, efficient communication between interactants. Given prevailing stereotypes about online identity—white, male, and heterosexual unless otherwise marked—all unmarked social conversation could easily be argued for as conversation between tech-savvy white users. Alternatively, I could have examined fringe white demographics such as the alt-right to center racism as a defining characteristic of white masculine identity. I could also have used less-charged markers of white racial identity to attempt to disambiguate white Twitter practice based on class, sexuality, or other demographics. In either case, I would have been susceptible to critics claiming that I had not properly considered the heterogeneity of white identity and digital practice, which is my point.

That Black Twitter is often portrayed as representative of the entire Black community despite the heterogeneity of Black culture speaks to the power of American racial ideology's framing of Black identity as monoculture. I deliberately omitted mention of the more egregious racist responses to Black Twitter, intent on presenting Black Twitter as the technological mediation of a specific cultural discourse rather than as the product of fevered online fantasies of degenerative Black online behavior. Although these fantasies are much more vivid and easily disparaged, focusing on them moves the gaze away from Black Twitter's creativity and tech literacy to white framings of Black activity. Examining egregious online racism while ignoring more subtle, structural forms of online discrimination is problematic; equally problematic is social science and communication research that attempts to preserve a color-blind perspective on online endeavors by normalizing whiteness and othering everyone else. It is my hope that this chapter sparks a conversation about both practices.

4

Black Online Discourse, Part 1

Ratchetry and Racism

> In the technological realm, creativity by African Americans is regularly dismissed as cleverness, instead of being interpreted as smart, ingenious, or innovative.
>
> —Rayvon Fouché (2006, p. 647)

> In societies where scientific rationality and objectivity claimed to be highly valued by dominant groups, marginalized people and those who listen attentively to them will point out that from the perspective of marginal lives, the dominant accounts are less maximally objective.
>
> —Sandra Harding (1992, p. 442)

> Who
> can be born black
> and not
> sing
> the wonder of it
> the joy
> the
> challenge
>
> —Mari Evans (1970)

The previous chapters recounted case studies of Black digital practice. This chapter and the one following represent my efforts to synthesize those chapters and earlier musings on Black technoculture into an admittedly incomplete conceptual framework of Black digital discursive practice. These chapters theorize Black digital practice through three interrelated frame[1] sets, all drawing on Black aesthetics: ratchetry, racism, and respectability. Ratchetry (the quality of being ratchet) here refers to digital practice born of everyday banal, sensual, forward, and "deviant" (Cohen, 2004) political behavior that is rooted in Black culture and discourse. Racism—here defined as a set of external practices and beliefs delineating and maintaining Black identity—is an inescapable context through which Black digital practice must be contextualized. I am not arguing that Black folk are racist,[2] as racism by definition incorporates structural discrimination that Black folk have little access to. Instead, racism—as a synonym for white supremacist ideology—is the milieu in which Black identity was created. As such, responses to racism are deeply interwoven into Black discourse and aesthetics even in digital spaces where embodiment is elusive and symbolic. Finally, respectability—drawing on Higginbotham's (1993) "respectability politics"—refers to uses and beliefs about "appropriate" Black digital practice and will be addressed in the next chapter.

In a sense, I conceived these three frames of digital practice in answer to Pursell's (2010) entreaty to look at what technologies *mean* and do—in this case, the meanings intended by Black folk when they do digital practice. They are also a preliminary answer to the larger questions posed throughout this book: How do Black aesthetics shape Black digital practice and discourses? Moreover, my approach engendered an unintended yet familiar claim for the Black academic: Should racism be considered a part of the Black aesthetic?

My argument for a libidinal economy of new media and information technologies incorporates the concept of pathos—specifically, Black pathos—to argue for the rethinking of Black digital practitioners' "nonproductive," "inefficient" online activities. I apply this concept to my three proposed frames of Black online discourse, beginning with the most voluble and, I argue, most misunderstood frame: ratchet practice, or ratchetry. Given Twitter's proficiency at ritual drama and catharsis, ratchetry—thanks to its unrestrained nature—lends itself to Black Twitter practice like no other discursive frame because of its cathartic use of libidinal tensions and expressions.

Racism also has a powerful libidinal tension, the expression of which powers and colors today's social and digital media. This chapter closes by examining racism's libidinal effect on Black digital practice. While the *practice* of racism online has received enormous attention from media and the academy, the *effects* of racism on Black digital practice have not been as thoroughly researched. These effects are not limited to microaggressions or internalized racism; instead, this chapter argues that racism-as-technology mediates digital discourses of Black interiority in the context of white racial ideology.

Taken together, I reason here for ratchetry and racism as competing tensions that overdetermine the discursive frame of respectability. This perspective is deeply beholden to Du Bois's double consciousness; indeed, it only works by taking his claim seriously. Mills (1997) states that the African American experience, culture, and worldview are "deeply motivated by the necessity of doing a critique *of* the dominant view" (p. 4; emphasis original). As such, ratchetry can be (incompletely) understood as influenced by and opposed to racism. My arguments for racism also draw on Mills's research—specifically, the fact that Enlightenment thinkers wrote extensively about universal equality while ignoring arguments for the complete elision of slavery present in the majority of Enlightenment philosophy. To exist, then, Black folk continually operate in a racist paradigm through affirmations of self-worth and personhood and the recognition of racism with a *militant* insistence that others recognize it too (Mills, 1998, p. 9). In its visceral expression, this militancy can be understood as ratchet behavior, which is often identifiable by the resigned annoyance of the Black middle class and the glee of Blacks who can relate. It is visible because of the context within which it exists.

Thus I have made the choice to address both ratchetry and racism together in this chapter. In doing so, I hope to uncover the interlocking set of tensions keeping both frames active. One cannot exist without the other; racism needs a shibboleth to justify its coercion, while ratchetry without racism is just Black libidinal agency. That is, would we need to define Black agency-as-incivility as *ratchetry* if there was no gestation of *Blackness* by white supremacist ideology? Finally, I recognize the fragmentary nature of reading in this digital age. Many readers will explore this book piecemeal, and because these two concepts cannot be separated, I examine them together in the sections that follow.

Ratchetry: The Online Politics of the Everyday

> Respectable anger calls lawyers; ratchet anger calls goons. Respectable anger throws barbs; ratchet anger throws bottles.
>
> —S. G. Benjamin (2014, p. 61)

> If you want to feel humor too exquisite and subtle for translation, sit invisibly among a gang of Negro workers. The white world has its gibes and cruel caricatures; it has its loud guffaws; but to the Black world alone belongs the delicious chuckle.
>
> —W. E. B. Du Bois (1940, p. 75)

I begin with ratchetry—the enactment and performance of ratchet behavior and aesthetics—to highlight the sensuality that is present in Black digital practice. For Black culture, the invocation of *ratchet* conjures up someone who has no filter or propriety; a condition that across American race relations has often been akin to a death sentence. Ratchet shares connotative space with *ghetto* but differs from *ghetto*'s aesthetics thanks to its enactment and performance of militant insouciance.

I appropriated the term *ratchet* to ground this frame in the banal, sensual, and outspoken aspects of Black expressive culture. A second and third reason for using the term lies within the technical and technocultural denotations of *ratchet*. Technically, a ratchet is a device that, once engaged, can only rotate in one direction, while technoculturally, *ratchet* describes a process that is changing irreversibly or deteriorating. The multiple dimensions of *ratchet* offer a directional, agentive, and technical identity that works well for this frame. Finally, it is my firm belief that before commodification and before resistance, Black folk enact their cultural identity online because they enjoy being Black; my definition of *ratchetry* thus includes a libidinal component of pleasure. In all cases, *ratchet* indicates a change agent—one that seems inexorable and unamenable once involved.

For example, reconsider the intersection of *Black* and *Twitter*. Neither has ever been considered technoculturally appropriate; neither has ever possessed much cultural or social capital with mainstream institutions. Twitter is historically and currently understood as a banal (or more recently, toxic) online space, and despite its acclaim as an agent for social justice, its utility is questioned daily. Similarly, while Blackness may have reached its peak approbation during the eight years of the Michelle Obama administration, it nonetheless stands as the signified cultural nadir for American whiteness—uncivilized, impure, and primitive. The modulation of Twitter by Blackness, then, should signal a desolate wasteland of incoherent technical and digital discourse, but instead, Black Twitter is considered the premiere use case for the microblogging service, with significant contributions to information and computer technology (ICT) practice as well as social activism.

I chose *ratchet* rather than *banal* to describe the energies expressed within everyday performances and practices of Black folk online. *Banal* is a diminutive, pejorative term meant to indicate the mundanity and irrelevance of activities denoted as such. *Ratchet*, on the other hand, is hypervisible thanks to its embodiment and its performance of agentive deviance—to external and internal social and cultural orders. To be ratchet in Black culture is not always intended as a compliment but is always indicative of agency. In online spaces, ratchetry should also be understood as the willingness to intentionally be Black and perform Blackness in spaces that are still uninterested in recognizing Black agency. For Black women and queer folk online, race is often no respite from in-group prejudice; being and performing Blackness is often met with Black male misogyny, sexism, and homo- and transphobia, but nevertheless, they persist.

Feminist media scholars have been interrogating ratchetry and ratchet behavior since the term entered the popular lexicon from 2000s-era Southern rap. *Ratchet* joins a long list of slang terms (e.g., thot,[3] basic) linking Black bodies—often female and/or queer—with "hood" or deviant behavior (Bradley, 2013a, 2013b; Cooper, 2012; Warner, 2015). From rap's perspective, ratchetry revolves around perceptions of crass materialism, promiscuity, rudeness, ignorance, inappropriateness, dishabille, and occasionally violence. Ratchet even has a digital practice component: the highest-rated definition of *ratchet* on Urban Dictionary includes the stipulation "owning a BlackBerry." Given the BlackBerry's one-time association with white professional culture, the Urban Dictionary's reassigning of the smartphone to a raced, gendered, technical identity is a signifyin' recognition of Black digital practice.

My aim here is to reconstitute *ratchet* as a positive force by positioning it as (uber)performative authenticity—as "'bout it," "real," and "doing the most"—which links implicitly with the technical definition of the ratchet as a one-way force. In this I am not alone; there are a number of cogent academic definitions as well. Stallings (2013) calls *ratchet* "the performance of the failure to be respectable, uplifting, and a credit to the race" (p. 136). Bradley (2013a) positions *ratchet* as a Black Southern cultural export—a form of expression intervening against the ways in which respectability politics denigrates women of color. I would add that ratchet folk are unapologetic about their Black identity, and even suggesting that it is performative would rub many the wrong way. I argue here that ratchetry's superpower is its refusal to apologize for or assimilate to out-group and in-group notions of appropriate behavior and aesthetics.

Ratchetry as Online Praxis

At this point, it is necessary to highlight the foundation of my framing of ratchetry as online praxis and Black digital practice: Cathy Cohen's (2004) article "Deviance as Politics." Defining *deviance* as "breaking the assumed agreed upon norms of socially acceptable behavior," Cohen argues that "in the space created by deviant discourse and practice . . . a new radical politics of deviance could emerge. It might take the shape of a radical politics of the personal, embedded in more recognized Black counter publics, where the most marginal individuals in Black communities . . . act with the limited agency available to them to secure small levels of autonomy in their lives" (p. 28). From here, it is but a small step to associate ratchetry with deviance; doing so invigorates deviance by deliberately associating it with Black (women's) bodies. "Small levels of autonomy" clearly refers to everyday moments when Black folk are able to assert agency despite the forces arrayed against them, not grand gestures of respectability or political solidarity (e.g., the choice to wear a purple weave as an expression of self rather than a relaxed hairstyle). For instance, the canonical hashtag #BlackGirlMagic, created by Twitter user CaShawn Thompson (@thepbg), is a beautiful example of the creative libidinal tensions present in ratchet embodiments of Black femininity. Finally, Cohen's phrase "the space created by deviant discourse and practice" anticipates Twitter beautifully a full three years before its creation and five years before Black Twitter began to be noticed. While Twitter fits this phrasing best thanks to its unconventional discourse practices, Cohen also describes Black digital practice—an unanticipated cultural intervention into a virtual space through discourse and technical skill. She adds, "It may be that through the repetition of deviant practices by multiple individuals new identities, communities, and politics are created and a space emerges where seemingly deviant, unconnected behavior might evolve into conscious acts of resistance that serve as the basis for a mobilized politics of deviance" (2004, p. 42).

My claim for ratchetry diverges from Cohen's definition of deviance to avoid equating Black deviance with "wrongness," which it incurs even in Cohen's generous interpretation. Recasting *deviance* as *ratchet* links my libidinal economic analysis of online Black deviant behavior and practice to expressions of joy, sensuality, and anger; some of these expressions might occasionally manifest as online politics and a counterpublic sphere. Where discourses of respectability tend to link ratchet with the hardcore strip club anthems of the 2000s or the scripted reality-show antics of Black women, I am suggesting an alternative perspective. Despite the constraints of the white racial frame (Feagin, 2013), Black culture as a whole is unabashedly, joyously, cathartically ratchet. Even enmeshed in white racial ideology, Black culture still manages to create agency through pathos, here defined as revels in sensuality and the erotic.

Similarly, linking deviance to the "most marginal individuals" undersells the capacity for acts of uncivil resistance across the entire Black community—for example, consider recent arguments for Black professional women's enjoyment of ratchet performances of Black womanhood on reality television (Warner, 2015). Given my arguments for libidinal tensions as Black pathos, I see ratchetry and ratchet digital practice as expressions of joy—as celebrations of self in defiance of norms that can be imposed by both external and internal forces. This is particularly evident in examining Black Twitter practice but also lives on in the visual expressions afforded by (Black) Instagram or Snapchat. These expert enactments of Black identity—as referenced by the hashtags #BlackGirlMagic or #BlackBoyJoy—are in and of themselves shows of defiance to a world that expects obeisance and victimhood. Thus *marginal* can only insufficiently describe the technical capacity or even the assets of Black digital practitioners.

For example, in communities where monopoly telecom providers extend lackluster broadband internet, mobile technologies and devices have propelled Black digital practitioners beyond multiple digital divides. Pew Internet reports that nearly 64 percent of Black users access the internet solely through smartphones, taking full advantage of mobile app development and broadband to be full participants in online and social media. The catch—and a basis for my arguments for ratchet digital practice—is that activities promoting the self are often seen as supplanting appropriate practices, such as "work" or "progress."

Benchmarking the Ratchet: Appropriate Digital Practice

To strengthen my argument for ratchetry as deviant digital practice, however, I must discuss "appropriate" internet digital practice. Given the wildly heterogeneous nature of the web, it seems disingenuous to suggest that there is a "right" way to internet. As I found in chapters 2 and 3, however, both white and Black internet users believe Black folk behave online in certain ways—practices, performances, and discourses—even as the different groups disagree along racial lines about whether those activities are appropriate for online spaces and devices. Thus it makes sense to argue for ratchet digital practice's deviance by benchmarking what appropriate digital practice might be.

The web's heterogeneity can be traced back to the epistemology of the hyperlink. Conceptualized by Tim Berners-Lee as content-agnostic, the hyperlink's design draws on Vannevar Bush's (1945) and Ted Nelson's (1974) arguments for connecting culture and information. Its function enables access to *any* media stored on remote servers via *any* client or protocol. This freedom has been extremely generative for the web, encouraging the development of an incredible variety of websites, applications, platforms, and services—enough so that many believe the internet has its own culture. However, race has never been fairly considered as a contributor to that culture. Whiteness is rarely understood as an element of internet culture(s) even though the vast majority of creators, coders, engineers, venture capitalists, and designers are white or white-adjacent. Their copresence in and proximity to the internet standardize their conduct as a norm for internet behaviors. Consider the activities of two former Google employees, James Damore and Kevin Cernekee. Damore was terminated for posting a ten-page manifesto arguing that women are less capable than men (Conger, 2017), while Cernekee was fired for proposing that his colleagues fundraise in support of white nationalist efforts (McKay, 2019; Copeland, 2019). These examples and other recent events illustrate that racism, sexism, and misogyny are long-standing practices in the tech community. The refusal to mark whiteness as an identity powers the concept that internet culture is raceless, that racism is a "glitch" (Nakamura, 2013), and that Twitter is the cause of internet incivility.

How, then, does Black embodiment—not just performance but enactment—manifest in online spaces? Earlier I suggested that ratchetry can be understood as a hypervisible, embodied performance of agentive deviance. Despite the absence of physical embodiment in online venues, Black folk have constructed, contested, and maintained cultural online places through symbolic means: online discourse—including images and memes—and the design of home pages and social media profiles.

Home Pages > Social Media

Consider the World Wide Web. Even before Black folk, with their deviant selves, were understood to be active in online spaces, Web 2.0 was argued for as a deviation from the hand-coded transactional and individual expressiveness of online practice (e.g., webrings or spaces like GeoCities) thanks to its narrowly tailored design principles, which served as aesthetic correctives to the chaotic design values of personal home pages. At the same time, others complained that the nascent movement was a continuation of mass media's hegemonic cultural apparatus due to the rapid capture of these new artifacts and platforms by investors and media companies. Nevertheless, Black folk turned to weblogs as spaces for personal and cultural expression in rapidly increasing numbers (Brock, 2007).

Personal website design in the Web 1.0 era largely consisted of hand-coded HTML, GeoCities templates, or BlackPlanet personal pages.[4] The freedom to experiment with fonts, text effects, graphics, and media players made the early personal web a cacophonous destination.

Blogging platforms such as Blogger or Typepad sought to address this—even as they lowered barriers for casual users seeking to build a web presence—by promoting a more uniform design. These sites read more like printed pages, with standardized internet fonts and a white space–oriented design aesthetic. When encountering Blogger, Typepad, or WordPress sites of this era, one knew to credit the platform rather than the individual user for the page's design choices. I argue that more than any other internet spaces, the blogging platforms encoded Web 2.0's focus on information transmission that was only lightly flavored by personal tastes. In short, these platforms helped establish what "appropriate" web design should be, an aesthetic later solidified by Facebook.

As mentioned earlier, BlackPlanet encouraged users to design their home pages and promoted designs on the portal's destination page. Omar Wasow and Gary Dauphin's initiative to embed HTML design tools and social affordances within BlackPlanet prefigured Web 2.0's digital sociality and personalization. Oh, but the designs. In addition to the excesses of Web 1.0—sparkling cursors, autoplaying media players—BlackPlanet was one of the first spaces where user-generated content featuring Black everyday culture was proudly displayed and promoted (Banks, 2005; Byrne, 2007). While BlackPlanet functioned as a portal site offering employment resources and news, its home pages often featured content that was intent on generating culturally based emotional appeals: alluring pictures of beautiful brown people; gospel, R&B, or rap music; and appeals for page votes as a marker of popularity were in vogue as early as 1999. BlackPlanet was ratchet long before Myspace or Twitter were understood as minority-dominated online spaces.

In danah boyd's (2009) canonical talk "The Not-So-Hidden Politics of Class Online" (later published in 2011 as "White Flight in Networked Publics? How Race and Class Shaped American Teen Engagement with Myspace and Facebook"), she argues that the design aesthetics of two early Web 2.0 titans—Myspace and Facebook—are linked to the cultural, even racialized uses of each site. She focuses on teens, and her argument is noteworthy for the ways in which the interviewees talk *around* race. The assertions boyd makes also hold true for BlackPlanet even though the site never gained the notoriety of Myspace or Facebook.

The lack of mainstream attention—perhaps in part because BlackPlanet's demographics skewed older—also helped BlackPlanet initially avoid the *ghetto* tag associated with Myspace, which like then contemporary social network services (SNS) Bebo and Xanga appealed to younger users.

Black culture, however, has never been considered as a natural space for information technology use and design. BlackPlanet's explicit focus on Black users led academics and the mainstream media to view it as a "niche" online destination, even hindering it from being considered as one of the first social networking sites. Indeed, Dauphin suggested that investors were reluctant to fund the site because they did not believe Black folk would be interested in creating or able to code their own home pages (Brock, 2007). These sentiments—that Black folk were not "serious" or rational internet users—also framed early commentary about Black Twitter use (Brock, 2012). I contend that the dominance of Black cultural content on Twitter has even led some to declare the "end" of Twitter (Topolsky, 2016; Romano, 2019; Schroeder, 2014) as investors and tech pundits scramble to explain why Twitter cannot continue in its current iteration. These prognostications and opinion pieces are driven by libidinal energies of antiblackness rather than political economy—that is, technocrats cannot conceive of a successful technological enterprise driven by Black pathos.

Although there is little consensus on whether today's mobile internet constitutes Web 3.0, there will always be arguments about what constitutes appropriate internet practice and design. Design privileges a certain type of user; from this perspective, Twitter has long been considered incoherent and inappropriate based on its design principles privileging personal contacts, terse content, and broadcast messaging. Few realize, however, that much of Twitter's interface and features draw on its originally conceived platform: the smartphone's short-message service (SMS). SMS was derided as inappropriate in the United States for years because teenagers took to it so quickly and thoroughly despite their lack of jobs or productivity. SMS (and the smartphone) should instead be considered as one of the first communication technologies linking digital use and embodied discourses. The next section briefly considers how mobility and connectivity in a Black digital context tie race (and often class) with information resources in ways that transform "inappropriate" digital practice.

. . . and Mobile Digital Practice

I began this chapter by appraising how race mediates website design; however, we must also consider the rise of the smartphone[5] as a deviant Black cultural and informational artifact. Black folk use cultural aesthetics to inform their mobile computing use—they are "on trend"—in ways that perform Black identity in a recognizable form while consistently gaining attention in (and in some cases, dominating) our crowded information spheres. While late 1990s and early 2000s arguments for Black digital technology adoption traded upon capitalism, desktop computing paradigms as "productivity," and respectability ideologies (e.g., community technology centers where Black folk could learn technology to get "good jobs" or code academies for today's minority youth), the mobile phone's interpenetration into everyday life meant that a new type of user was reshaping information technologies in their own image. I don't just mean poor Black folk either: Black and Brown parents overindexed on home-computer ownership during the aughts (Smith, 2010a) to ensure that their families would have access to these new information resources, which were largely unrestricted—unlike historically segregated institutions, such as the library or the academy.

Smartphones, introduced in the United States in the early 2000s, are high-end variants of mobile (née cellular) telephones. Whereas cell phones were first deployed in 1994 and were primarily designed to connect to a cellular radio system to provide mobile telephone service, smartphones employ an operating system featuring mobile applications as well as a suite of features, including higher-resolution color screens, more powerful processors, multitouch interfaces, web access, multimedia technology and playback, and GPS navigation. Smartphones overlap and extend both the personal data assistant and the Pocket PC phone era (e.g., Windows CE, BlackBerry, and Palm phones and devices); these devices, characterized by resistive touch screens, physical keyboards, and styli, enacted a digital and ideological commitment to productivity and enterprise software needs and interfaces. I should mention an additional category of cell phones, the feature phone, which allows voice calls, limited internet browsing, and text messaging but offers few other features. These phones were once mainstays of prepaid and lower-cost cellular subscription plans, but low-cost Chinese smartphones have largely supplanted them. This means that smartphones are employed by an ever-growing number of users who are boxed out of more expensive postpaid plans.

Smith (2015) notes that a greater percentage of Blacks and Latinx (70 percent and 71 percent, respectively) own smartphones compared to whites (60 percent). Smith also contends that Blacks and Latinx have higher rates of smartphone dependency—that is, they have fewer alternative ways to access the internet. This dependence can be attributed to a number of economic, social, and technical factors, including the deregulation of the landline telephone industry, the disinvestment in landline telephone access in underserved communities (and thus broadband access), the inability to afford unmetered data use cellular subscription plans, and the falling prices of computational technologies.

The initial uptake of the smartphone by early adopters—a small set of technological, cultural, and economic elites—furthered technocultural beliefs about mobile information technology as a productive, efficient artifact and practice. For example, for several years, the BlackBerry was the preferred communication device of industry, medicine, government, and tech elites. Indeed, President Obama was loath to give up his BlackBerry device upon assuming the Oval Office, as its security features and material affordances were familiar to him even though it was not fully supported by the woefully underprepared White House information technology infrastructure.

Although governments and enterprises rapidly adopted BlackBerry phones and Windows CE–based phones, mobile computing has long been considered less competent than desktop-based computing thanks to multiple technical, aesthetic, and technocultural constraints (e.g., display technology, interface design, and beliefs about productivity). Mobile devices are commonly derided as lifestyle products even with advances in connectivity, increases in screen size, and leaps in computational power. This dismissive attitude gained strength with Apple's introduction of the iPhone (2007) and iPad (2010), as Apple is commonly seen as a "fashion" or "lifestyle" brand instead of a "serious" computing manufacturer like Palm, RIM, and Hewlett-Packard.

From a digital divide perspective, mobile broadband access has significantly increased the number of Blacks online. Rainie (2016) notes that only 55 percent of Blacks enjoy home broadband access, while nearly 80 percent of Blacks access the internet using smartphones and mobile devices. When media reports on these surveys claim (Riley, 2019; Marriott, 2006) that Black smartphone usage signals the closing of the digital divide, counterarguments—particularly those referencing the lack of "desktop-class" apps or the use of "lifestyle" appliances—are quickly deployed to dismiss these assertions. These counterarguments are made not only by whites; they are also deployed in the service of respectability by well-meaning, progressive, and technophilic Blacks for whom the current statistical dominance of smartphone ownership is not a marker of progress precisely because of the libidinal and banal practices (i.e., "consumption" or "distraction") Black folk engage in while enacting Black identity online.

From a libidinal economic perspective, what are the consequences of having an internet-connected, social network–connected, high-powered computational and video device in one's pocket every day (and night)? Claims about mobile productivity and use must be reevaluated, as the smartphone serves as the genius loci around which one's communicative life revolves and as a witness for many mundane activities up to and including sleep. For Black smartphone users, these devices reduce social isolation in unfriendly spaces through their capacity to share culturally relevant content and connect with other, often isolated Black others. Smartphone affordances, such as instantaneous communication, the ability to record moments of everyday life, and the transmission of these moments and communications to already-identified affiliative cultural group members, offer Blacks a virtual third place similar to that defined by Oldenburg (1999) or Nunley's (2011) African American "hush harbors."

The Smartphone as a Digital Third Place

I have argued for Black online spaces as third places before (Brock, 2009), but it's worth reconsidering the differences between an online third place and one anchored by the materiality of the smartphone. According to Oldenburg (1999), third places offer

- a home away from home, where
- conversation is the main activity and
- playfulness is the prevailing mood.

Let's unpack these characteristics to see how they work as digital affordances.

Neutral yet Intimate

A desktop-based online third place is always anchored to a specific computing location: your living room, the library, a college campus, or the office. Even as one spends time in a virtual location with friends, she is also geographically present in either a home or a work space. By contrast, smartphone usage can and does happen anywhere—particularly on the go, in the street, or in "inappropriate" spaces, such as the bathroom and the car. For Black and ratchet digital practice, smartphones allow the recording and sharing of activities—impromptu dances, risqué behavior, and moments of hilarity (or violence)—that couldn't take place in more proscribed environments. Thus there is an uncoupling of technology use from appropriate behavior. Moreover, Black discourses once located in private spaces, such as the barbershop (Steele, 2016, 2018) and beauty salon (Nunley, 2011), have been extended to group chats, discussion threads, and other messaging applications.

The smartphone's portability is based on the ergonomics of the hand—and to be held and used at arms' length—as well as its small[6] screen size. Together, these attributes concentrate the user's visual and cognitive focus on a small area held in close physical proximity. Smartphone use thus affords aspects of "personal space" to invoke intimacy while simultaneously connecting the user to (and disconnecting from) a wider world. Whereas webcams present the video creator in an intimate, personal space, thanks to technical features, embodied locations, and environmental aspects, smartphone video retains physical proximity while transferring intimacy to spaces outside the home. As such, the smartphone becomes nearly as much a domestic locus of identity as the home itself; so much of our intimate activities and social relationships occur in the space between screen and self. In doing so, the smartphone supplants the telephone's capacity to forge intimate virtual spaces, bringing conversations that were once held in our bedrooms or on our comfortable couches into public spaces.

Ratchet digital practice benefits from the smartphone's public intimacy. One benefit is catharsis: the smartphone modulates an intimate space where the affronts and excesses of American racial ideology can be shared with other Black folk. These cathartic moments are not just postencounter but, importantly, also preencounter. A jarring example of postencounter catharsis would be the Facebook Live video testimony of Diamond Reynolds following the murder of her boyfriend, Philando Castile, by a Minnesota police officer during a random stop. Reynolds narrated the events immediately preceding the video, maintaining her composure with great difficulty. While her video was not enough to convince a jury of the police officer's malfeasance, her recording stands as a powerful example of Black digital practice transforming information technology into a wailing wall, reposted thousands of times across the social web.

To explain preencounter catharsis, consider two comedy routines in the legendary concert movie *The Original Kings of Comedy* (Harvey et al., 2000). The first is philosophical: comedian Cedric the Entertainer muses on differences in racial epistemologies of progress by arguing that white folk "hope," while Black folk "wish." He gives an example of seating arrangements at a concert: late-arriving white folk *hope* no one is sitting in their seats, but Black folk *wish* "a muthafucka *would*" be sitting in their place. This dialogic longing for confrontation as a corrective to deliberate misunderstandings of humanity and entitlement can be understood as ratchet discourse. It also allows the interlocutor to build energies from both their performance and the reaction of the audience, creating a precatharsis moment.

The second instance from *Kings of Comedy* is Bernie Mac's canonical ratchet grammar exercise, where he articulates Black uses of the word *motherfucker*. A description doesn't do it justice, so I have reproduced it here as best as I can to honor Bernie's diction and intensity:

> When you're listening to one of our conversations, you might hear the word MOTHERFUCKER about thirty-two times. Don't be afraid of the word MOTHERFUCKER. . . . Imma break it down to ya. . . . If you're out there this afternoon and you see like three or four brothers talkin', you might hear a conversation, and it goes like this:
>
> "You seen that MOTHERFUCKIN' Bobby? That MOTHERFUCKER owes me thirty-five MOTHERFUCKEN' dollars! He told me he gone pay my MOTHERFUCKIN' money last MOTHERFUCKEN' week. I ain't

> seen this MOTHERFUCKER yet! I'm not gonna chase this MOTHERFUCKER for my thirty-five MOTHERFUCKEN' dollars.
>
> "I called the MOTHERFUCKER four MOTHERFUCKEN' times . . . but the MOTHERFUCKER won't call me back. I called his momma the other MOTHERFUCKEN' day . . . she gonna play like the MOTHERFUCKER wasn't in. I started to cuss her MOTHERFUCKEN' ass out, but I don't want no MOTHERFUCKEN' trouble.
>
> "But I'll tell ya one MOTHERFUCKEN thang . . . the next MOTHERFUCKEN' time I see this MOTHERFUCKER . . . and he ain't got my MOTHERFUCKEN' money . . . I'm gonna bust—his—MOTHERFUCKEN' head! And I'm OUT this MOTHAFUCKA!"

The ratchetry within this extended utterance happens on multiple levels: the denotative and connotative profanity of *motherfucker*, the aggressive energy of the invocation, the repetition, and the audience. These two examples highlight the signifyin' practice of the "woof" or "wolf ticket"—that is, "barking but not going to bite." They establish agency through the performance (not the enactment) of verbal violence.

While the connection between these comedy bits and the digital might seem tenuous, I link these two cases of preencounter catharsis to digital and mobile practice to support my arguments about the digital's mediation of offline Black discursive practices. The smartphone recasts these activities as Black discursive identity, broadcasting their libidinal tensions to a virtual space and audience. These are crucial affordances for those of us who are "the one Black person" in primarily white environments. Instead of expressing these cathartic sentiments to those with institutional or social power over us, we can preserve our sanity by relating them to those who understand the need to vent in safety. Where once these conversations had to wait until one returned to Black enclaves or the home, now they can take place in a neutral yet intimate third place.

Conversational

This is the easiest point to support, given that the smartphone's raison d'être is communication. The smartphone benefits from its telephonic origins as a precomputation virtual space, where intimate conversations could (and did) take place away from visual feedback. Its audiovisual capabilities add additional bandwidth to intimate conversations and activities (e.g., Yo Gotti's "Down in the DM" and Snapchat's mix of visuality and ephemerality). Additionally, the smartphone's capacity to record and store video or images at any time adds archival affordances to libidinal digital practices, like sharing intimate pictures. The smartphone's maturation as a social networking device—particularly for near real-time networks like Twitter, Snapchat, and Instagram—encourage discursive interactions. Finally, the rise of group chat applications—for example, GroupMe and Facebook Messenger—should dispel beliefs about the smartphone as an alienating, isolating device, since group conversations connect dozens of intimates (or associates) while demanding virtual presence and participation to prosper.

Playful

The smartphone's ability to distract the user from his geographic surroundings leads to my final quality: playfulness. The device's capacity for play and, by extension, pleasure contribute to technocultural beliefs about its inappropriateness as a social and productivity artifact. I am avoiding the smartphone's capacity for gaming as playfulness because that is a facile distinction, and smartphones are not yet considered "true" gaming devices like desktop computers or consoles. I will, however, discuss the link among leisure, playfulness, and distraction.

Smartphone use affords a lesser-known aspect of playfulness in digital spaces, one that is often granted to proponents of uncivil and hurtful behaviors, such as trolling (Phillips, 2015)—namely, spectatorship. This is the recognition, acknowledgment, and sharing of the joy of people *like me* captured by the smartphone's camera. It differs from voyeurism in that I am not viewing the activities of strangers. It's also not consumption, although new media researchers have studied social media as second screens for media consumption (the television is the first screen) and building online community (Williams, 2016; Lee & Andrejevic, 2013). Instead, the metrics of digital platforms interpellate spectators as users, audience members, and participants. Where sporting event ticket sales and Nielson Media Research use quantitative data to determine audience size and composition, the digital metrics of views, likes, shares, reposts, and quotes define spectators as vital components of playful moments that are shared to social media. Accordingly, gaming scholars such as Gray (2016) document how internet-protocol television has empowered spectatorship as a viable part of the gaming community through participatory personal game streaming and online-only coverage of digital gaming competitions, lending credence to this argument.

Consider the smartphone's function as a music player. It neatly usurped radio, the Walkman, and even the vaunted iPod's place in American culture as the avatar of portable entertainment, communication technology, and leisure, but "leisure," mediated by the smartphone, has significantly changed in representation and practice. Radios were depicted in popular media and in advertising as a source of musical pleasure for physical gatherings and even as catalysts for enabling leisure spaces in unlikely physical locations (the stoop, the street corner, etc.). There are even racialized representations of the radio: transistor radios for white youth versus the canonical boom box for Black and Brown youth. As a music player, the smartphone is often depicted as an isolating activity thanks to a lack of quality speakers.[7] Indeed, smartphone music listening is represented through racialized shorthand. For example, Apple's white EarPods signify the upper class, whiteness, and leisure, often modulated by Black bodies for rhythmic, soulful emphasis. Similarly, prior to their purchase by Apple, Beats by Dre headphones were argued for as a sign of lower-class and nonwhite identity due to their bass-heavy sound profile and association with Andre Young, a canonical hip-hop producer and rapper.

The smartphone as music player, then, encourages a reconsideration of leisure as digital practice. After all, leisure requires time and attention; it is not idleness or simply distraction. While leisure is often defined as sociality, many find pleasure in solitude and isolation. The isolation that the smartphone-plus-earbud combination provides often masks, if not alleviates, the frenetic chaos of urban living. Moreover, the smartphone affords the music or podcast listener the capacity to enjoy—not just endure—the unavoidable tedium of work, long commutes, and extended exercise sessions. Thus an inappropriate digital practice can contribute to leisure and to quality of life.

To return to ratchetry, the smartphone's capacity for creativity-as-play is also a component of inappropriate digital practice. Burgess and Green (2009) argue that everyday content creation should be understood as social network formation and collective play. Gaunt's (2015) work on twerking, mobile phones, and YouTube provides an illustrative example. Twerking, Gaunt argues, is a "kinetic orality" (p. 247) that draws on a genre of dances across Africa and the African diaspora featuring the rotational isolation of the hips. Given the Western racialized and gendered pejorative association of a woman's hips and posterior with libidinal erotic energies, twerking is deemed an inappropriate activity. Although it came to mainstream attention through the shenanigans of Miley Cyrus, it has a nearly twenty-five-year history that is tightly tied to Black women's bodies and southern rap music. Gaunt deftly unpacks YouTube's capacity for the expression of Black girls' and women's kinetic and artistic creativity in dance; she argues that the recording, broadcast, and sharing of Black women's dance videos breaks social and spatial boundaries for Blacks and non-Blacks. To this, I add that the smartphone's uncoupling of videography from the semifixed lens of the webcam and the expense of high-definition video cameras and studio settings has contributed to Black women's digital expertise in video production and dissemination. The smartphone also lends the user mobility, detaching intimate, celebratory, and energetic Black cultural performances (like twerking) from the domestic sphere and moving them into less "appropriate" spaces. Smartphone videos even recast the domestic sphere as a public space, as twerk videos are often posted from home, enabling women to simultaneously express the freedom to be on their own terms in public *and* in private. In a similar vein, Bragin (2015) determines that "hood dance" challenges assumptions of where and how dance can be performed as improvisational practices teaching hip-hop aesthetics of freestyle and rhythm.

To recap: smartphones can be understood as digital networked Black cultural third places. The interactions in these virtual gatherings draw on libidinal expression—sometimes violent, sometimes pleasurable, but always sensual—in the context of computer-mediated communication, leading to my characterization of the smartphone as a ratchet, often inappropriate device.

Ratchet Digital Practice

After that lengthy preamble, let me offer examples of ratchet digital practice. In keeping with the connection between digital practice and computer-mediated communication, my first exemplar reflects my admiration of the creativity of Black Twitter display names, which often follow a long Twitter tradition of embodied, libidinal Black online user names. These inventive pseudonyms have received short shrift, as they should be properly considered discrete, ephemeral snippets exemplifying the playfulness of Black discourse and culture. Let me explain: Twitter, like many other online services, allows users to identify themselves through a unique username. For example, countless profile generators use an email address to authenticate and identify the account holder. In recent years, developers have begun to understand that personalization creates a deeper bond between the user and the technology and thus encourage users to proffer their "government name"[8] or nickname. These names, rather than the username or account number, often serve as a marker[9] for the user's account profile.

Twitter differs from most services; it also allows users to create a pseudonymous display name to be displayed *alongside* the username.[10] Twitter user names, which serve as profile links, addresses, and account identifiers, have historically been limited to fifteen characters and do not allow spaces. Usernames were originally counted as part of a tweet's 140 characters[11] even as their use diminished the space available for the message.[12] Display names, however, could be up to 20 characters long; this was recently expanded to 50 characters and can include spaces, emoji, and other Unicode characters. Many users set their given names as their display name—especially verified users—which lends legitimacy and authority to their Twitter practice. Display names can be changed at any time; Black Twitter users often take advantage of this to display affiliation, cultural knowledge, and more.

I argue that Twitter's extended display name feature eschews utility while affording Black Twitter users cultural specificity, their allegiance to Black culture, and the performance of style and aesthetics in ways that are not always possible on other digital spaces. Moreover, Twitter's prominence to the mainstream exposes these display names to audiences who have never encountered Black culture elsewhere. To redress the lack of attention to this Black digital practice, I offer an incomplete list of Black Twitter display names gleaned from my timeline as avatars of Black agency in digital spaces. These names are all from public accounts. Rather than decode them, I present them in their unaltered, signifyin' glory as a way of acknowledging the ratchetness they perform:

- Gucci Ma'am
- Auntie Hot Flash Summer
- Wikipedia Brown
- Fatniss Collargreen
- BitchesLoveLibraries
- DarkSkintDostoyevsky
- coochiechagulia
- skeptical brotha
- Tardy B
- Blanket Jackson
- y'all dont read
- Zora Neale Hustlin'
- Mercury in microbraids
- kin klux klan
- Ho, Ho, Hotep!
- Durags & Dialectics
- Optimus Fine
- Swole Porter
- lupita's sideburns

I will not sully the ritual, inventive signification of these display names by attempting to unpack their symbolism or their connections to Black culture. I should note that display name creativity is a common feature shared by all Twitter users, not just Black Twitter; in many cases, users coin creative and imaginative pseudonyms to mark their accounts. However, the names listed here share Black cultural commonplaces, articulated in a limited space, to construct Black discursive identity in digital spaces. These names anticipate the libidinal, signifyin' Black Twitter content that these users post, making it clear that style, rather than efficiency, is a productive method of communication.

Ratchetry in Action

An interesting example of ratchet digital practice occurred while I was writing this chapter. On March 6, 2016, Nancy Reagan, former first lady of the United States, passed away at the age of ninety-four. The next day, "David D" created a Change.org petition asking that then popular rapper Fetty Wap perform his breakout hit "Trap Queen" at the first lady's funeral. While Fetty Wap—born William Maxwell II—would not be the first African American artist asked to perform at a state funeral, the petition goes far beyond quotidian uses of Black culture to commemorate government actors. The vulgar song directly criticizes US drug policy by addressing the devastating effects of that policy on minority communities.

This ratchetry works in multiple dimensions. From a digital practice perspective, Change.org is a privately run nonprofit website where users create online petitions to advance social causes; it is similar to other public policy–oriented websites that follow the principles of crowdsourcing, such as MoveOn.org. One of its most popular petitions, with more than two million signatures, argued for the conviction of George Zimmerman during his trial for the murder of Trayvon Martin. Change.org petitions have been signed by political figures such as President Obama, and the site has been acknowledged as a change agent. Change.org is not, however, the same as the White House–sponsored petition site We the People (https://petititions.whitehouse.gov), where petitions that meet a certain threshold of participation may be reviewed by the White House administration and even engender an official response.

What's ratchet about a petition website? A banal (but not ratchet) We the People petition in 2014 garnered nearly three hundred thousand signatures to ask the US government to deport Justin Bieber because he was "dangerous, reckless, and drug abusing" ("Deport," 2014). The White House responded to the petition by promoting immigration reform but declined to take action to deport the young singer. While this example says much about Americans' professed distaste for popular and Black music—and also reveals a hint of xenophobia—it's not ratchet.

David D's petition achieves ratchet digital practice in use, content, and intent. It was created *using* an online service to subvert political activism through deviant means: the critique of public policy using hip-hop. This is particularly evident in the choice of *content*; rather than suggesting an appropriate artist from an appropriate genre to provide a musical tribute for a sober state occasion, David D selected a rapper whose song specifically references inappropriate libidinal topics: drug dealing and the objectification of women. Fetty Wap's[13] debut single, "Trap Queen," was released in 2014 and reached the number-two spot on the Billboard Hot 100 Chart in 2015. Julianne Escobedo Shepherd (2016) describes the song as a "loving ode to a woman uniting with a man in emotional, spiritual, and economic matters, the latter of which involves cooking crack cocaine . . . an excellent song that perfectly melds romance with nihilism." Finally, David D's *intent* links the positive connotations of "Trap Queen"—despite its negative depictions and negative context—to Nancy Reagan, who David D describes as the "biggest Trap Queen ever." Despite Reagan's ostensible intentions to curb drug use in minority communities, the "Just Say No" campaign had little effect during the 1980s, as it merrily glossed over the conditions under which the drug trade flourishes, including environmental and educational inequality, racially biased enforcement, and economic policies intended to punish minorities for being poor.

The petition garnered more than seven thousand signatures at the time of this writing; it doesn't have a snowball's chance in hell of exerting any influence over the former first lady's interment ceremony. But the outcome isn't the point—it's the performance. In speaking out of turn while violating boundaries of propriety and civility, David D's petition achieves ratchetry through the hypervisibility of digital media used to signify through libidinal Black cultural critique.

Discussion

This section has done significant work in connecting libidinal economy to digital practice but at the expense of omitting more outrageous, visceral examples of ratchet behavior. This omission includes a dearth of profane, obscene, or violent ratchet digital practices, such as the meme "WorldStar!" referencing the hip-hop site WorldStarHipHop, which is notorious for posting uncensored street fight videos. I take my cue from Judy's (1994) pronouncement: "The human can be designated a phenomenal thing of the slave experience, *nigger*, but never *is* a nigger"

(p. 217; emphasis original). Given America's fascination with Black deviance, I could have easily turned to Antoine Dodson's viral interview, which ignited the Auto-Tune sensation "Hide Yo Kids, Hide Yo Wife," or Kimberly "Sweet Brown" Wilkins's viral interview and her Black commonplace catchphrase "Ain't nobody got time for that." Moreover, it is far too easy to highlight social media memes about "things respectable Black folk don't do," including posing with guns on social media; "thots," thirst traps, and fuckbois;[14] twerking; and wearing outrageously colored hairstyles, sagging pants, or grilles.

I use these examples to illustrate my own discomfort with ratchetry; they show that the problematics of ratchetry largely lie in the perceptions of those worried about being seen as ratchet. Selecting instances guaranteed to offend those who are even slightly interested or invested in respectability would have short-circuited my arguments for ratchet digital practice. Similarly, choosing more visceral examples of Black folk behaving "badly" would have obscured my efforts at constructing a nuanced definition of ratchet digital practice.[15] Ratchetry is often interpreted by the mainstream—and middle-, upper-, and working-class Blacks—as the only behavior of (often poor) Black folk. That is, pejorative perspectives of ratchetry are shaped by (1) the mainstream racist frameworks in which ratchetry takes place as well as (2) the effects of that racist framework on Black folk.

In making this claim, I am guided by Du Bois's (1940) description of Black middle-class attitudes toward working-class Blacks. Observing Blacks and their "peculiar social environment" (p. 61) from a sociological perspective, Du Bois writes, "The American Negro, therefore, is surrounded and conditioned by the concept which he has of white people and he is treated in accordance with the concept they have of him . . . if in education and ambition and income he is above the average culture of his group, he is often resentful of its environing power; partly because he does not recognize its power and partly because he is determined to consider himself part of the white group from which, in fact, he is excluded" (p. 173). This concept—the veil from *Souls of Black Folk*—is not internalized racism; instead, it should be understood as Black interiority within American supremacist ideology. Du Bois here offers a cogent example of the heterogeneity of the Black community, but he also addresses the complicated nature of a communal identity constructed from histories of oppression and discrimination. Thus the second frame, *racism*, addresses the "peculiar social environment" that technology affords white racial ideology while ratcheting up the libidinal tensions on Black digital evocations of interiority.

Racism and Reflexive Digital Practice

> Like a nightmare on the brain of the living.
>
> —Karl Marx, as cited in Joe Feagin (2006, p. 7)

Reflexive digital practice often works hand in hand with ratchet digital practice to read, shade, or celebrate Black everyday life through sensuality, humor, or anger. Racism implicitly and explicitly compels reflexive digital practice; while the explicit is egregious and shocking, the implicit is more damaging across time. To illustrate this, historian Kevin Kruse (2018) posted a Twitter thread discussing lynchings in the American South in the early 1900s. Throughout the thread, Kruse reiterates in nearly every tweet that *only* twenty-eight lynchings occurred in the 1930s—but each served as a signifier to Black folk that their lives were forfeit to a white supremacist regime. The threat of lynching was nearly as debilitating as the lynching itself, serving as a coercive, disciplinary measure to keep Blacks "in their place."

Focusing on racism as a frame for Black identity, however, seems deterministic. After all, not every Black activity is subject to—or determined by—the racism Black folk experience through daily or systemic macro- or microaggressions. Nevertheless, given the structural inequalities that have been levied on Black folk and that are endemic to American culture, any research into Black online culture must address how technocultural racism has shaped Black digital practice (Daniels, 2009, 2013; Feagin & Elias, 2013). In the previous section, I referred to Du Bois's "veil"—and its articulation of the effects of internalized racism—as *Black interiority*. From a libidinal perspective, Black interiority is powered by the libidinal tensions of *reflexivity* as a response to the multilayered elision and hypervisibility of Blackness online; this may come in the form of catharsis or concerns about online representation or digital visibility.

George Yancy (2005) argues that racism's power lies in its enforcement of a logic foreclosing the possibility of Black bodies body from being anything "other than what was befitting [their] lowly station" (p. 219). This imprisoning, epidermal logic is required to support the invisibility of the negative relation—the elision of Blackness—through which whiteness is constituted (p. 219). This imprisonment is reproduced in digital environs as well. Consider the archetype of the "default internet user" who is white, male, middle class, and heterosexual. Based on this default, interfaces were designed, content was created, and networks were structured, leading to the seemingly inevitable conclusion that minorities are on the "wrong" side of the digital divide. However, this reasoning ignores the deliberate environmental, geographic, educational, and economic discrimination underlying the deployment, decisions, and designs of internetworks and digital media (Straubhaar, 2012). Thus the carceral libidinal economy of Western technoculture deliberately obscures the Black digital practitioner. Black internet use is obscured by whiteness; as such, it is difficult to apprehend, much less credit with anything more than unproductive, "playful" engagement with information technologies.

Racism-as-frame is steeped in Black historical narratives, awareness, and responses to egregious acts of racism, like the burning of Tulsa or the New York City draft riots. It is also indebted to early online social justice activist moments, such as support for the Jena Six or Shaquanda Cotton. Here, however, my focus is on the smaller, distributed, more insidious effects of structural racism on Black online life. Racism as a libidinal frame references Black online discourses engendered by micro- and macroaggressions—from the algorithmically driven social media sharing of Black death at the hands of the state, to the constant reality of being surveilled and judged, to the reflexive pleasure and pathos involved in eating fried chicken in public spaces.

Racism as a frame of Black digital practice operationalizes Yancy's (2005) assertion that "Blacks . . . possess a level of heightened sensitivity to recognizable and repeated [racist] occurrences that might very well slip beneath the radar of others" (p. 6). He continues by noting that such perception might indicate that Blacks are part of an epistemological community where the very culture is an ongoing master class in the critical interpretation of a reality that film director Jordan Peele (2017) has evocatively described as "the Sunken Place." These perceptions—apprehension over the implied violence heralded by racism and racists—also work as a *ratchet*, applying more and more tension to further complicate Black interactions with the world.

Nakamura (2013) explains the centrality of racism to digital practice, arguing that racism online is not a "glitch" but a feature. Instead of being engendered by internet practices such as anonymity and a lack of physical feedback, racism is as old as the network itself. Nakamura adds that online "content that includes people of color often becomes part of a technosocial assemblage that produces racism and sexism" (p. 1). This aligns with the infrastructural nature of everyday digital practice, where implicit racism is encountered in the mainstreaming of the white racial frame through appropriation and representation in online media. Simultaneously, explicit online racism toward Black culture has found its most pungent, mediated expressions in comment sections and social media feeds. Social media provides evidence for Black epistemologies of racist ideology through the continual reproduction of racist practices, representations, and discourses, which are in turn driven by algorithm-based digital media, social sharing, and individual affronts. This evidence, taken together with Yancy's (2005) contention that the world systemically and systematically destroys Black dignity while reducing Black folk to a state of nonbeing, supports my argument for pathos as an epistemological standpoint.

Online spaces contribute to—and are, in some ways, more susceptible to—the fixity of Black identity and representation. For example, the 2014 Gamergate campaign created sock puppet Twitter accounts of social justice activists featuring Black women avatars and Black slang. These tactics were emulated by Russian botnets in the 2016 presidential campaign. It was even reported that a prominent and influential Twitter account supposedly helmed by a Black Lives Matter activist was actually a Russian troll account (O'Sullivan & Byers, 2017; Parham, 2017). Also consider Natasha Tiku's (2018) recent findings about Netflix's algorithmic machinations to surface Black televisual representation on video streaming services. Tiku uncovers that the streaming service shows content thumbnails featuring Black actors in otherwise mainstream white movies to certain viewers, although Netflix does not require subscribers to provide their racial identity. While Netflix responded by saying that the service only determined content offers from users' viewing history, they acknowledged that these decisions stemmed from a recently implemented machine-learning approach to subscriber retention. From these examples, we can see that just like in offline spaces, online Black positionality vis-á-vis the white racial frame is reified by space and context.

The algorithmic racialization of Black-oriented digital content is a new and unexpected phenomenon given the historical paucity of Black representation in mainstream television, film, and the arts. As mentioned earlier, Anderson and Hitlin (2016) of Pew Internet Research conducted a study that investigated the types of content Black and white users encounter online. They found that Blacks are more likely than whites to see race-related content on social media. The researchers also found that over a fifteen-month period, only .04 percent of all tweets published on Twitter mentioned race. This time period included the mass shooting of nine churchgoers in Charleston, South Carolina; the findings of an inquiry into the death of Sandra Bland; and the unrest in Baltimore following the death of Freddie Gray. Pew addresses this startling finding obliquely by noting that Blacks are nearly twice as likely to *post* on race and racial matters than whites but the authors of the study did not venture further.

The digital gives additional weight to arguments for racism as a structural quality, as social beliefs are encoded within these technologies as meaning-making strategies for developers and users alike. Gray's (2012) research on multiplayer gaming demonstrates that users bring explicit racial ideologies to digital interfaces and practices; similarly, boyd's (2011) research on racial attitudes and social networks provides an example of how technological aesthetics can be racialized. Whereas Dinerstein (2006) argues that whiteness powers Western technoculture, I argue here that racism is a libidinal technocultural norm. As such, it has an inordinate influence on Black online technoculture.

With this in mind, racism-as-frame operationalizes Black digital practice as an *awareness* of racism and its enveloping effects on- and offline, generating a marked libidinal digital interiority. This awareness shapes digital practice through pathos, leading to—but not limited to—acts of political agency and resistance. It works hand in hand with ratchet digital practices to call out racial and social microaggressions not only through catharsis but also through sensuality and humor. The following section investigates how Black activity online responds to racialized and racist content in order to frame reflexive Black digital practice as an evocation of an epistemological community in libidinal tension with white supremacist ideology.

Reflexivity, Interiority, and the Digital

In *Souls of Black Folk*, Du Bois argues that white people often ask Black people, "How does it feel to be a problem?" (1984 [1903], p. 43). Black responses to this question are often interpreted as resistance in cultural studies or social science research. However, a libidinal economic perspective affords the contention that resistance is powered by the emotional energy engendered by *reflexivity*. That is, to resist white supremacy, Black folk must evaluate both the ontology and the epistemology—the *what* and the *why*—of that racial ideology as well as how the methodology of white supremacy affects them on a daily basis. From this standpoint, Black offline existence in the American racial regime requires constant reassessments and adjustments in order to not run afoul of the existing order. This is particularly true for racial microaggressions, which require daily vigilance to assure that one's sanity has not been compromised or to ensure that one has not fallen afoul of some new, previously unknown discriminatory policy.

Black online existence as digital practice articulates reflexivity under a slightly different set of circumstances. Consider, for example, racial microaggressions happening in offline spaces. Much of their offensive power lies in the recipients' sudden awareness that within a certain physical space, they are not considered as equals or even as existing within a "good, moral, and decent society" (Sue, 2010). Likewise, racial microaggressions' covert, often subtle nature induces isolation, self-doubt, exhaustion, and frustration (Solorzano, Ceja, & Yosso, 2000). In online spaces—thanks to a communicative infrastructure of voracious, always-on websites demanding content, combined with a twenty-four-hour news cycle needing spectacle to drive viewership and the private(ish) publics of social media services—microaggressions have been elevated from individual experiences to widely broadcast, reverberating moments experienced by many Black digital practitioners.

For example, in describing the stress associated with articulating Blackness as a journalist with an extensive online portfolio, Cord Jefferson (2014) writes, "My anger over each new racist incident is now rivaled and augmented by the anger I feel when asked to explain, once more, why Black people shouldn't be brutalized, insulted, and killed. If you're a person of color, the racism beat is also a professional commitment to defending your right and the right of people like you to be treated with consideration to an audience champing at the bit to call you nothing but a nigger playing the race card" (para. 10). Here Jefferson expresses the libidinal consequence of claiming that "Black lives matter" in a space that is predisposed to minimize the presence of nonwhite bodies. Without the internet, stories about racial animus would be restricted to local newspapers and talk radio shows or and even disregarded entirely by non-Black-owned media companies. But online, the cumulative effect of these microaggressions—encountering multiple incidents that are happening to others like you—can be understood as *racism-without-racists*, or online microaggressions facilitated not by individual actors but by the internet's capacity for distributing information bolstered by SNS' mechanisms for sharing information to affiliative groups. In response, Black digital practitioners have co-opted online spaces and services to engage with microaggressions or overt racist incidents through *reflexive digital practice*. The most attention-grabbing reflexive digital moments tend to be cathartic and political, addressing macro- and microaggressions in ways that assert the humanity of Black folk while decrying injustice.

Weak-Tie Racism

Jefferson's response, as a journalist, to the continual demands of having to professionally articulate his humanity in digital spaces can be understood as racism's generative capacity for reflexive digital practice. But absent institutional coercions to articulate the racialized self, how do mundane Black folk become interpellated into online racism-without-racists? Consider offline racism: in the course of everyday life, Black folk cannot avoid racist institutions or incidents, as racism is integral to American culture. Similarly, despite the internet's vaunted freedom to provide individualized, personalized content, Black folk must still deal with racism in online spaces.

To address the mechanisms through which Black folk respond to and reflect on racist and racialized online content, I developed the concept of weak-tie racism. This phenomenon draws from tightly-knit networks of Black digital practitioners combined with the internet's need for content and its capacity for effortless distribution, leading to a pronounced libidinal framing of Black online interiority, or reflexive digital practice. The term refers to the relationships among user, machine, and ideology—that is, the networked libidinal tensions arising from the diffusion of racist and racialized content through social media practice, connectivity, and algorithmic publishing.

Weak-tie racism is an extension of Granovetter's (1973) explanation of the generative sociality of weak tie relationships, arguing that the "emphasis on weak ties lends itself to discussion of relations *between* groups" (p. 1360; emphasis original). In my formulation, the machine, network, and/or algorithm is the distancing catalyst *and* the bond between entities, demanding its own interaction and reciprocity to sustain the relationship between user and network (Haythornthwaite, 2002). Granovetter (1973) states, "The strength of the tie is a combination of the amount of time, the *emotional intensity*, the *intimacy*, and the reciprocal services which characterize the tie" (p. 1361). Many researchers have equated intimacy and emotional intensity with *friendship*, which allows them to distinguish a (presumed) positive comity for strong and for weak ties. I argue instead that racism, as a marker of relationships between Blacks and whites, similarly includes qualities of intimacy and emotional intensity.

Weak-tie online racism, then, is racism that is indirectly experienced through digital representation and the distribution, interactivity, or algorithmic repetition of antiblackness directed toward a specific Black body or bodies but abstracted through social media participation. It has no author; instead, racism is enacted through digital networks of social interaction. Weak-tie online racism is not individually performative; it operates as a signifier of racist ideology that is structurally manifested through digital means. Weak-tie racist activities are often minimally interactive; they are likes, shares, reposts, and retweets—especially if the account sharing the content has a wide network of followers. This does not mean the account holder is racist, although that occasionally is the case. Rather, the account's reach and visibility allow for the imposition of indirect racism through dissemination on social media.

Finally, weak-tie racism is a computational manifestation of microaggressions (Sue et al., 2007; Solorzano, Ceja, & Yosso, 2000); the differentiator is the indefinite, amorphous originator or interlocutor. When one sees a racist tweet receive thousands of likes, is the platform the antagonist? Sue (2010) cogently notes that microaggressions can be environmental, a characterization that explains to some extent the virtual spaces in which weak-tie racism is encountered. Weak-tie racism also harms through accretion—that is, the "text is only experienced in an activity of production" (Barthes, cited in Ott, 2004). Nixon (2011) describes this as "slow violence," or "a violence that occurs gradually and out of sight, a violence of delayed destruction that is dispersed across time and space, an attritional violence that is typically not viewed as violence at all" (p. 2). The act of liking a video can be influenced by the already-present signifiers of virality (e.g., number of comments, likes, or reposts) but is (correctly) not assumed to be in and of itself a racist act; yet its contribution to virality can often be understood in the aggregate as weak-tie racism.

Weak-tie racism is the means rather than the ends; perhaps the best way to describe it is as a hate-speech act as opposed to hate speech itself. Likes and reposts alone are not microaggressive acts even though they may denote affiliation or recognition in a social space that is counter to one's own beliefs or affiliations (*pace* hate-watching[16]). When the aggregation of likes causes one's feed to be populated by racist content, however, this demonstrates that weak-tie racism occurs through the reproduction of banal social signals that are deemed important through minute traces of social interaction promoted by algorithmic means.

Through the aggregation of and interaction with hateful content, white and machinic articulations of racism present intimate, intense libidinal tensions bonding the out-group and the in-group. When presenting this work as it developed, my canonical example of weak-tie racism was whiteness as antiblackness—for example, the social media impressions of police shooting videos broadcast by mainstream news outlets, where the institutional imprimatur of the "fourth estate" authenticated the content shared as content over unaffiliated sites, such as

Facebook and YouTube. However, the best example I could never have asked for occurred during revisions: weak-tie racism vis-à-vis the libidinal intensities of Donald Trump's social media activity while campaigning for president and since his inauguration. While it was immediately clear that racism (and xenophobia) were the elements driving his social media popularity, I was bemused to see that media outlets and the academy constantly misconstrued the libidinal element of Trump's social media content as "economic anxiety" to explain white folks' allegiance to the Republican candidate. I find vindication in the recent findings about the roles Facebook and Twitter played in disseminating and promoting racist misinformation using likes and retweets (rather than actual comments) posted by Russian content farms, such as the @Blacktivist account mentioned earlier.

Black folk (the in-group) can and do similarly bond over their awareness of racism, their positionality to racism, and their responses to racism regardless of intensity. Libidinal Black digital clapbacks to weak-tie online racism create affective and intimate in-group bonds that are responsive to racist ideology but not solely constituted by racism. These acknowledgments are characterized by interiority, riposting to (weak-tie) racism as a "hail," or the catalyst for a cathartic or emotional rejoinder.

This section has repositioned weak-tie theory to emphasize the emotional intensity and intimacy of racism. The resultant application to algorithmically driven social media feeds predicated on libidinal tensions reveals that computational technologies can serve as both conduits and agents in the formulation of relationships. Where weak-tie theory has been used to examine the utility of weak ties in allowing individuals access to information from disparate networks, this perspective offers a way to understand how a negative informational interaction can create loose relationships between ostensibly oppositional entities. Weak-tie racism, then, can be understood as *machinic racism*—absent individual contribution—promoting an atmosphere of social death to be experienced thirdhand by Black internet users.

I have been careful to limit my argument for weak-tie racism to online milieus, as is appropriate for the overall argument of this text—that is, I strive to be cognizant of the mediating effects of digital media and tech on Black culture and identity. From this position, weak-tie racism manifests through digital and online media's affordances for sharing information, including, but not limited to, algorithmically presented social media content. A large part of digital practice is textual and discursive even as digital visual technologies have become a larger part of everyday communicative practice. Code occupies some of this textual space, shaping the interfaces, mechanics, and protocols through which digital practice can happen.

Similarly, algorithms are also discursive forces. Gillespie (2014) notes that "algorithms need not be software: in the broadest sense, they are encoded procedures for transforming input data into a desired output, based on specified calculations" (p. 167). In this inquiry, by *algorithm*, I am referring to data-mining processes that attempt to infer patterns of human activity. Algorithms are similar to actuarial tables, which are used by financial entities (e.g., insurers or banks) to predict risk based on the statistical analysis of data sets of observed social behaviors. Their similarity rests on both processes' efforts to uncover "related attributes or activities or potential proxies for outcomes" (Barocas & Selbst, 2016). This is potentially problematic. As mentioned previously, out-group behavior is not the sum of its traits, appearance, or practices. Actuarial tables have a long history of discriminatory intent toward Black folk; their assessment of racial group characteristics as "risk" tends to encode difference as a negative stereotype using eugenic theory, speculation, and ideology (Wolff, 2006). Algorithms have not escaped these biases, for all their technological and technical sophistication. For algorithms, which infer patterns[17] from historical instances of a decision problem, Hardt (2014) observes, "Race and gender . . . are typically redundantly encoded in any sufficiently rich feature space whether they are explicitly present or not. They are latent in the observed attributes" (p. 1).

Ott (2004) offers a valuable way to understand algorithmic contributions to weak-tie racism. Citing Barthes, he argues that "the Text is experienced only in an activity of production" (p. 202) in the name of pleasure. Consider that many videos of extrajudicial killings are captured by governmental devices (e.g., body cams and dashboard cameras) as documentary moments but not as evidence (or culpability). Their meaning and authorship change when they are posted and distributed to a wider audience on social media—often prefaced by an exclamatory catharsis or heralded as "objective" news reporting. Each iteration—reposts and shares—is yet another moment of production;

each interactant has a different interpretation. Thus the algorithmic post is a multidimensional collaboration among the corporation, the computer, the network, the content, the post's originator, and the audience. Far from being a single-authored artifact, the algorithmic feed is an intertextual moment for all, inscribing meaning on the viewer while deprecating his or her understanding of self as a unified subject (Ott, 2004). Returning to the libidinal economy of information technologies, I offer that weak-tie racism, as evidenced in algorithmic social media content, is a libidinal tension powering Black interiority and reflexivity. Without a need for a single author or an individual racist, social media algorithms become evidence of the (infra)structural forces elevating prejudice to racism.

Reflexivity: Racial Battle Fatigue

Theorizing weak-tie racism offers the potential to reframe discussions of online racism to focus on the *effects* rather than the incidents of racism and the digital. One such possibility lies in the examination of how online contact with racialized and racist content over time mediates Black digital practice. Smith, Yosso, and Solorzano (2006), in examining the impacts of constant racial strife and stress on Black academics, coined the phrase *racial battle fatigue* (RBF). RBF refers to the harmful psychophysiological symptoms resulting from living in racist environments. The symptoms arise from the cognitive and emotional effects of decoding microaggressive subtleties: sufferers struggle to decide whether to acknowledge and how to respond to these affronts. Similarly, my colleagues, friends, and associates of color have attested to fatigue and anxiety upon viewing yet another racist incident posted online, served up by social media algorithms designed to surface content that has been algorithmically determined to be of import to the reader.

That Black folk experience RBF in online spaces serves as a compelling example of weak-tie racism's libidinal effects. Black digital fatigue and stress accumulate not only from direct racist posts or comments but also from repeated exposure to televisual and textual racial affronts that are displayed as a result of the algorithmic mechanism of social media feeds, shares, or indirect contact with well-meaning non-Black others.[18] The most visceral examples of online RBF can be found in

Black reflexivity about continual exposure to police shootings of Black folk shared across social networks. RBF also manifests through social network relationships with non-Black folk who are unwilling to engage with their own relationships with whiteness and white racial ideology.

Another indicator of RBF is the articulation of online Black interiority. These practitioners reflect on existing in the mundane world of white supremacist ideology and on having to coexist with the pain of people like them yet not them. Novelist Brit Bennett (2014) wrote about RBF on Jezebel in an article titled "I Don't Know What to Do with Good White People." For Barnett, weak-tie racism came in the form of a hashtag—namely, #CrimingWhileWhite, which was created by well-meaning white people responding to Michael Brown's execution at the hands of Darren Wilson. After a grand jury declined to charge Wilson, Barnett wrote, "Over the past two weeks I have fluctuated between anger and grief. I feel surrounded by Black death. What a privilege, to concern yourself with seeming good while the rest of us want to seem worthy of life" (2014, para. 8). The weak-tie affront here is not about explicit racial confrontations; Barnett even says, "Sometimes I think I'd prefer racist trolling. . . . A racist troll is easy to dismiss."

For Jefferson (2014), online writing about race leads to overexposure driven by weak-tie racism. In "The Racism Beat," Jefferson recounts his experiences as a journalist of color working "the race beat"—that is, stories that are intended to illustrate the lives of nonwhites in the United States and elsewhere. He writes, "When another unarmed Black teenager is gunned down, there is something that hurts about having to put fingers to keyboard in an attempt to illuminate why another Black life taken is a catastrophe, even if that murdered person had a criminal record or a history of smoking marijuana, even if that murdered person wasn't a millionaire or college student." His frustration and pain at absorbing Black tragedy from online media only to translate it for outsiders can be understood as an example of Black interiority and pathos. In particular, Americans' ongoing fascination with antiblackness leads Black digital practitioners to rationalize and debate the humanity of the victims to those "born not to know" (Saadiq et al., 1988)—those tied to them through the aggregation of social network affiliations.

Finally, in her long-form essay "Treading Water," Dionne Irving (2016) writes, "The malaise and nausea I feel when I recognize the rhetoric of racism and privilege coming out of the mouths of people whom I have confided in, brought into my life, whom I work with and respect, keeps me off the Internet. . . . It visits me with the symptoms of a depression so deep and so all-consuming that I have, more than once, closed my office door in the middle of the day to cry. I cannot eat, cannot sleep, cannot write, and cannot think" (p. 52). Irving's essay is not about being Black on the internet; it is about the difficulties of being Black in spaces that are resolutely white, such as the Midwest. Irving explains how racism taints intimate and social relationships—perhaps doing more damage over time than casually tossed off slurs from unknown passersby or random store employees. Irving explores how incidental racism—expressed as privilege by non-Blacks—debilitates her digital practice and leads to spiritual, cognitive, and emotional distress.

I have written elsewhere about the role the internet plays in relieving the isolation of being Black and male in the Midwest (Brock, 2012), but "Treading Water" adds a metaphysical aspect to internet usage that I had not considered. Irving is of Caribbean descent, and the essay is permeated with her island-engendered love of water and swimming. Water is also a long-standing metaphor for those experiencing the internet; Netscape Navigator was one of the first popular web browsers, for example. We also talk about traversing the web as "surfing," and many of us speak of "drowning" in information. Irving's essay, however, specifically references how water and the act of swimming rejuvenate her—water serves as her space for rejuvenation and psychic hydration.

I believe reflexive digital practice can also rejuvenate Black digital practitioners. Rather than withdrawing from the digital spaces where they are exposed to constant trauma, reflexive digital practitioners reshape otherwise banal internet content to include cathartic discourses. In the process, they gain support for navigating the everyday contexts of white supremacist ideology from others sharing similar experiences.

Reflexive Digital Practice: A Military SNAFU

Reflexive digital practice is not always cathartic or political; it is sometimes irreverent and decidedly not respectable. Even under the smothering blanket of racism, Black folk find pleasure and seek leisure opportunities. Consider a tweet issued in error—and subsequently deleted in less than twenty minutes—by Yahoo! Finance in January 2017, which promoted an article on the Navy's financial budget wish list for the incoming Trump administration (figure 4.1).

Deleted tweets are inaccessible, but unfortunately for Yahoo Finance, Archive.is captured the tweet, "/r/BlackPeopleTwitter" moderator Dawood16 pinned a screenshot of the tweet to his subreddit, and smart Twitter users took screenshots of the offending item. BuzzFeed News (Griffin, 2017), in an article describing responses to the tweet, credits the resultant hashtag #NiggerNavy to Twitter user JeSuisDawn, who caught the mistake at 11:09 p.m. Soon after, Black Twitter awakened, stretched its muscles, and began to signify.[19] Many of the first responses by Black Twitter users were image macros and GIFs expressing disbelief or outrage, but then things got funny. Their responses evoked Black cult humor to darkly critique labor practices, social protocol and etiquette, Black parenting strategies, and much more. Although not depicted here,

Figure 4.1. Yahoo Business' No Good, Very Bad Day. Tweet by @YahooFinance, January 5, 2017. Screenshot by author.

many tweets contextualized the hashtag with photos of Black celebrities and Black media culture, all mediated by the call-and-response functions of Black Twitter hashtag practice (figures 4.2 and 4.3). Notice the pungent yet affectionate tone of these tweets. I argue that they should not be understood as ratchet digital practice even though they expose elements of Black culture that are unfit for respectability paradigms to the mainstream gaze. Instead, these tweets are an exercise in Black interiority—a celebration of Black everyday life that is rarely captured on the screen or stage. Moreover, consider the responses in figures 4.4 through 4.7:

Figure 4.2. "What you ain't gon do." Tweet by @Blike_Dante, January 5, 2017. Screenshot by author.

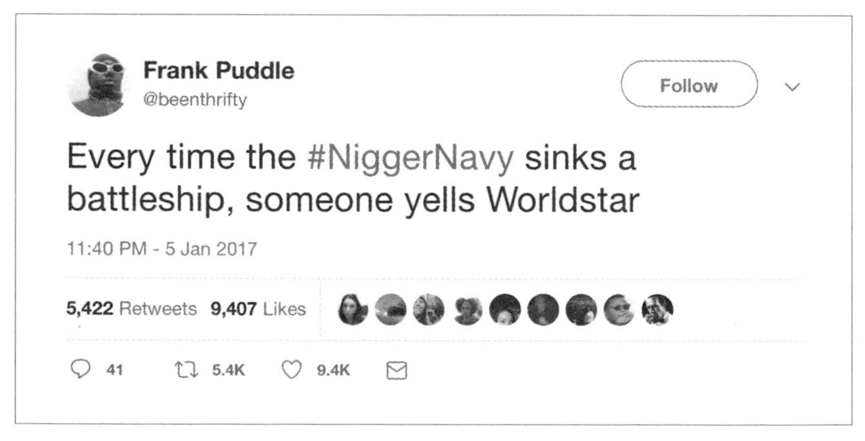

Figure 4.3. "WorldStar!" Tweet by @beenthrifty, January 5, 2017. Screenshot by author.

Figure 4.4. "White people react to #NiggerNavy." Tweet by @tuckerfooley, January 6, 2017. Screenshot by author.

Figure 4.5. "Trending for what?" Tweet by @jadande, January 6, 2017. Screenshot by author.

Figure 4.6. "Token labor." Tweet by @Keelectric_Lady, January 5, 2017. Screenshot by author.

Figure 4.7. "The only thing." Tweet by @CamJugg, January 6, 2017. Screenshot by author.

This image macro originated from the "BlackPeopleTwitter" subreddit, but it was soon joined by Black Twitter reflections on the intersection between white and Black social media propriety. This is also Black interiority as reflexive digital practice—where the reclamation of a disparaged word, *nigger*, becomes discursive agency through digital practice, inventiveness, and humor. As a moment of Black digital practice, #NiggerNavy is a demonstrative moment about the complexity and joy of Black culture in response to a machinic generation of racist ideology. Black online practitioners refused to be rendered invisible by weak-tie racism or the white racial frame. They did so using absurdity and empathy, which supports my claim that reflexivity powers resistance.

Reflexive Digital Practice: Communitarian

As I wrote earlier, pathos can be sensual, joyful, or erotic. Reflexive digital practice allows for the addition of another characteristic: communitarian. A final example of communitarian pathos can be found within one of the gentler instances of reflexive digital practice. In November 2018, the hashtag #ThanksgivingWithBlackFamilies (#TBF) became a widely discussed topic across my section of Black online culture. The hashtag evoked humor about kinship, holidays, and food culture. It was contextualized by photos of Black celebrities and Black media culture, mediated by the call-and-response functions of Black Twitter. Although much of this activity took place on Twitter, the hashtag was picked up by other Black online media outlets who curated "best of" moments. In doing so, they facilitated additional social media sharing (e.g., on Facebook), opening up the conversation for their commenters and allowing their readers to participate at their leisure (figure 4.8).

But you may ask, How is the reflexivity articulated in #TBF related to racism? Returning again to the concept of weak-tie racism, I ask you to consider the online (and offline) media barrage about the "values" of Thanksgiving in America. Depending on one's online media habits (and habitats), visual representations of Thanksgiving center on portrayals of white families in middle-class contexts gathered around a large table preparing to dine on clichéd food items. Multiply these media representations times the advertiser-sponsored content, and these portrayals are easily understood as the default cultural vision of

Figure 4.8. "You better speak." Tweet by @_JTHenderson, November 24, 2015. Screenshot by author.

a problematic American holiday. Prior to digital media, representations of Black folk celebrating the holidays were primarily relegated to Black print and televisual media. These depictions drew heavily on respectability politics, showing "ideal" Black families as a way to counter mainstream narratives about Black deviance (figure 4.9).

#TBF serves as a riposte to these early representations across multiple dimensions. It is simultaneously

- a response to erasure (the implicit racism inherent in representing Thanksgiving as a white holiday),
- a response to the effects of racism without having to go full ratchet,

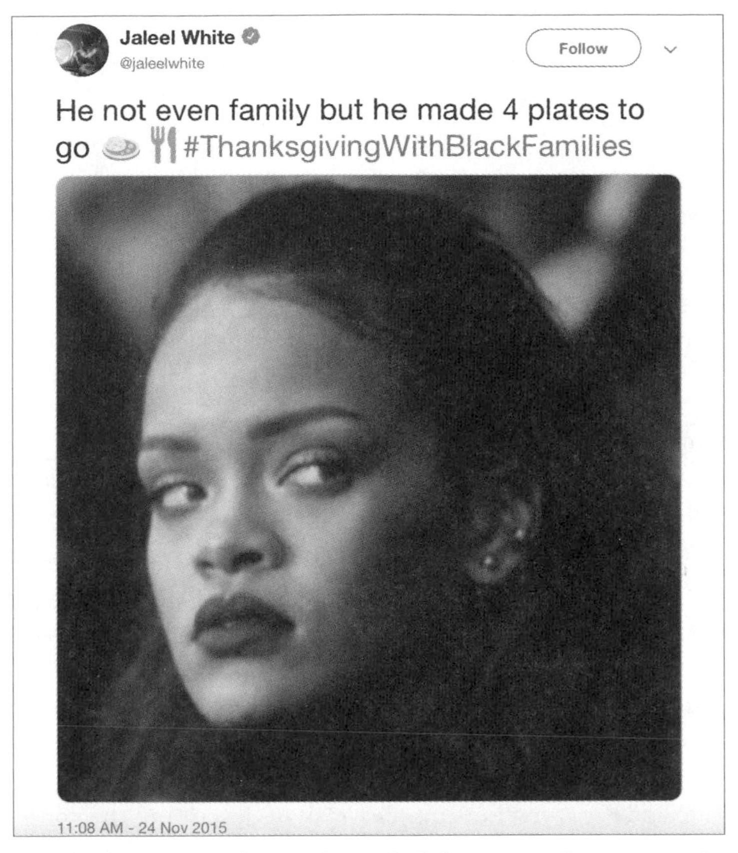

Figure 4.9. "Taking a plate!?" Tweet by @jaleelwhite, November 24, 2015. Screenshot by author.

- an empathetic representation of an event from a Black cultural perspective without actually displaying the typical iconography of the event as offered by the mainstream media, and
- a response that was only possible through digital media's affordances of media display and distribution plus social media's affordances for sharing.

As a moment of Black digital practice, #TBF is an example of the complexity and joy of Black culture amid the reductiveness of American racial ideology. Its practitioners recast the mainstream representation of Thanksgiving as a nuanced libidinal enactment of extended family relationships, Black food culture, and the clash of class status endemic to limited opportunities for economic success. As opposed to the #NiggerNavy participants, these practitioners rebuff the mainstreaming of Black culture through the respectable depictions endogenous to Black media outlets. Both efforts are accomplished through humor and empathy, leading to my claim for reflexivity powering resistance.

On to the Next One

At the beginning of this chapter, I argued that ratchetry and racism should be considered in concert rather than separately. In doing so, I wrote this chapter to decenter Black resistance as the appropriate manifestation of Black online identity. Linking ratchetry and racism as a facet of double consciousness highlights that Blackness employs multiple, interlocking strategies to manage the matrix of American white supremacist ideology. Without the environmental context of racism, the visceral yet banal energies of ratchet digital practice would simply be considered digital practice. Similarly, the interiority performed by reflexive digital practitioners demonstrates a hyperawareness of public perceptions of Blackness, leading to a deliberate eschewal of the discursive register of ratchetry to articulate the libidinal effects of online racism.

This chapter essayed the complex task of describing the confluence of ratchetry and racism and identified aspects of "appropriate" beliefs of Black culture affecting digital practice. I now turn to the frame of respectability on Black digital practice to examine the effects of that ideology on the politically and economically able Black folk who believe they must coexist within its confines.

5

Black Online Discourse, Part 2

Respectability

> It is an error to think that being negro existentially (i.e., being a Black human) results from a particular set of morally determined social decisions and acts.
>
> —Ronald Judy (1994, p. 230)

> Who's more racist? Black people or white people? Black people. . . . You know why? Cause we hate Black people too! Everything white people don't like about Black people, Black people really don't like about Black people.
>
> —Chris Rock

Figure 5.1. "Too absorbed." Tweet by @RyanTheHoly, January 11, 2018. Screenshot by author.

Despair and Dogma

In the previous chapter, I argued for ratchetry and racism as competing, carceral libidinal tensions overdetermining discourses of Black respectability. Racism coerces the expression of Black life by demanding the expenditure of libidinal energies to avoid danger or manage stress. Ratchetry is agentive and cathartic in practice, but many Black folk demur from ratchet practices because they wish to avoid reinforcing stereotypes of Black deviance held by the mainstream as well as by members of their own community. Higginbotham (1992) describes it better: "An enormous division between black people and white people on the 'scale of humanity'; carnality as opposed to intellect and/or spirt; savagery as opposed to civilization; deviance as opposed to normality; promiscuity as opposed to [sexual] purity; passion as opposed to passionlessness" (p. 263).

Historically, respectability politics has sought to modify embodied, sensual, and "deviant" Black behaviors toward standards of middle-class whiteness, rendering it curiously racist in both its depictions of Black female deviance and its valorization of whiteness for political gain. It is worth considering that much of the libidinal energy powering respectability politics originates from denial: denial of prevailing stereotypes of Black women, denial of the libidinal energies of Black folk culture, and a curiously aware denial of the consequences of assimilating to white middle-class standards. From this perspective, what happens when respectability is performed in digital milieus?

The libidinal tensions powering Black online respectability can be understood as *despair*—despair over the perceived pathologies of Black morality intertwined with fears of being left behind in Western technoculture through "inappropriate" digital practice. It is difficult to argue against respectability politics as a positive ideology given the legal and economic gains that its storied proponents have fought for and won, but one must acknowledge how certain Black folk are "thrown under the bus" to achieve respectability's gains. Like others (Gaines, 1996; Higginbotham, 1993; Hine, 1989; White, 2001; Morris, 2014), I consider Black respectability a carceral ideology, but I am reluctant to label its libidinal energy as such. Instead, I consider Black respectability to be *dogmatic*, legislating the behavior of Black folk in the hopes of creating a "good,"[1] moral person who is subject to a "governmental habit of thought" (Judy, 1994).

Thus *dogmatic digital practice* describes Black online discourses that promote a specific set of moral virtues that are enacted in and around digital practice. These practices take place in digital spaces and across social media, couched in terms of "uplift" or, in more extreme variations, as "hotep" or "ashy." They pathologize ratchet activity and unproductive digital behavior, with the goal of getting Black folk to assimilate to white Western technocultural norms and aesthetics. While dogmatic digital practice powers online Black respectability, its digital nature actually alienates respectability's potential for social change.

Black Respectability Politics: An Overview

To buttress these claims, I must first offer a criminally brief overview of respectability, which is here presented as shorthand for "Black respectability politics." This section pulls from W. E. B. Du Bois's work; I also draw on the writings of Evelyn Brooks Higginbotham, Darlene Clark Hine, and Farah Jasmine Griffin. In writing about Black women's struggle to garner and retain political and economic agency in the face of a "clearly hostile white, patriarchal, middle class America" (Hine, 1989, p. 916), these Black feminist scholars offer an intersectional perspective on gender, race, and respectability through their critiques of white supremacy and Black men's misogyny, economic exploitation, and sexism.

Du Bois (1940) writes that the Black community is ever vigilant in policing itself, voicing in private spheres a "bitter inner criticism of Negroes directed in upon themselves" (p. 91) while remaining critical of the context in which such policing is necessary. From this perspective, drawing as it does on Du Bois's concept of double consciousness, Black respectability politics is the performance of a specific version of Black culture for two audiences: Blacks who should be "respectable" and whites who needed to be shown that Blacks could be respectable (Harris, 2003). Cohen (2004) argues that Black respectability politics polices, sanitizes, and hides nonconformist behaviors of certain members of African American communities and individuals, but Higginbotham contests that even in doing so, it assumes a "fluid and shifting position along a continuum of African American resistance" (1997, p. 187).

Sanitation and hygiene, as markers of modern society, represented two of the most visceral sources of respectability's technocultural libidinal tensions—especially for Black women. Educated, professional women expected that they (and other women) would have to renounce sexual expression to gain economic, reproductive, and sexual autonomy (Hine, 1989, p. 919) with the hope that their sacrifice would lead to increased social capital in Black and white communities. While these beliefs seemed to reinforce the civil ideal of marriage as the appropriate vessel for sexuality and reproduction, Morris (2014) notes that Black women found ways to subvert the carcerality of marriage. Similarly, Higginbotham, referencing Darlene Clark Hine's work, mentions Black women's "culture of dissemblance." Referring to Black middle-class women's intent to protect a sexual identity from the vicissitudes of white racial ideology, dissemblance was the practice of "reconstructing and representing their sexuality thru its absence—through silence, secrecy, and invisibility. In so doing, they sought to combat the pervasive negative images and stereotypes" (1992, p. 266).

Higginbotham draws a clear link between dissemblance and ongoing Black political movements of the late nineteenth and early twentieth centuries (e.g., "race work"), which equate Black normality, individual success, and group progress with conformity to white middle-class models of gender roles and sexuality. She notes that reformers worry about the decreasing influence of the Black church as well as the rise of urban cosmopolitanism and consumer capitalism. Respectability politics emphasizes the reform of individual behavior and attitudes both as goals in themselves and as strategies for the betterment of American race relations (Higginbotham, 1997). These reforms include, but are not limited to, changes in dress codes, expressive culture, music, speech patterns, and public etiquette. Failure to conform to these politics of "respectability" was equated with deviance or pathology and correlated by Blacks and whites alike as the rationale for racial inequality and injustice.

Respectability as Authority to Speak

> Such a discursive rendering of race counters images of physical and psychical rupture with images of wholeness.
>
> —Evelyn Brooks Higginbotham (1992, p. 270)

To clarify the connection between respectability and digital practice, I would like to redirect this analysis toward respectability as the quest for authority to speak to the white American public sphere (Ward, 2004). Ward makes this argument with respect to the then burgeoning growth of radio as a broadcast medium, but it transfers well to the internet as a space for public discourse. Where once social movements appealed to sentiments of equality and human dignity, Black respectability's embrace of modernity—including the use of print, broadcast, and now digital media—offers "technical" fixes to gaining the franchise and economic parity. This strategy is undergirded by the proven path to gaining access to American social acceptance, identity, and enfranchisement: the deployment of antiblackness. This strategy works well for native-born poor whites and immigrant groups (Black and non-Black). In using radio, periodicals, newspapers, and now social media, Black respectability movements reinvented Blackness for the technical manifestations and representations needed for those media.

Unlike European and white American respectability movements, the Black community could not rely on the use of state power to enforce their norms (White, 2001). Thus Black respectability proponents warily employed private media resources—Black newspapers, periodicals, and radio—to promote their goals. Rhodes (2016) adds that after World War II, Black cinema "race movies" also provided representations of respectability to coerce Black folk into modernity as it was depicted on the silver screen. Discourses about Black respectability privatized the practice as individual behaviors in the service of a Black ideal. Even when they intersected with capitalism, respectability proponents were much more likely to acquiesce to capital's need for labor and service, policing Black bodies into becoming durable and servile workers. In this manner, Black respectability created a counterhegemonic discourse that reproduced white racial ideology's representations of Black culture (Griffin, 2000; Higginbotham, 1993).

Assimilation, Abnegation, and Information

Suffrage, civil rights, and labor movements altered (but did not eliminate) racial and gender roles. Early modernity reified and commodified the "private sphere" introduced by bourgeois nationalism (White, 1990) while creating institutions that identified and controlled people. The introduction of information technologies expanded these institutional capacities, leading to "social reflexivity" (Giddens & Pierson, 1998, p. 115), or reflexive modernity, where the world is increasingly constituted by information rather than "pre-given modes of conduct," and one must constantly reassess one's relationship to and information about reality. When evaluating the role radio and televisual media played in airing Black political grievances against governmental, civil, and individual transgressions during the civil rights era, we can understand the reflexivity that was demanded by these new media as another way to enact Black culture: informational Blackness. That is, in the absence of physical bodies, this combination of information technologies and cultural content made possible the distribution and reception of Black culture in ways that were previously only possible in face-to-face settings, which were often clandestine in response to white domestic terrorism. I highlight the influence of radio, television, and film on the display and performance of Blackness during this era to excavate their technical and technocultural effects on the enactment and transmission of cultural identity and as a hermeneutic for understanding the influence of digital and networked technologies on Blackness in the present day.

In the enactment of informational Blackness, Black radio and television often reified the aims of respectability proponents. Middle-class Black professionals and elites invoked antiblackness to distance themselves from Black culture's reputation as a "low-class undifferentiated mass" (Du Bois, 1940), distinguishing themselves as able interlocutors with modernity and with white American culture. Antiblackness takes on multiple aspects for Black elites; their political goal of Black community uplift ameliorates to an extent the two facets of antiblackness that I apply to informational Blackness here. The first aspect to consider is assimilation. By conforming to a specific set of white cultural norms, Black respectability proponents felt that an emphasis on "home training" and service-sector employment would demonstrate the capacity to rationally address whites regarding the inequities confronting the Black community. To this end, they put into action assimilation discourses of technology as modernity, social control, and domination—surveillance, near-eugenic reproductive control, disparagement of libidinal folk culture, and techniques of personal and environmental hygiene to achieve their ends—ensuring that "formal technical rationality [turned] into material political rationality" (Marcuse, 1964, p. 10).

A second aspect of respectability's antiblackness is abnegation—that is, the denial and disparagement of Black folk culture. Abnegationist beliefs were initially directed toward minstrelsy, popular culture artifacts, and media depicting stereotypes of lazy, immoral Blacks. But abnegation can also be understood as encompassing emergent Black cultural forms of jazz, ragtime, slang, dance halls, and other urban entertainments. Black respectability equated nonconformity and Black popular culture with the enablement of racist behavior *against* Blacks, in the process suturing the modern quality of "rationality" to race through privatized racist discourses (Higginbotham, 1993). Griffin (2000) cogently notes that respectability politics "fails to recognize the power of racism to enforce itself upon even the most respectable and well-behaved Black people" (p. 34). Thus middle-class Blacks measured their "modern" national identity in a similar way to whites: by deploying negative images of Black others to induce social control over Black culture.

Assimilation and abnegation undergirded performances of Black respectability on the radio in the first half of the twentieth century, presaging arguments made here about the internet and dogmatic digital practice. Spinelli (1996) argues that radio and the internet share some compelling characteristics, noting the transcendent, utopian early rhetorics promoting radio's ability to shift the consideration of life possibilities from an everyday physical space to an "ethereal, magical one" (p. 3). The possibilities of advocating embodied concerns from a disembodied space held great appeal to institutions such as the National Urban League, the National Association for the Advancement of Colored People, and the Johnson Publishing Company (i.e., *Ebony*, *Jet*). Many felt they could use radio's virtual assembly and geographic reach to espouse assimilationist strategies for Black education and cultural aspirations.

Many historically Black colleges and universities used radio in its early days to promote assimilationist aims. Moreover, many Black churches (particularly in the South) saw radio as an opportunity to minister to Black (and white) churchgoers (Ward, 2004, p. 92), deploying a "militant gradualism" to cautiously advance progressive aims. Ward notes that many of the programs developed under this rubric prized the Black exhibitions of standard American diction—and classical oratory, long a prerequisite of American education through the Second World War—over a distinctively Black vernacular style (p. 81). Black radio personalities who could speak standard English had greater opportunities in the segregated world of radio, where audiences couldn't see their faces. Ward argues that this technocultural capacity reinforced the sense that assimilation and respectability were linked to upward social and economic mobility (p. 82).

From an abnegationist perspective, radio announcers and programs using a distinctively Black vernacular style—such as the hugely popular Amos 'n' Andy and the breakthrough Black deejay Al Benson, who creatively manipulated and disassembled standard speech—were troublesome. Respectability proponents associated Benson's verbal gymnastics (and the deejays who continued this new pattern of technocultural engagement) and Amos 'n' Andy's performance of rural, premodern, folk discourses as racial problematics that displayed the community's inability to conform to modern standards of civil discourse and communicative practice. These attitudes flourished even as these vernacularly gifted radio personalities demonstrated qualities that were understood as status markers and social skills in Black communities—linguistic fluidity, sharp wordplay, and communal, sensual discourses—in the course of demonstrating mastery over a modern communication service, medium, and form. Moreover, Black radio broadcasts led by these performers promoted the breakout of jazz, blues, and even gospel music as popular forms of American culture to white audiences. At one point, one educator even complained that political discussions of "Negro Rights" were subsumed by entertainment shows (Ward, 2004, p. 110).

Digital Assimilation and Abnegation

Returning to the digital: online media provides a useful (if not powerful by conventional metrics) venue for Blacks to contest their exclusion from the public sphere. For example, consider Black online responses to media representations of "looters" and "refugees" during the disastrous relief efforts following Hurricane Katrina. Concurrently, high rates of smartphone adoption and corresponding broadband access have led to greater visibility of the Black public sphere alongside a greater awareness of Black digital expertise in enacting online cultural and political activity. Thus information and communication technologies have aided in revealing the "appropriate" humanity of Black folk across electrical, electronic, and digital information networks, eschewing embodiment for distributed discourses about Black bodies. Moreover, these cases are considered the "best" Black cultural uses for information and computer technologies, as they align with the political and cultural goal of achieving recognition in American national culture.

While the assimilationist educational and political aims of respectability radio make for a compelling narrative of Black resistance using technology, it is just as important to consider the failure of abnegation strategies. Despite exhortations to "do better," many more Black (and white) radio listeners tuned in to hear the Black music and entertainment that reformers felt demeaned Black culture by playing into stereotypes. Livingstone (2005) notes, "Private leisure is scrutinised and judged . . . for its potential or actual contribution to the public sphere" (p. 31). She questions whether audiences have a moral responsibility to critique and resist the problematic yet taken-for-granted assumptions of media messages (p. 30). Similarly, while the internet allows respectability proponents to disseminate their ideas to like-minded folk, it provides many more opportunities to experience, create, and enjoy content that rebels against the patriarchal, assimilationist aims of respectability politics. Thus even as communication technologies were harnessed by respectability proponents to promote hegemony and modernity, they had to also contend with communication technologies affording libidinal energies of pleasure, joy, pain, and catharsis for their audiences.

Dogmatic Digital Practice

> The Black community becomes the police in order to not give the police [state] any reason or cause to violate it.
>
> —Ronald Judy (1994, p. 221)

Digital and social media exacerbate respectability's libidinal tendencies toward ideological control (Douglas, 2006) of information about Black aesthetics and culture while diminishing control over the culture itself. *Dogmatic* digital practice can be understood as coercive online discourses and practices (posting, publishing, etc.) that draw on concerns about inappropriate bodies. These discourses are occasionally also imbricated with concerns about inappropriate digital practices. From this perspective, one can argue that online respectability may be informationally fruitful and sometimes provocative in its exhortations for moral improvement and technocultural assimilation. However, its carceral and abnegationist perspectives are undermined by digital and social media, precipitating a loss of engagement with many of the people for whom respectability proponents ostensibly speak.

Despite the fervid attention dogmatic digital practice receives from Black media, which leads to high levels of engagement for their websites, its content rarely achieves the virality of ratchet or reflexive digital practice. This can be attributed to a number of factors, one being that dogmas of Black respectability are often invoked by Black cult figures (Warner, forthcoming) with whom mainstream audiences have little or no familiarity (e.g., Michael Baisden, Tariq Nasheed).[2] In addition, dogmatic digital practitioners operate in an infosphere that is saturated with white racial ideologies of Black pathology; their only value to the twenty-four-hour information cycle is their use of racial affinity to warrant the white coercion of Black bodies. While some dogmatic digital content is picked up and amplified by white conservative and alt-right personalities, pundits, and internet and social media commenters, these contexts and personalities reify white supremacy instead of Black communal unity.

Where ratchetry and reflexivity are dialectical alternatives to white racial imaginaries of Blackness, respectability can be understood as an inability to perceive Blackness outside of the confines of modernity, whiteness, and capitalism—that is, as a failure of imagination. It is the ratification of Black life as social death spoken from Black faces. From this perspective, it is easy to see why dogmatic digital practice does not directly respond to white racism online; its preferred discourse is antiblackness, or the chastisement and discipline of Black bodies and

Black digital practices. Moreover, given that mainstream online milieus had little need for additional antiblack content during and after Barack Obama's presidency, the memetic dogmas of respectability do not cause the same stir as the other Black libidinal digital practices.

Inappropriate Tech and Respectability

As I mentioned in the previous chapter, appropriate digital practice involves information and interface design, which must be efficient and productive. The information created and transmitted should be devoid of opinion (or rather, in alignment with a specific political-economic one) and easily digestible to audiences and users of a particular culture. For example, my line brother once confided that he allows his children to use their smartphones to send text messages *if and only if* they compose their messages using complete sentences, correct punctuation and capitalization, and no slang. He was apprehensive that the brevity and informality of short-message services (SMS) would corrupt his children's ability to write term papers, essays, and other necessary productive texts.[3] His fears for his children's economic prospects coupled with his assimilation to white perceptions of Black technological deviance can be understood as dogmatic digital practice.

Assimilation and abnegation are present in dogmatic digital practice in forms that speak to the cultural mediation of information and communication technologies. For example, mobile technologies are often depicted as inappropriate digital artifacts, services, and content, providing warrants for online respectability discourses. Respectability discourses about mobile device use are abnegationist—that is, proponents argue against the smartphone's affordances of social connectivity, playful information use, and nonproductive communication because they see smartphones as encouraging the libidinal articulation of Black folk culture, intimacy, and embodiment. Thus dogmatic digital practice can be understood as a rebuke of ratchet digital practice, since ratchetry transgresses the norms of respectable behavior *and* appropriate digital practice. Dogmatic digital practice expresses anxieties about Black folks' morality; it sees the expression of inappropriate Blackness as evidence of an inability to assimilate to the modern, rationalist, capitalist desires of Western technoculture.

From an assimilationist perspective, digital divide discourse provides signposts toward a digital route to respectability. The 1996 Telecommunications Act's definition of *universal service* reshaped beliefs about information and communication service by legislating remedies for inequalities in telephone service, which was necessary at the time to access the nascent internet and World Wide Web. Cognizant of antiblackness as a rationale for telecommunication companies not fully deploying "plain old telephone service"[4] to Black communities, Black technologists, academics, and politicians were at the forefront of calls to "transcend" the digital divide. They argued that a lack of access to the burgeoning information society signaled a loss of economic opportunity for Black communities even as the digital divide traded on images of poor illiterate Blacks. Thus Black respectability politics is often driven by the desire to make Black folk *modern* despite (or perhaps because of) the assimilationist equivalence of modernity with white middle-class norms. Giddens and Pierson (1998) argue that modernity is often invoked to discipline folkways, embodiment, and sensual aesthetics. Although Black activists and elites did not have control of mainstream institutions, communication technologies, or popular culture, they used the available discourses and technologies—the church, the Black press, Black cinema, and Black radio—to articulate modernity as encapsulated by the cultural and social ideologies of that era.

Similarly, dogmatic digital practitioners do not have control of modern "technologies of power" (i.e., twenty-four-hour cable news networks, telecom providers, and technology companies). As digital practitioners, they use the subversive technologies at hand—social networks, memetic content—to enact and perform modernity. By comparison, Black Lives Matter's online activism draws energy from Black Twitter's reflexive and ratchet digital practices. Even (or perhaps because) while doing so, these activists are accused of not practicing embodied politics—Gladwell's (2010) critique of them "not having boots on the ground" comes to mind—at the same time garnering accusations of slacktivism (Christensen, 2011). Still, Black Lives Matter is more evocative of political resistance than dogmatic digital practice simply based on online metrics of participation. Dogmatic digital practice will *never* be understood as liberatory online activism; its antiblack exhortations and patriarchal misogyny reduce its libidinal power over those who are already empowered by the medium.

To its credit, Black respectability politics is ethically and politically subversive in its discursive reclamation of Black bodies from the violence of the white racial frame, using social-scientific discourses to chivvy Black folk along. Unfortunately, dogmatic digital practice lacks the subversive nature and stature of historical respectability politics due to the digital's means of media production and dissemination. Instead of relying on historically significant Black institutions (e.g., the church and education) and their means of coercing moral behavior, dogmatic digital practice trades on social network visibility, affinity networks, performance, and memes. Whereas historical respectability depended on the ethos of Black excellence (for good or for ill) as a warrant for cultural change, dogmatic digital practice is handicapped by Black folks' expanded access to and individualization of social media.

While social media can augment and amplify the pillars of Black respectability—celebrity and professional accomplishment (e.g., the Beyhive and Ta-Nehisi Coates)—its two-way performative nature abridges the moral *private* space that Black respectability once laid claim to. Where peccadilloes and misdeeds of Black icons were once only whispered about or discussed in local third places, social media and entertainment blogs encourage Black folk to comment openly about the behaviors of the Black elite using the same affordances, memes, and affinity networks used by dogmatic digital practitioners. Moreover, through this two-way performative discourse, dogmatic digital practice becomes nearly indistinguishable from color-blind and racist technocultural rhetorics in its embrace of embodied propriety *and* neoliberal notions of digital practice. This marks dogmatic digital practice—and modern respectability with it—as different from previous incarnations of respectability politics. The petit bourgeois, youth, queer folk, and other Black subcultures can speak back—publicly and vituperatively—to respectability proponents in ways that were unavailable to them even twenty years ago.

Dogmatic Digital Practice: Slut Shaming versus Callout Culture

In the guise of respectability, Black pathos, or the epistemological standpoint of Black culture, is often framed as Black excellence but conflicting internal libidinal tensions can derail its engagement with issues that affect the community. An example of dogmatic digital practice in this vein can be found in the discourses of race, colorism, sexuality, and class generated by a social media post by a wealthy Black woman and the reactions it engendered around the Blackosphere. Let me introduce you to Ayesha Curry—professional chef, lifestyle blogger, television personality, and wife of two-time NBA Most Valuable Player Stephen Curry:

> The Currys are the NBA's royal family. If I had to compare them to a real royal family, it would probably be The Royal Family, the Middletons. Just look at the parallels: royal dad (Steph); two cute, highly photogenic kids (Riley and Ryan); and the wife-mother-future queen, who keeps the photo firmly in place in the family scrapbook. Much like Kate Middleton's, Ayesha's job, at least according to a certain strain of people, is to excel at *wifehood*: look beautiful, produce heirs, be relatable in a basic sort of way while remaining engaging enough, especially on social media, to help support the narrative. That story is that Steph is rewriting the basketball rule book; he is a golden boy and a family man with a perfect wife and adorable kids. Ayesha was very good at that job, the best, probably. (Davis, 2016, para 11)

This description appeared on The Ringer, a sports culture website led by veteran sportswriter and ESPN personality Bill Simmons. It is unmistakably a puff piece—but not in the service of enhancing the reader's understanding of an elite athlete's excellence or training regime. Instead, the superlatives fashion Curry's spouse as a "perfect wife" and are firmly rooted in American cultural beliefs of modern womanhood, focusing on a heteropatriarchal role for women and the nuclear family. The piece is also curiously absent of racial modifiers.[5]

Prior to this glowing description, on December 7, 2015, Ayesha Curry posted this tweet in figure 5.2:

Figure 5.2. "The good stuff." Tweet by @ayeshacurry, December 5, 2015. Screenshot by author.

Curry's motherhood, her cooking show, and her low-profile demeanor encouraged Black men (and women!) to associate her with purity and faithfulness. Her public profile, reified by her social media postings, is a sterling enactment of the modern Black wife, mother, and entrepreneur. However, with this tweet, she became an avatar of Black respectability, a tool for pitting women against one another, and a shibboleth to chastise Black women to be used by more extreme respectability proponents (e.g., the hoteps).

This tweet is clearly Curry's opinion, which she has every right to express. But it is also an encapsulation of Black respectability politics, and given the medium, it should be understood as dogmatic digital practice. In conversation with her followers, Curry promotes a personal style decision while subtly criticizing those who do not subscribe to her aesthetics. Earlier I argued that dogmatic digital practice is the libidinal expression of despair over the plight of the "unenlightened." However, there are a number of considerations associated with this tweet that elevate Curry's offhand musing to the level of respectability politics. For one, Curry has a public persona: her widely publicized "appropriate" relationship with an extremely popular and talented athlete as well as her growing reputation as a lifestyle social media personality has led to a large following on Twitter and Instagram. Thus any social media utterance she makes will be publicly scrutinized and interpreted as an indicator of her ethos, regardless of her initial intent. Her contribution serves as a dog whistle for the tenets of respectability politics: sexual agency only for those with the appropriate partner and control over Black women's embodiment warranted by her marriage, her wealth, and her religious beliefs.

Ebony (Pickens, 2015) reported that Curry's post went viral over the next twenty-four hours as overlapping circles of Black Twitter users retweeted and liked to their affiliative networks. While Curry's social media following would ordinarily seem to be women of color and lifestyle aficionados, I believe the tweet's virality is due also the reception by the overlapping audiences of Black men, sports fandom, and sports websites covering NBA culture. Curry, who has 375,000 followers, even briefly became a national trending topic, with the post garnering approximately 72,000 retweets and nearly 100,000 likes. There are three types of responses (out of dozens) to be discussed here: those of Curry's supporters, those of Curry's detractors (both categories include Black online media outlets and social media commentators), and those of white mainstream media outlets. I begin with the mainstream media outlets, as they directly critique Black digital practice in ways that the Black-authored tweets and responses do not.

Sports and Black Culture

I examined two types of media websites: sports culture websites and general interest websites. The sports culture sites are relevant to this inquiry because apart from their interest in the Currys, their commentary touches on appropriate social media use and Black digital practice. For example, Micah Peters (2015), writing for *USA Today*'s sports subsite For the Win (FTW), considered Curry's tweet a "harmless, if unsolicited opinion." In response to the social media reaction Curry received, Peters suggested the "rules of Twitter":

- don't react
- never tweet (para. 3)

These anodynes were offered as counteractants to the reactions of "half of Twitter," though Peters never mentions Black Twitter by name.[6] He does, however, implicitly recognize Black Twitter users' command of the service's affordances of attention and visibility. In turn, this admission plays into the long-standing American conception of Black hypervisibility-as-threat (Mowatt, French, & Malebranche, 2013), where more than three Black folk in any environment renders that setting as "overrun." It also recalls an old chestnut my sociology professor offered about Black bodies in a formerly white space: "more than three is a crowd." By this, my professor meant that the Black body is often hypervisible when it is seen as impinging on a protected space or resource. While he was referring to housing desegregation, I believe this aphorism also applies to mainstream perceptions of Black Twitter (and Myspace before this; see also boyd, 2011). Despite composing only a small percentage of all online users, Black digital practices can signal certain previously "unmarked" spaces as Black due to digital and cultural signifiers of race.

Peters also references an internet phenomenon called the think piece. The term refers to long-form online writings that purport to be critical, intellectual responses to events; however, it is deployed in Peters's article as a pejorative. Peters's mention of think pieces highlights a number of considerations for this text:

- the distributed nature of Black digital practice
- the limitations of Twitter as a place for lengthy, nuanced conversations
- the perceived irrationality of utilizing the productive capacity and resources of information technology for a conversation about aesthetics and moral propriety

By *distributed*, I mean that people responded to Curry's tweet in situ—online—in volume and intensity. The post was also embedded and discussed across a spectrum of Black-authored media, from media websites, to personal blogs, to Tumblr sites. Although I will not cover these additional spaces here, I mention them to highlight the multimodality and distribution of digital practices that Black folk engage in to articulate Black identity. The second point speaks to Twitter as a space where conversations are kindled but rarely explored in depth; this is simultaneously a strength and a weakness.

Respectability proponents' critique of information technology is illustrated through the third point: Twitter (more so than other social network services [SNS]) has long been considered as an irrational technology because it does not fit neatly into technoculture's productivity paradigms. Twitter's brevity and network affiliations strongly favor expressions of pathos, leading to charges that Twitter encourages a "mob mentality" among irrationally emotional users. When combined with racial beliefs about technology users, Black Twitter discourse becomes recast as a "mob mentality"; this concern is augmented by the perceived irrationality of Black embodied existence. While think pieces are often produced outside of Twitter, Peters's critique can be understood as a dismissal of Black rejections of dogmatic digital practice.

Over on another sports culture website, SportsGrid (part of the *Complex Magazine* web portal), Tanya Ray Fox (2015) discusses the cultural and gendered contributions of Twitter, offering additional examples of technically oriented dogmatic digital practice. Fox, who is white, begins her coverage of the internet's response to Ayesha Curry's tweet by praising Curry's marriage, financial stability, and children. She argues that Curry's post is "completely acceptable" and that the response to it is only "manufactured Twitter 'outrage.'" Fox further characterizes the response as originating from "a bunch of women [who] got their panties in a twist trying to defend something that wasn't under attack." Similar to Peters, Fox never explicitly references Black Twitter, but she links women, feminism, and "outraged Twitter" together.

Fox highlights a few of the more passionate rebuttals to Curry's tweet but dismisses them by saying, "Mrs. Curry is living the high-life right now and shes [*sic*] feeling herself." Of particular note for this analysis, Fox turns to "sensible Twitter" and features responses that she feels reflect appropriate internet usage. See figure 5.3 for one such embedded tweet:

This post ends by obliquely referencing the "keyboard warrior" (KW). An insult that is older than the World Wide Web, KWs are defined by their tendency to get involved in emotional, irrational online arguments; their addiction to being online; and their inappropriate use of technology (Brock, forthcoming). If this sounds familiar, that is because these charges have been leveled at "social justice warriors" as well. Moreover, both internet archetypes are considered to be insincere and attention-seeking. Thus we can understand Fox's embed of JayJazzi's

Figure 5.3. "She already sleep." Tweet by @JayJazzi, December 5, 2015. Screenshot by author.

post (figure 5.3) as offering a double dose of social status checking, disciplining technical behavior, and dogmatic digital practice.

Social media represents a new, more immediate way for sports fans to engage with multimillionaire athletes and declare fandom. That sports websites would report on the social media activities of a player's wife is reflective of ESPN's influence and the demands of a twenty-four-hour news cycle, but there's another aspect to this. Despite not being exclusively dedicated to reporting on Black celebrity culture, sports websites depict Black athletes as examples of American excellence and of Black deviance. Since Jack Johnson, Black sports figures have simultaneously represented the best of Black culture and the problematics of being Black in American culture. This can be seen in the deification of many such athletes in Black cultural outlets throughout the last century—some for their breaking of segregated color lines, some for their physical prowess, and some for their domination of their chosen sport. Black athleticism, then, has always involved an element of modernity and, because of their success in sport as a triumph over structural white racial ideology, of respectability.

Even still, some might see reporting on the social media activity of an athlete's wife—even if the wife of a reigning NBA MVP—as a diminishment of sports journalism in particular and journalistic credibility in general. Ayesha Curry's tweet was a banal moment involving someone who is arguably peripheral to the activities on the court. However, the involvement of Black Twitter—its networked, visible, cultural reproach *and* support—is the exigency that elevates Curry's tweets to reportable events for these sports websites.

This exigency allowed sportswriters to critique Black culture—in its guise as a social media public—rather than American sports culture, supporting my claim for respectability as a dogmatic digital practice. Black Twitter fails the respectability test, as it is critiqued for both its rambunctious digital practice as well as its reproach of Curry.

Black News and Entertainment

When I looked to Black media websites to address the complexities of Black respectability in Ayesha Curry's tweet and in the online responses to it, I found both supportive and critical posts. I selected The Root, a Black cultural and news website owned by the Spanish-language media conglomerate Univision, as the exemplar for Black media, although other hybrid Black-owned media (*Ebony*, *Essence*) and online-only Black media (Hello Beautiful, Madame Noire, This Week in Blackness) also addressed the controversial tweet. My choice of the site is not accidental: The Root is currently the closest thing to a mainstream media Black-interest news outlet as is possible in today's media climate.

I mentioned the Black press as a disseminator of respectability politics through the "modernization" of Black folk earlier in this chapter. While outlets like the *Chicago Defender*, the *Pittsburgh Courier*, and the *New York Amsterdam News* flourished throughout the twentieth century (Gallon, 2009), few Black newspapers were able to make the jump to the emerging World Wide Web. This was not necessarily a technical problem; many smaller news organizations struggled in the 1980s and 1990s as advertising and subscription revenues dried up. In my dissertation on Black online identity in the aftermath of Hurricane Katrina, I found that online Black press coverage of the disaster was largely provided by radio personality Tom Joyner's BlackAmericaWeb. Black culture periodicals and newspapers had little to no online content at the time, largely because many still treated the web as a place that would cannibalize existing audiences and thus reserved their news content for print editions.

The Root, originally founded in 2008 as a partnership between Henry Louis Gates Jr. and the *Washington Post*, neatly fits into my arguments for modernization and respectability in online spaces. It was initially pitched as a "Slate [online magazine] for Black readers" (Romanesko, 2008), or as the *New York Times* reported, "a more highbrow, political alternative to established magazines like *Ebony* and sites like BlackAmericaWeb.com and BlackVoices.com" (Pérez-Peña, 2008). The Root's managing editor added that articles posted to the site would "not have an explicitly Black angle." This informational and cultural positioning is significant; Gates's previous online endeavor, Africana.com, grew out of his *Encyclopedia Africana* project as a respectable academic and cultural portal for Black folk. In keeping with Gates's background and interests, at the time of its launch, The Root featured a genealogy section, which was intended to highlight its "serious" nature compared to other Black entertainment or cultural websites. This genealogy section in particular should be understood as a Black technocultural artifact, as the DNA testing provided by a Gates-owned company enacts race-as-technology (Chun, 2013) as an additional warrant for modern Blackness and identity (Nelson, 2016).

In the late 2000s, there were few online spaces in which Black internet users could find news speaking to their perspective. Gates's previous online cultural venture, the web portal Africana.com, was sold to Time Warner in 2000 and incorporated into America Online (AOL). Joyner's BlackAmericaWeb was still extant, as was radio personality Lee Bailey's EURWeb[7] (both sites still operate as of this writing). BlackVoices, which at one point was funded by the Chicago-based *Tribune* company and operated as a Black news and entertainment portal, was sold back[8] to AOL in 2004 and subsequently deprecated. BlackVoices was resurrected in 2011 as part of the AOL-owned *Huffington Post*'s ethnic vertical, Voices. Despite Black Entertainment Television's (BET's) long history of web initiatives—who can forget MSBET?[9]—the network primarily used the internet as a second screen for its entertainment programming even during their brief heyday in the early 2000s as a news network featuring Tavis Smiley and Ed Gordon. The Grio, originally launched by NBC News in 2009, was purchased by an entertainment studio in

2016. BlackWeb 2.0, founded in 2007, is largely restricted to technology-industry news and web trends that are pertinent to Black culture.

The Root, meanwhile, following its purchase by Univision in 2016, now operates as a weblog presenting information on Black news and culture. This move, which entailed adding the site to the Gawker Media properties as well as the Kinja publishing platform, reshaped The Root into a space for long-form commentary and opinion pieces rather than news reporting. This restructuring also added an ethical journalistic dimension to the site's content, given Univision's purchase of Gawker Media following the troubling demise of that company at the hands of Peter Thiel and the subsequent removal of articles that could be considered offensive (or libelous). Thus The Root cannot engage in the aggressive journalistic style that Gawker was once known for; the critiques read as personal evocations rather than as articles from a Black journalism institution operating on the principles of the fourth estate. The website trades on an ethos of affront and upright cultural critique as a warrant for its content, recasting The Root's response to Ayesha Curry's tweet as an online invocation of Black individualism and respectability.[10]

Let me provide an example of The Root's shift from Black fourth-estate journalism to lifestyle and cultural-critique reporting. Since its genesis at the *Washington Post*, The Root sought to tap into and report on the growing Black presence in the STEM disciplines, in the tech industry, and on social media and the influence of Black social networks. This includes efforts like the feature "The Chatterati," which lists trending topics across various social networking services. They also publish The Root 100, an annual list of Black influencers between the ages of twenty-five and forty-five who "excel across multiple disciplines." The criteria considered for the award include celebrity, political or cultural achievements, media mentions, social media metrics, internet mentions, contributions to the Black community over the last twelve months, and a "mathematical formula to determine the substance of their work" (The Root, 2018). The list, as expected, is top heavy with celebrities, politicians, activists, and entrepreneurs. Respectability, by this assessment, becomes about putting on an appropriate performance of Black modernity that must be ratified by the instrumental measures of social media. I must, however, give The Root 100's list credit where credit is due: much of the lower half of the list is dominated by Black folk in various information and new media industries. There the measure is not overdetermined by social media reach—many of the tech honorees have relatively low Twitter follower counts.[11] Instead, technical savvy and mastery of social media are the qualifying factors for their inclusion.

Black Websites and Respectability

The Root articles examined for this chapter appear to fit the definition of think pieces. Earlier I noted that think pieces

- display the distributed nature of Black digital practice;
- highlight the limitations of Twitter as a place for lengthy, nuanced conversations; and
- demonstrate the perceived irrationality of utilizing the productive capacity and resources of information technology for a conversation about aesthetics and moral propriety.

Contributor Demetria Lucas D'Oyley (2015) voices support for Ayesha Curry's social media posts, arguing that those who were responding negatively were "adding in layers that weren't in Curry's original tweets." She continues, "There are no Hotep respectability politics telling women that if they cover up, they'll get what she has" (p. 2), which refers to an online faction of Black Twitter notorious for its misogynistic and patriarchal version of Black respectability. Arguing from an individualist perspective, D'Oyley glosses over Curry's digital practice. She asks, "Why are so many people acting as it's wrong for a woman *not* to put her whole body on display . . . are we really trying to argue that dressing with your ass and breasts out should be called 'classy,' too? Really?" (emphasis original).

D'Oyley continues by contextualizing Curry's tweet through Curry's conformity to respectability and dogmatic digital practice norms, arguing that her marriage gives her the right to opine about women's fashion ("what her husband likes") and that people on Twitter have no right to "twist her words"—here a vague reference to Twitter's potential for miscommunication through misinterpretation. She closes by wondering "if the real issue [is] . . . what Curry represents in our culture" (p. 2). This last point is key. D'Oyley writes,

> [Ayesha Curry is] a young, black, happily married mom of two. She and her media-friendly, Christian husband project what some might think of as the perfect relationship. They're always posting goofy family videos of them loving on each other and the kids. She has something that a lot of people wish they had, and for that, some people have been looking for a reason not to like her. In some baffling way, they think that her recent set of tweets are a solid reason to rally against her and that doing so will hide their envy of her life. (p. 3)

Unmentioned is Curry's hustle as a media influencer, which is built on the digestible, respectable aspects of her personal life that D'Oyley valorizes. As an influencer, Curry's follower counts across her social media presence recursively serve as a validation of her ethos while also demonstrating her technical expertise. To a lesser extent, these social media metrics also serve as indicators of *Black digital virtue*—that is, an implicit marker of esteem, credibility, and ethos. D'Oyley neglected this aspect of Curry's digital practice in her argument for those critiquing Curry as envious and as without having those aspects of respectability in their own lives.

D'Oyley's colleague at The Root, Diana Ozemebhoya Eromosele (2015), provides a counterpoint to the Curry tweet and Twitter responses. She begins by referencing an earlier social media incident involving respectability politics. Black cult figure Tamera Mowry, a former child star and current respectability advocate, posted to Twitter about her desire to dress modestly while simultaneously criticizing rapper Nicki Minaj for her often revealing fashion choices. Eromosele also references Black digital virtue, implying that while social media users can own and express opinions, once they become influential, their engagement measures—follower counts and platform visibility—warrant a higher standard of discourse. She notes that Curry's tweet encouraged misogynistic and patriarchal elements of Black Twitter to rationalize Black woman bashing, particularly with respect to enforcing control over Black female sexuality and eroticism. Eromosele addresses Black digital practice by noting Twitter's affordance for distributive discourse, grounding her critique by embedding tweets that support her arguments. She highlights three feminist-leaning tweets to support her argument about Curry's misplaced critique, closing the article with an admonition to Curry to refrain from passing judgment on others.

Both D'Oyley's and Eromosele's articles provide paratexts from which to examine dogmatic digital practice. Their presence on The Root constrains discursive possibilities for both authors. Given The Root's position as an "appropriate" space for Black news and entertainment, it is not surprising that Eromosele and D'Oyley focus on moral propriety, female aesthetics, and social media etiquette. Both expand on the possible connotations and interpretations of Curry's tweet, lending an additional discursive layer to the original exigency. Finally, both articles practice dogmatic digital practice by chastising digital practitioners for their social media use.

I earlier categorized both articles as think pieces. As such, they are valuable examples of Black digital practice, offering insight into the influence of Black culture on Black online content. Institutional long-form analyses of Black culture from a Black cultural perspective are rare in mainstream media, so their publication on The Root signals a validation—at least for the purposes of abnegation—of Black social media activity. Moreover, posting these critiques of digital practice on a website that is more technically and culturally accessible to a wider audience is valuable for understanding the heterogeneity of Black digital literacies and Black online culture. This assertion is based on the premise that these digital pieces extend Twitter conversations to those who might not be as invested in the Twitter ecosystem, allowing non-Twitter users to also participate in the conversation. Indeed, Eromosele's article attracted more than one hundred comments, which further extended, interpreted, and deconstructed the author's points as well as Ayesha Curry's tweet. Thus despite the disdain Peters expresses for think pieces, I find that they are valuable elements of Black digital practice.

Finally, this approach shows that online cultural exigencies are not limited to the originating platform; in many ways, filter sites like The Root, Madame Noir, and the *Huffington Post* are the first spaces where the broader public can engage in the discourse. I mentioned in the previous section that expanding Black cultural conversations outside of the insular engagement of social media highlights the heterogeneity of the Black community, but simply publishing Black content to a Black media site doesn't guarantee a robust conversation. Conversation and dialogue are touted as important features of the internet; pundits and academics argue that interactivity is key to information access and a robust public sphere. However, the comment sections where those dialogues could happen are a fraught endeavor in today's media environments; many large sites have disabled their comments thanks to inappropriate community behavior or pernicious bots and spamming by bad actors. Meanwhile, smaller sites face long-standing issues of discovery due to the massive amount of information available online, so the initial task of building a commentariat is difficult, and conversations are hard to sustain. The Root enjoyed—but never actually cultivated—a modest online commentariat while it was a standalone site. The site's move to Gawker's Kinja publishing platform, however, both removed comments that were posted prior to the move and introduced the authors to a more racially diverse setting.

Meanwhile, over on Twitter . . .

I mentioned earlier that Ayesha Curry is a social media influencer; as of this writing, her Twitter account has 765,000 followers, her Instagram account has 4,800,000 followers, and her official YouTube channel has 470,000 subscribers. Moreover, the tweet sparking this discussion of respectability politics and Black digital practice had 70,000 retweets and 93,000 favorites—a considerable body of data by any measure. While these numbers can be argued for as a measure of popularity, I argue that Curry's "influence" across these networks and platforms draws on her performance and evocation of respectability politics for Black audiences, which translates as civility, modesty, and adherence to patriarchal definitions of gender and sexuality—or appropriate behavior—for more mainstream viewers.

However, this chapter doesn't directly examine Curry's Twitter (or any other of the social networks she inhabits) posts or interviews. Instead, I've spent some time exploring how her discursive performance was received *outside* of the social networks she posts to. This is a methodological move; this text employs critical discourse analysis, where *discourse* includes utterances from multiple actors across various platforms, apps, and networks. Method can also be seen as a discursive move: by focusing on reception rather than the original utterance, I show that the post's uptake by other Twitter users decenters Curry's authorial intent and vivifies alternative libidinal readings.

That said, Twitter provides its own discursive mediation of Black discourse, and this section addresses how Twitter illustrates and extends dogmatic digital practice. I am not examining seventy thousand retweets, though! In keeping with my framing of this exigency as a discourse operating across multiple media, I instead examine the tweets that were selected by FTW, SportsGrid, and The Root to illustrate the debate about aesthetics and sexuality. Twitter's mediation of dogmatic digital practice became clearer as I recovered the original tweets for archival purposes. The mainstream and Black cultural websites all made reference to the impassioned Twitter responses sparked by Curry's posts but did not have the capacity to provide examples. Here I begin with the tweets published by the Black writers on the sports-oriented websites.

For example, Peters's (2015) article on FTW embeds three decidedly banal tweets (figures 5.4–5.6) from a California Sports Network reporter recounting Steph Curry's opinion about his wife's Twitter activity: These tweets are not in and of themselves products of Black Twitter, however nebulously organized it may be. Properly considered, they are the responses that a famous Black athlete gave to a Black reporter—who may occasionally participate in Black Twitter practice—from a regional

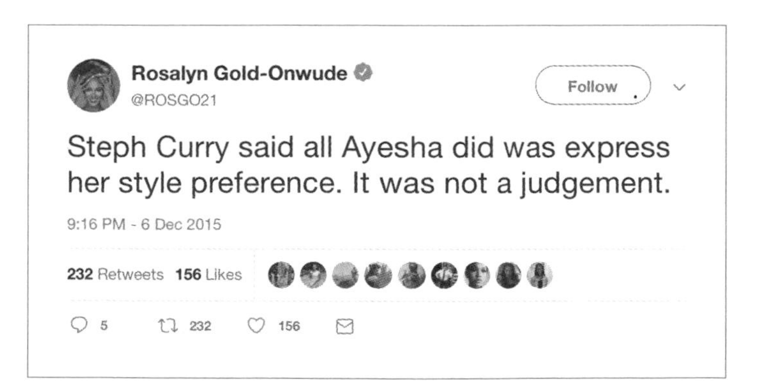

Figure 5.4. "Steph said." Tweet by @ROSGO21, December 6, 2015. Screenshot by author.

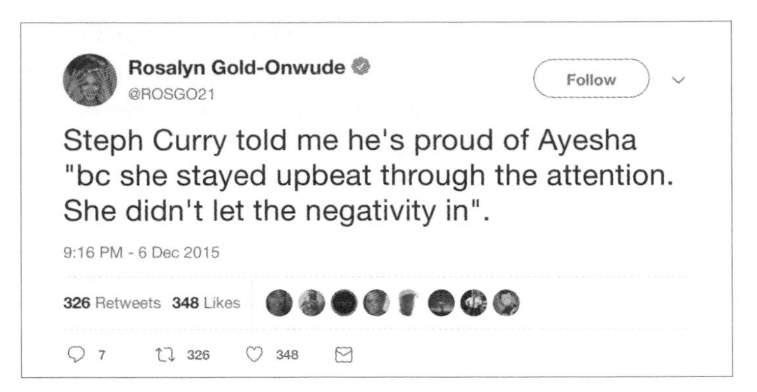

Figure 5.5. "Steph's proud." Tweet by @ROSGO21, December 6, 2015. Screenshot by author.

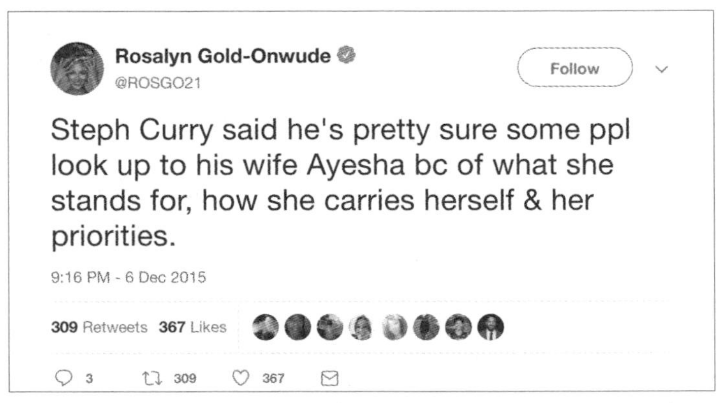

Figure 5.6. "Ayesha carries herself well." Tweet by @ROSGO21, December 6, 2015. Screenshot by author.

sports network. These embedded tweets are completely in keeping with the purpose and ethos of "For the Win," a *USA Today* online vertical focusing on sports entertainment; they are simultaneously news and culture artifacts that are relevant to the social domain of sport. They also illustrate that while Black Twitter may be the most visible Black community online, there are multiple Black subcommunities on Twitter that also draw on Black culture and commonplaces. This seems like a banal pronouncement, but in an era when Black Twitter has become nearly synonymous with Black digital practice, it is worth pointing out that Black digital practice on Twitter happens in multiple ways (see also Freelon, McIlwaine, & Clark, 2016).

Finally, even though these tweets are not content issued by a "certified" Black Twitter user,[12] they represent an evocation of dogmatic digital practice on Twitter. In particular, the third tweet quoting Steph Curry on the "negativity" of Black Twitter's responses reads as a coercive move to silence online dissents rather than a husband's defense of his spouse's social media activity. Peters published this tweet to buttress his argument that one should avoid engaging with Black Twitter, which is an odd statement to issue from a sports website catering to sports fans—but not strange at all when viewed through the lens of Black respectability.

On SportsGrid, Tanya Ray Fox embedded a number of tweets pungently replying to Ayesha Curry's original post. Fox correctly categorizes these responses as "backlash" and adds that it was "predictably louder and more abundant" (para. 7). This implicit jab at Twitter's facility for fostering unproductive, contentious conversations is in line with popular conceptions about Twitter's role in diminishing online civility. I should point out that Fox never explicitly refers to Black Twitter; nevertheless, I consider her critiques of Twitter practice as a critique of Black Twitter digital practice. Her observations speak to my arguments for dogmatic digital practice as a strategy designed to discipline inappropriate interlocutors attempting to critique respectability. Fox embedded the tweets below (see figure 5.7) and characterized them as "women . . . using feminisim [*sic*] to back up their various gripes" (para. 8).

To reference more appropriate Twitter behavior, Fox also posts tweets originating from "sensible Twitter." Earlier, I referenced the tweet she posted chastising those responding to Curry for spending too much time on the internet—a common technorational retort for those seeking to delegitimize emotional responses to online content. Twitter offers a unique context for the long-running archetype of the keyboard warrior (KW) / social justice warrior (SJW), which was also mentioned earlier. "Appropriate" digital discourse valorizes dispassionate, rational dialogue as the standard for online discussions of any sort. Dogmatic digital practice, as used by Fox, levies an intersectional critique against Black Twitter. By this I mean that the capacities of Twitter for immediate, dialogic interactivity are inveighed against as stifling reflexive, unemotional discourse. The false objectivism of normative internet discourse is tied to norms of whiteness, masculinity, and patriarchy and warranted by claims that "everyone knows" or "it's common knowledge."

Figure 5.7. "Don't shame others." Tweet by @KiranOpal, December 6, 2015. Screenshot by author.

Figure 5.8. "Better than?" Tweet by @felicianista, December 6, 2015. Screenshot by author.

Figure 5.9. "Consumer goods." Tweet by @felicianista, December 6, 2015. Screenshot by author.

Moreover, Blackness is associated with a surfeit of passion and sexuality. Thus when nonwhites, women, queer folk, or other subcultures employ Twitter to dispute Curry's respectability—often in detail with evidence, citations, and anecdotal experience—they are labeled as SJWs or, in this case, as making inappropriate Black responses.

Their arguments are rejected as being too emotional or, in an inversion of technical expertise, as a product of them spending too much time on the internet. It's interesting to see this rationalist, technocultural insult being levied at Curry's detractors, as it unintentionally ratifies the sentiments—rather than the practice—behind Curry's statement to normalize an elite opinion while delegitimizing responses using the same medium.

Black on Both Sides: Rebukes to Respectability

As I wrote previously, social media's two-way discourse—not quite democratic but closer to the flat hierarchy that is common to third places as defined in Oldenburg's (1999) *The Great Good Place*—affords discursive agency to the targets of respectability's coercion. Contra Oldenburg, however, these discourses are not playful; instead, the libidinal tension that is most visible is reproach. I argue for *reproach* rather than *rebuke* because these rebuttals of respectability ideology still seek to maintain Black community membership with respectability proponents. These reproaches expand the discourse space within which respectability proponents claim authority by recognizing the intersectionality and heterogeneity of Blackness. Moreover, they "pull the card" of respectability proponents by highlighting both problematic takes and the antiblackness of the proponents' discourse. Occasionally, online reproach blossoms into "cancel-culture initiatives," where social media influencers and the like loudly proclaim their refusal to recognize folk promoting coercive respectability takes (e.g., Erykah Badu's argument that young women should dress modestly to avoid sexual harassment led many folk to argue she should be canceled). Cancel-culture initiatives could properly be considered a rebuke, but recent events on Twitter indicate that canceling folk on social media is ineffective (again referencing social media's two-way nature) and, in the end, just as carceral as respectability initiatives.

All social media, by definition, allows for direct and indirect interaction between interlocutors, but Twitter in particular lends itself best to both the promotion and diminution of respectability ideals. Unlike Facebook, where respectability posts like Curry's ferment in shared circles of subscribers, Twitter's public broadcast model allows unaffiliated others to chime in. These users can interject themselves into conversations by directly addressing the content (quote retweet) and the original poster (reply), offering skilled practitioners (and bad actors) multiple opportunities to reauthor, divert, and reinvent topics and arguments. While Instagram's changes to its discourse mechanisms (e.g., expanded sharing mechanics and increased commenting space) have increased discursive space, its image-centric format tends to sharply delineate possibilities for wide-ranging conversations. Moreover, hashtags and trending topics accelerate conversational expansion—as well as the derailment or distillation of dialogue—by encouraging weak-tie engagement through likes, follows, and in- and out-platform sharing. Twitter's attention economy exposes a much wider audience to respectability posts than other social networking services in part because of these weak-tie affordances increasing the visibility—but importantly, not the reception—of respectability content. The same weak-tie connections also increase the vulnerability of respectability ideology by exposing it to possible dispute—if not outright antagonism.

To support these claims, I turn to the only examples of Twitter discourse that were offered by the Black cultural websites I investigated, as neither of The Root's think pieces included actual tweets. The first article examined, by Demetria Lucas D'Oyley, only summarizes Twitter users' reactions to Curry's tweets. Her interlocutor, Diana Ozemebhoya Eromosele, chooses a different route by embedding tweets by Twitter user felicianista to illustrate the problematics of Ayesha Curry's tweets (figures 5.8 and 5.9).

Both tweets highlight how informational Blackness deprecates respectability's command over media representations of appropriate Blackness. Felicianista contests Curry's moral and discursive authority to dictate "appropriate" Blackness, feminism, and sexuality. While it is entirely possible that Curry never saw her responses, the uptake by sites outside the Twittersphere indicates that felicianista's retorts made cogent points. Her measured responses are certainly more civil than other retorts to Curry's sentiments, which probably determined the inclusion of these tweets in Eromosele's piece.

Black Memetic Subculture: Man Crush Monday and Woman Crush Wednesday

In the process of analyzing Curry's tweets, Fox also criticizes Black digital practice indirectly by embedding an additional set of tweets calling out

Black Twitter memetic subgroups. Internet memes have been an object of academic study for some time (Shifman, 2013; Milner, 2016), but there is surprisingly little research on race and internet memes. Fox calls out hashtag memes that are heavily employed by Black Twitter, such as Man Crush Monday (#MCM) and Woman Crush Wednesday (#WCW), among others, to critique the Black cultural impulses behind them. Fox's critique of this aspect of Black digital practice is of interest because of its deployment within a respectability—cultural and digital—context.

As digital practices, #MCM and #WCW can be understood as gendered displays of unrequited attraction and affection that are often but not always sexualized.[13] Florini (2019) notes that these hashtags "mark a space of play where heteronormative rules don't apply," arguing that the practice allows many users to express same-sex affection without being seen as queer. The meme consists of an image paired with either a hashtag or a descriptive caption; posting the acronym provides practitioners an opportunity to share or reveal a person, personality, or celebrity that they find attractive. These memes are part of a larger digital cultural practice: Twitter users developed alliterative day references (e.g., #FollowFridays and #ThrowbackThursdays) to share something of interest with their followers and to the public. These references are *not* exclusive to Black Twitter or indeed to Twitter itself; they have also found purchase on Instagram and Pinterest.

Shifman (2013) describes internet memes as "units of popular culture that are circulated, imitated, and transformed by individual internet users, creating a shared cultural experience in the process" (p. 367), but this definition lacks cultural specificity. When it comes to Black memetic culture, I propose that Black memetic digital practice invents, transforms, and signifies upon units of Black and mainstream culture to create a shared social and cultural experience.

This definition draws on Blackness as informational identity, sharing a number of commonalities with signifyin' discourse. Signifyin' practitioners have always taken great pride in using language for invention, transformation, and sharing of cultural phenomena and objects, a practice that predates internet culture. More specifically, signifyin', like Black life, is exquisitely social (Moten, 2013) and requires a participatory audience; these qualities transfer easily to social media sharing. While an astonishing number of internet memes originate from the anonymous inventive chaos that is 4chan, Black memetic culture is often nearly as popular (e.g., the "Kermit sipping tea" image macro). In addition to being hilarious or pointed, it can be purposive, reflexive, and coercive, which reads differently from the "just for the lulz" of 4chan (Phillips, 2015; Milner, 2016).

Shifman proposes an analytic framework to evaluate the instigating phenomena of meme culture based on a schema of content, form, and stance—which also deserve some unpacking. She argues for *content* as "the ideas and ideologies" contained within the memetic text, whereas *form* is the "physical formulation of the message perceived through our senses" (p. 367). This arrangement doesn't go far enough to emphasize *where* memes happen. Drawing on critical technocultural discourse analysis (CTDA), I argue that the social, networked, and technical capacities of the platform on which a user chooses to display a meme should feature in any analysis of that meme. Moreover, technocultural belief is applicable to memes in both form and content, particularly with regard to the perceived utility of the content's dissemination. Some online spaces are more conducive to the interplay and invention necessary for memetic culture by allowing participants to play with meaning, form, and reception of their memes.

Furthermore, Shifman urges researchers to consider imitation as the primary element to be observed, but this only makes sense if one gives primacy to the authorial intent of the original post. If we are to understand memes from the Black cultural signifyin' tradition, I argue that the audience's *reinterpretation* of the original content is the initial force driving memetic transmission. Invention is necessary to repurpose the meme-as-boundary object, referencing the original signification while repurposing it to fit into the kairotic moment. In an information landscape where sensemaking pulls from the encoding strategies one uses every day, one's libidinal (re)imagining (Ott, 2004) of the possible meanings of online content will bring greater attention and appreciation than mere imitation. Thus invention should be prominent in meme analysis, rather than deducing what the original content might have been trying to promote.

Given the reproductive capacity of the digital, where multimedia content is constantly re-created in exact form across multiple platforms, the question for meme (and new media) researchers should be "Why here?" While an exegesis of the original content is necessary, the analytic focus of memes should be on how they are repurposed—rather than simply imitated—to suit a different rhetorical exigency proposed by the interlocutor.

Shifman's (2013) third framework dimension is *stance*, which she defines as the "information memes convey about their own communication," focusing on how "addressers position themselves in relation to the text, its linguistic codes, the addresses, and other potential speakers" (p. 367). This definition includes three additional aspects: participation structures, keying, and communicative function. Shifman's conception of stance addresses a small part of my concerns about the technical dimensions of memetic content by ostensibly addressing who can participate and the tone and style of the address. These linguistic and communicative dimensions are important, but they do not address the social and cultural constraints on and affordances of discourse that stem from the online venue in which the meme is posted. This can be particularly important when the meme leaves behind the platform in which it is originally posted, bringing us back to the question "Why here?"

With all of the above in mind, figures 5.10 through 5.12 are screenshots of the tweets Fox posted. These tweets are signifyin' upon memetic Twitter subcultures, and their indirect approach is part of the critique here. In my discussion of subcultures, I refer to Freelon, McIlwain, and Clark's (2016) multimodal study of Black Twitter, in which they identify several "community hubs" of Twitter users that power Black Lives Matters's information machine. One such was Young Black Twitter (YBT), whose practitioners often post about "topics and communication styles that appeal to Black youth: hip hop music, culturally relevant jokes, fashion, sex and relationship advice, and Black celebrities." I bring this up because some of the subgroups identified by Fox overlap and expand on the interests expressed by Freelon, McIlwain, and Clark's YBT community.

The tweets I selected reference the following:

- Black women promoting their pride in their male offspring and Black masculinity

- Black women pledging New Year's resolutions for affirmation
- Black women who have not been validated by social media attention but don't need it for self-affirmation

I link them to Black Twitter, Black culture, and to practices of targeting Black women because of the subject matter of the post in which they are embedded but more specifically because of how Black femininity

Figure 5.10. "My son is my MCM." Tweet by @spikereed, December 6, 2015. Screenshot by author.

Figure 5.11. "Got them heated." Tweet by @RedNationBlogga, December 6, 2015. Screenshot by author.

Figure 5.12. "Nobody's WCW." Tweet by @spikereed, December 6, 2015. Screenshot by author.

is imbricated in Fox's critique of digital practice. Despite their lack of African American vernacular, I am marking them as Black Twitter discourse (Brock, 2012) and as a variant of dogmatic digital practice because of their subject matter, their signifyin' discourse style, the poster profiles, and their inclusion in the Ayesha Curry debate.

In addition to the "crush" callouts, the tweets Fox selected include mocking references to female self-help and self-affirmation devotees. These posts are examples of dogmatic digital practice because they rebuke certain Black digital practices—particularly, those of Black women. While these tweets do not reach the extremism of "Hotep Twitter,"[14] their masculinist and technorationalist perspectives are nonetheless dismissive of various digital feminist and womanist digital discourses, ostensibly in support of a Black woman. That they are being cited as examples of "sensible Twitter" offers additional support for my argument for the dogma of "appropriate" digital and cultural practice.

Must Be Two Sides: Respectable Blacks as and versus Informational Blacks

Twitter and other social networking services enable Black community members to articulate a modern politics of respectability, utilizing digital means to police the on- and offline behaviors of Black folk. Not quite cyberbullying, occasionally humorous, but in its fashion evocative of the statement the "personal is political," Black Twitter's dogmatic digital practice simultaneously illustrates, incites, and performs coercive behaviors. Although there has been little research on the actual effects of Black Twitter's policing, I optimistically argue that it is a communitarian action rather than solely a punitive one. As such, Black Twitter's policing is emblematic of a satellite public sphere. A growing number of researchers are now interested in examining Twitter's surveillance capabilities and arguing for the platform as a coercive, invasive space, but I ask you to consider Twitter's cultural capacity as a coercive force as well, mediated by Twitter's specific affordances.

6

Making a Way out of No Way

Black Cyberculture and the Black Technocultural Matrix

> Take up the challenge posed by Pursell: to look more at context and impact than at actors and objects. In this case, answering his deceptively simple questions—What do [technologies] do? What do they mean?—led me to acknowledge the presence of race.
>
> —Carolyn de la Peña (2010, p. 931)

> Black life . . . is irreducibly social.
>
> —Fred Moten (2013, p. 739)

Throughout this book, I have framed Black online identity and Black digital practice as Black cyberculture, an awkwardly named construct incorporating *cyberspace* (itself a dated term) and *technoculture*. As mentioned earlier, technoculture can be understood as the relations between, and politics of, culture and technology. Dinerstein (2006) argues that "technology is the American mythos" (p. 570). When defined this way, however, *technoculture* often tricks upon the racial identity of whiteness, and white racial ideology and technological beliefs become the norm. That obviously won't do! Black technology users are not white (even if they are Western), so it becomes necessary to interrogate how Black people make sense of their existence as users and as subjects within advanced technological artifacts, services, and platforms. This final chapter is that catechism, firmly placing Black folk at the center of information and communication technology use. I offer this interrogation not as a summary of the previous chapters but as a provocation for those who are interested in centering Blackness as digital practice.

Reorienting technoculture to incorporate Blackness invites an inquiry into the possibilities of Blackness as technology—not Black bodies (been there, done that) but Blackness as technology—in the same way that Blackness often stands in for the best of American entertainment and culture. I am not arguing for minstrelsy and blackface here, to be clear, even though those representations of Blackness are as American as apple pie. Nor am I suggesting that Blackness is a nonserious use of technology; indeed, technology use for Blacks often occurs from the margins of society, where survival, joy, and resistance intertwine uncomfortably in the everyday. Chun (2013) contends that race-as-technology "posits a comparative equality or substitutability—but not identity—between the two" (p. 8). Chun goes on to probe how whiteness incorporates science and technology to build technologies and institutions of race—a helpful formulation for antiblackness and technology but not as necessary here. Instead, I would like to begin from the introduction's discussion of "technology as text" to build out from the possibilities of Black thought into a concept of Black technoculture. From there, I will discuss Afrofuturism as an analytic for Black technology use and time and Black technoculture. Finally, I close with a foray into a libidinal framework of Black technoculture.

Technologies as Cultural Texts

My argument here centers on the digital's networked and distributive capacity for banal, everyday Black information and computer technology (ICT) practices, but others have argued similarly for artistic and technical artifacts (Fouché, 2006; Ebo, 1998; McGahan, 2013; Weheliye, 2002). "Technology as text" has multiple postulations for distributed Blackness and for Black technoculture:

- code (interface and practices)
- the digitally distributed content generated by and mediated by that code
- signifyin' and other cultural discourses of Black digital practitioners

The first two are instrumental and organizational; think of the possibilities for art and discourse that were introduced by Grandmaster Flash's innovative technique of scratching records as part of a musical performance. The last marks the generative relationship between the first two, revivifying the noncommunicability of Blackness into a mediation for the production of Black life and thought. From this perspective, code, digital discourse, and language-as-culture can (and do) constitute racial identity. Adding technological mediations of discourse (Herring, 2001) allows one to examine computer-mediated communication and digital practice as racial identity as well.

It is vital, however, to *not* incorporate the digital's technocultural alienation (drawing on whiteness's Manichaean separation of mind and body; Dyer, 1997) into my formulation of online Blackness. I wrote the previous sentence long before I read Wilderson (2010), but his words advance my claim: "As an accumulated and fungible object, rather than an exploited and alienated subject, the Black is openly vulnerable to the whims of the world and so is his or her cultural 'production'" (p. 56). Here Wilderson states that because Black folk have no legible stature in the West as political agents, they have no inalienable rights to Black cultural production. Thus Blackness (in online spaces and elsewhere) is immediately captured by Western culture, leaving little possibility for emancipation from that framework. I agree: while I recognize possibilities for emancipation through radical and decolonizing digital practices, my pressing concern for Black technoculture is to make manifest the vitality and joy of Black uses of ICTs. While these libidinal impulses may become commodified or surveilled, they are paraontological—that is, the embodied cognition they express preexists the platforms on which they are published, visible, and deemed appropriate for consumption. The digital mediates culture—in this case Blackness, but otherwise typically white Western—in ways that allow for sociality despite commodification. The next section reviews other researchers' takes on Black technological practice, which I then extend to specifically examine digital practice.

Thinking through Blackness and Technoculture

Rayvon Fouché's (2006) concept of Black vernacular technological creativity (BVTC) offers additional touch points for conceptualizing Black technoculture. Fouché writes that technology as material oppression is not the only way to analyze Black experiences with tech (p. 641).

Anticipating many of the claims made throughout this text, he defines BVTC as "innovative engagements with technology based on Black aesthetics" (p. 641). By asking how Black folk see, view, feel, understand, and interact with technology from their own perspective, BVTC offers a praxis-based, three-point perspective on Black technoculture:

Redeployment is the process by which the material and symbolic power of technology is reinterpreted but maintains its traditional use and physical form, as with blues musicians extending the perceived capability of a guitar without altering it.
Reconception is the active redefinition of a technology that transgresses that technology's designed function and dominant meaning, as in using a police scanner to observe police activities.
Re-creation is the redesign and production of a new material artifact after an existing form or function has been rejected, as in the case of DJs and turntablists developing new equipment (p. 642)

BVTC is ontologically compelling thanks to Fouché's avoidance of the dichotomy of arguing for Black technological use as either appropriate or inappropriate. Instead, he conceptualizes it as a relationship among Blackness, American racial ideology, and the technologies themselves. Fouché also takes up the vernacular—a concern I share—as the generative source of Black cultural production.

My Black cyberculture concept diverges here from BVTC. While Fouché (2006) describes BVTC as being informed by a Black vernacular aesthetic that includes, but is not limited to, the production or performance of music, dance, literature, visual art, and sport (p. 641), I have chosen to redirect my focus on the vernacular to linguistic performance, enactment, and discourse, particularly as computer-mediated communication expresses an engagement with the everyday in virtual spaces through digital practice. My approach differs from examining performances of "black-informed expressive or aesthetic representations of technology" (Fouché, 2006, p. 642) and from the "technology of stylization" that BVTC addresses. The Black banal and the everyday may occasionally rise to the level of art or politics, but its value lies in the unalloyed libidinal expressions of joy and catharsis that arise from interactions with others and institutions.

I also differ from Fouché (2006) in my conceptualization of the materiality of interfaces and interface practices. Fouché points out that BVTC engages with material artifacts; his elements of reconception and recreation prioritize Black technologists' capacity to have hands-on access to their chosen technologies—something that is much more difficult to achieve with digital services and practices.[1] While there have been Black digital initiatives encouraging users to gain coding or design literacies (most significantly, BlackPlanet), digital environments are typically less amenable to the types of agentive technical virtuosity Fouché outlines.

Black folks' lack of material (and financial) control over digital infrastructure can be visualized within the evergreen complaints of Black social media mavens. Many, like April Reign (@reignofapril), creator of #OscarsSoWhite, and Cashawn Thompson (@thepbg), creator of the viral catchphrase and hashtag #BlackGirlMagic, have agitated to be fairly compensated for the pithy content they generate, which is often repurposed into corporate and nonprofit marketing campaigns for lifestyle, media, and consumer brands. Social media content distribution rights are typically retained by the service; these power users have little control over their virtuosic social media practice. Like other social networking services, Twitter's (n.d.) terms of service note, "Such additional uses by Twitter, or other companies, organizations or individuals, may be made with no compensation paid to you with respect to the Content that you submit, post, transmit or otherwise make available through the Services."

The plight of these Black women social media creatives is summed up in Fouché's (2006) observation that Black technological practice is dismissed as "cleverness" rather than as sustained, creative engagements with the institutions and strategies of technology. Black digital practitioners and auteurs with far less reach than Ms. Reign or Mrs. Thompson are even more susceptible to this dismissal; they also labor under the restrictions of unavailable content, uninteresting interfaces, and unaffordable (in terms of time, attention, and economics) service. These obstacles have been tangentially addressed by the continued falling prices (if not costs to the end user) of ICTs as well as increased access to digital services (e.g., blogging platforms, smartphone videography). Black digital practitioners can thus enact their cultural identity in the interstitial spaces of commercial platforms, where they seek the communal presence of others like them in the racialized institutional and technological "desert of the real" (Baudrillard, 1981).

Thus to understand deficit narratives of Black technology use, one must consider Black exclusion from the capitalist economies of social media. However, limiting inquiry to the inequity (and iniquity) of the mainstream reception of Black creativity offers Black digital practice limited space or opportunity to flourish. Instead, it can be better appreciated through an analysis of the material and symbolic character of digital technologies. Such an analysis prioritizes an inquiry into the libidinal, virtual, and communicative aspects of everyday Black digital practice. For many scholars, Afrofuturism has been such an inquiry.

Afrofuturism and the Black Postpresent

As a framework for Blackness and technology Afrofuturism has rightfully been praised as an alternative path to analyzing Black technoculture. In truth, Alondra Nelson's groundbreaking special issue on Afrofuturism in *Social Text* provides the theoretical impetus for this manuscript. Nelson describes Afrofuturism as "African American voices with other stories to tell about culture, technology, and things to come" (2002, p. 8); this work owes a great debt to that formulation. Like many second-wave race and digital researchers, I resonate with Nelson's frustrations with Blackness's oppositional place in technocultural narratives of "progress"—or as she writes, "Forecasts of a utopian (to some) race-free future and pronouncements of the dystopian digital divide [as] the predominant discourses of blackness and technology in the public sphere" (p. 1).

Eshun (2003) uses Afrofuturism to analyze three partially intersecting spheres: mathematical simulations, informal descriptions, and "the articulation of futures within the everyday forms of the mainstream of Black vernacular expression" (p. 293). The last is valuable to this research, but Eshun's reliance on the Middle Passage as the foundational moment of Black alienation—"the constitutive trauma of slavery" (p. 299)—leaves me wondering how Black joy and pleasure can be understood in digital practice, leading to my incorporation of libidinal economy for this analysis.

In writing on Black feminisms of the future, Morris (2016) argues, "People of the African diaspora are continuously creating culture and radically transforming visions of the future. . . . These visions are necessarily transgressive and sub verse in relation to dominant discourse" (p. 33). She cogently ties together Black feminism and Afrofuturism, but her claims still draw heavily on themes of resistance and on reimagining Black bodies as agents of the future. Morris graciously allows for Afrofuturistic possibilities that are not moralizing or utopian, but her argument inevitably returns to "progress" as a feature of Afrofuturist epistemology. In this, Morris inadvertently privileges the desires of Black respectability proponents—in this case, through futurist artworks and artists. That position is not compatible with the aims of this book.

Similarly, Yaszek (2006) extends Nelson's formulation of Afrofuturism to define it as "not just reclaiming the history of the past, but about reclaiming the history of the future as well" (p. 47). This is a compelling position on Blackness and technology, but it also falls prey to utopian sentiments. Like Morris, Yaszek moves through art and literature to unpack Black cultural engagements with futures and technologies that are unintended for Black use, arguing that Black alienation is exacerbated rather than alleviated. The utopian angle arises when Yaszek suggests that Black disruptions of technological futures are "harbinger[s] of a new and more promising alien future" (p. 48). The possibilities of navigating the present moment of Blackness and technoculture seem distant from these pronouncements of future Blackness.

If it is not already clear from my analysis of the above works, I am not a champion of Afrofuturism-the-analytic. In the introduction to this work, I glibly proclaimed that Afrofuturism was unsuited for analyzing Black digital practice despite its utopian aims for the recovery of Black aesthetics, paired with a transgressive, resistive politics. For example, Afrofuturists are often virtuous even in (or perhaps because of) their weirdness. Consider Sun Ra, George Clinton, and Janelle Monae; Octavia Butler and Samuel Delaney; or Kool Keith, ATLien-era OutKast, and DJ Spooky. These artists' willingness to imagine a technologized, futurist Blackness through music is laudable, but they do not speak to existing in the present. While upon reflection my claim seems dismissive, I do not mean to refute Afrofuturism-the-project.

Instead, I resonate with Stallings's (2013) writings on the Black ratchet imagination. Stallings describes "failing, losing, forgetting, unmaking, undoing, unbecoming" (p. 136) as the ratchet's performance of the failure to uplift. Stallings's deft explanation of postwar imagination and antiwar activities provides generative power for the evaluations of Black digital practice throughout this manuscript. It is simply not futurist enough for Black thought to progress along the lines of Western technoculture. Instead, the digital has afforded online articulations of the explicit, the sensual, and the precarity of Black culture, similar to how hip-hop artists in the late 1990s and early 2000s celebrated "corporeal orature" (Defrantz, cited in Stallings, 2013, p. 138).

This chapter also takes up Alexander Weheliye's laments about the "literal and virtual whiteness of cyber theory" (2002, p. 21) in his criminally underutilized Afrofuturist essay "Feenin." His examination of Black cultural engagement with information technologies begins with a critique of the "white liberal subject in techno-informational disguise"—an aim with which I wholly sympathize. Weheliye's reading of Sylvia Wynter is especially generative for this text. He notes that Black culture denaturalizes "the human as a universal formation while at the same time laying claim to it" (p. 27). This figuration translates clearly to the digital enactment of Blackness. Indeed, Weheliye conjures the separation of Blackness from Black bodies by arguing that Black musical genres make their virtuality central to their texts: "Black subjectivity appears as the antithesis to the Enlightenment subject by virtue of not only having a body but by being the body" (p. 28). Where Weheliye is concerned with aural technologies and their capacity for Afrodiasporic politico-cultural formations, his assertions in "Feenin'" anticipated my direct engagement with computer-mediated communication, such as social media, digital practices, and online discourses.

Throughout this book, I have been careful to take heed of Nelson's (2002) admonition to those using Afrofuturism as a frame. She states that researchers must pay attention to "how selves are differently situated both within and outside of this network" without limiting Black digital identity to the "technical construction of selves over a distributed network" (p. 4). I find, however, that the literary and artistic objects analyzed to argue for the futurism of Afrofuturism warrant a technocultural respectability premised primarily upon the high-culture activities of surrealists, artists, and the politically resistive. I admit that my critique of Afrofuturism (but not its proponents!) could be seen as unfair; literature, the arts, and the academy are durable artifacts that capture and disseminate visions that differ from the dreary everyday. There have been few methods that encapsulate how average folk argue for themselves and their own futures—but the digital is one such method and space. Thus this text's interest in the banality of Black Twitter and other spaces where ratchet digital practice is enacted reinvests futurity into present uses of the digital rather than in possible Black cyborg or Black magical futures. In other words, Blackness is neither posthuman nor interested in being so.

Blackness, Technoculture, and Kairos

Whereas Afrofuturism seems preoccupied with reimagining a future history of Blackness and technology, Black cyberculture is better argued for as the "postpresent"—particularly as it is constructed and contested through Black cultural digital spaces and practice. By *postpresent*, I mean that Black folk in digital spaces are constantly engaged with the moment, or kairos. I am tricking off[2] of theories of postmodernity, postracialism, and information technophilia here—not to interrogate the increasing precarity of labor or the spread of surveillance and commoditization but to present how Black digital practice invests energies into *being*, a celebration of the now that incorporates past iniquities and future imaginings. This position is particularly indebted to Afro-optimism; Moten (2013) argues that Black thought is thought itself.

Black kairos is simultaneously racial performance or enactment, discursive invention, and appropriate, timely engagement within a communicative and cultural context. Although my use of this concept draws on my analysis of digital and communication technologies, I am careful not to limit Black kairos to digital practice. One way—for many, the only way—to understand Black kairos in the American context (e.g., racial ideology) is through the frame of respectability, as discussed earlier. Another limited possibility for viewing Black kairos through a political-economic lens, where Black digital activity can only be understood through its commodification, capacity for surveillance, and economic potential. From that perspective, however, libidinal tensions of control and coercion are still deemed to be the only aspects worthy of examination, while the erotic and kairotic properties of Blackness are elided. For this reason, my gaze remains riveted to moments of Black pleasure and catharsis. The preceding chapters have expanded on Black performance and invention, but the concepts of time and engagement deserve attention as well.

Timeliness (or the lack thereof) is a significant aspect of Black discursive identity. The concept of "colored people time" describes a joyous disregard for modernity and labor capitalism—for example, the aphorism "I might be late, but I'm always on time." As I deploy it here, kairos refers to the immediacy afforded to Black discourse by network protocols, communal structures, and the instantaneity and archival capacities of information networks. Similarly, while considering the rhetorical canon of delivery as an essential element of the art of digital communication, Porter (2009) notes that distribution and circulation, access, and interaction have been undervalued elements of print culture since the invention of the printing press.

The temporality of Black kairos is apparent in the riposte and swagger of face-to-face interactions, but historically, it has been much less visible in ICTs. While television and radio featured performances of Black kairos, everyday Blacks could only interact with these mediums at a remove (e.g., telephone call-ins). The internet—especially the introduction of bulletin-board systems and other discourse-oriented modalities—offered an ever-growing cross section of participants to create their own mediated discourse styles and mechanisms. Early on, computer-mediated communication researchers studied the synchronous and asynchronous aspects of time on digital discourses, but they often left unexamined nontechnical cultural understandings of time and discourse. Even as more researchers examined Black online communities with the rise of Web 2.0, only a few prescient scholars (Banks, 2006; Byrne, 2007) interpellated Black discourse traditions with digital discourse communities. It is only in the last few years—as social media has supplanted the World Wide Web as our communicative infrastructure—that investigators have started to understand cultural discourses as constitutive of digital practice.

For example, "showing the receipts" is one Black postpresent discursive digital practice that situates past transgressive behavior (often recorded in the form of digitized documents, but occasionally in visual or multimedia testimony) in the now (usually via social media) to be "read" as evidence in the moment. Similarly, one can see the Black postpresent within Black feminist, womanist, and queer Twitter's digital mobilization to agitate against perceived unjust phenomena and people, also known as "callout culture." Because of callout culture's desire for debate and its willingness to affront, it is derided by white feminists and technologists and color-blind internet pundits. The callout, originally a practice of Black women signifyin', has occasionally been mistaken for Twitter's "mob mentality," but it is qualitatively different: it is often a critique of systemic inequality rather than an attack against specific, individualistic transgressions. Kairos should not be construed as being limited to Black Twitter, however. It is equally in place on the Black "Gram,"[3] in threaded commenting communities such as Very Smart Brothers, or in the forums on Nappturality. While kairos is an important piece in the puzzle that is Black technoculture, I should perhaps revisit and expand on what I mean by (Western) technoculture before going deeper into conceptualizing Black technoculture.

Technoculture, or Race as Technology

At the beginning of this chapter, I referred to Dinerstein's (2006) contention that technology is the American mythos. Mosco (2005) writes that one of the primary sources of a myth's power is elasticity, which has a dual meaning for digital Blackness. First, the digital enacts virtuality through simulation. This is an expansion of the virtuality afforded by older information technologies (e.g., the telegraph, electricity, radio, television, telephones, and even the computer). The digital's elasticity resides in its capacity to simulate multiple possible virtual spaces through code, multimedia, and computational power. Moreover, the varied meanings digital practitioners ascribe to such virtual spaces afford even identical instances of code (e.g., subreddits, blogs, and PHP bulletin boards) the elasticity necessary to identify those spaces as heterogeneous in content yet similar in design. Second, and more important, the mythic elasticity of technoculture is denied to nonwhites and women. In Western ideology, the elasticity of being becomes fixity when nonwhites enter the picture; Africans and indigenous folk are "primitive," whereas Asians are "spiritual" (Eglash, 2002). This consideration becomes even more complex when one considers that whiteness is limned but not bounded by its aversion to, denial of, and love of Blackness. Thus the elasticity of technocultural myth is always already enframed by whiteness's interpretive flexibility.

Mosco (2005) adds that cyberspace-as-myth "transcends the banal, day-to-day worlds of time, space and politics" (p. 13), but this perspective is less than a stone's throw away from many Enlightenment philosophies of man and society that were conceived during the era of European slavery. Our understandings of time, space, and sociality are never exempt from libidinal or mythic beliefs about them; they are inescapably informed by them. My research on Black experiences in digital spaces contradicts Mosco's mythic claim; indeed, distributed Blackness is articulated through pathos about everyday life, centered on embodiment, and mediated by the digital. Furthermore, the 2016 US presidential election revealed how social media beliefs mediate everyday whiteness, from liberal and conservative white fragility on Twitter (i.e., "snowflakes"), to racist screeds on Gab, to libertarian individualism on Reddit.

I should note that there is significant overlap between beliefs about the computer and beliefs about the digital and internet, but there are also key distinctions. For example, consider a computer without an internet connection and one with an internet connection. The former contains and allows for the creation of virtual, immersive spaces, simulations, and multimedia. The latter includes those features (e.g., MMORPGs like World of Warcraft) but expands the virtual space to include social and relational connections between other computers and other computer users. Fundamentally, a standalone computer is an isolated imaginary; sharing the content or code generated therein can be done but is not inherent to the artifact. The networked computer, however, has sociality built into it. This last aspect is foundational to the concept of distributed Blackness—that is, Black sociality has been digitally networked and computationally mediated.

Glitching the Matrix

Stepping away from myth, let us consider technoculture as the interweaving of technology, culture, self, and identity. Dinerstein (2006) offers a compelling matrix of six elements that underpin Western technoculture:

1. Whiteness
2. Masculinity
3. Religion
4. Progress
5. Modernity
6. The future

While he does not describe them as libidinal, these elements certainly evoke libidinal tensions that influence how technology is understood in the West. Dinerstein's arguments for technoculture are not the first—the linkage among the West, religion, and technology has been explored by David Nye (1996), Leo Marx (2000), and James Carey (1984)—but he makes his signal contribution to technocultural theory by assigning a racial valence (whiteness) to American and Western technical identity. Dinerstein finds that technology is both the rationale for and the artifact of European and Euro-American imperialism and modernity, bolstering his claim that technology as an abstract concept functions as a white mythology (2006, p. 570).

Though I have cited, alluded to, and shouted out Dinerstein's (2006) matrix at every presentation and in most of my publications, I have not always clearly positioned it to either interrogate information and communication technologies or unpack the relationship among Blackness, Black bodies, technology, and technoculture. As an intermediate step, then, let us consider the immanence of Dinerstein's matrix aspects in the digital, networked space I am arguing for as distributed Blackness. The matrix works with technology as an abstract concept in order to tease out the libidinal tensions that are ordinarily unseen; Dinerstein eventually dials in on biotechnology as encapsulating his matrix. Similarly, this text limits "technology" not only to the digital—which is certainly a nebulous concept—but, more specifically, to information technologies used for communication, such as the computer and the internet. While these two artifacts have been mediatized, I draw directly from computer-mediated communication and social informatics research instead of solely from media and new media theories.

Three aspects of Dinerstein's (2006) matrix are relatively uncomplicated to map onto the digital. *Religion*, for information and communication technologies, draws on the technological sublime (Nye, 1996; Carey, 1984). It works as a paean to the spiritual power of information and the digital as a balm for social ills. Rather than putting faith in the works of a supreme being, religion recenters technology as a source of ineffable blessings *and* ills—either a digital utopia where speech is free and virtual spaces are democratic or a hellscape of incivility, terroristic acts, and violations of the informational self. Religion also is a grounding for the digital's links to transcendence; where the body is rendered in 1s and 0s while eschewing the bonds of material existence. *The future* can be understood as whiteness's (and the West's) quest for omniscience, where informational control over bodies (surveillance) and the material world (networks and datafication) is directly linked to spiritual, economic, and political gain. Information technologies are always seen as futuristic, drawing as they do on beliefs about control of the spirit and on the abstract reason of mathematics. *Progress* is closely tied to the future, as it is measured by the increase, reliance on, and deployment of computational solutions to social problems.

The informational capacity of *modernity* arguably originated before the Industrial Age with the advent of written culture (Giddens, 1984; Ong, 1982), but I refer to industrial modernity here: the command of space and time through networked communication, which in the process reworks relationships between the self, commerce, institutions, and technology. For example, consider the plantation. While it is relatively simple to consider it as an agricultural institution, the plantation depended on webs of trade, the datafication of the enslaved body (Reynolds, 2018), imperialist state policies of conquest and communication, and renegotiations of the state's and the individual's relationship to Black bodies. Modernity's contribution to the mythology of information and communication technologies, then, differs little from its contribution to technoculture overall: reflexivity.

By *reflexivity*, I mean that modernity's mythic capacity depends on our awareness of and reflection on how our lives differ from premodern (or even recent) social and cultural conditions. In this, modernity is deeply tied to progress and the future, further cementing the role of technology as the "spirit" of the West. I agree with Giddens and Pierson's

(1998) argument that through modernity, trust and risk have supplanted belief and fate (p. 102) as the predominant ways in which we informationalize our relationships with others and the world. Trust and risk, in Western technoculture, depend on our valorization of rationality, the scientific method, and logic as the most appropriate avenues to understand the world and our place in it. This becomes increasingly clear upon reading public and academic paeans to algorithms and big data, which are promoted as being trustworthy precisely because of their informational and computational capacities to model "reality" without bias. As is becoming increasingly clear, however, neither algorithms nor big data sufficiently model or account for the cultural qualities that are inherent to their design, leading to ethical and moral problems.

In keeping with the intersectional tendencies of this text, it is important to consider Dinerstein's technocultural categories of *whiteness* and *masculinity* as a set of relationships rather than as separate categories. Try a thought experiment: How do you visualize technology's relationship with white women? With Asian men? With indigenous folk of any gender? Masculinity, whiteness, and technoculture are coconstitutive—so much so that it is difficult to visualize any other group in relation. When we reveal whiteness and masculinity within frameworks of technocultural belief, we can see the libidinal energies that power our modern institutions, technologies, and infrastructure.

As mentioned previously, *whiteness* lends technoculture an interpretive flexibility—a quality that is magnified by ICTs. De la Peña (2010) notes that race is an "epistemology at play in all technological production and consumption" (p. 923), so interpretive flexibility, as whiteness, denotes the capacity to be simultaneously understood as individual and everyone—as the universal representation of humanity. Consider yesterday's web browser, ubiquitously placed on every PC desktop while harboring an infinite variety of web content. More recently, look to today's premium smartphones and tablets: they are "smart" precisely because of their interpretive flexibility. The entire screen fills to focus on one app and one app only despite an operating system that offers instant access to all other apps as well as the entire internet. Even still, mobile devices are considered less capable than today's desktop-class devices (including laptops), which embody interpretive flexibility in a frame of productivity and efficiency through their presentation and containment of multiple apps in one screen.

Masculinity, meanwhile, must be identified as heterosexuality and as sexual energy, especially given recent revelations about sexual harassment in the tech industry (e.g., the #MeToo movement). Dyer (1997) is especially helpful in this regard, writing, "White men are seen as divided, with more powerful sex drives but also a greater will power. The sexual dramas of white men have to do with not being able to resist the drives or with struggling to master them. . . . Dark desires are part of the story of whiteness, but as what the whiteness of whiteness has to struggle against. Thus it is that the whiteness of white men resides in the tragic quality of their giving way to darkness and the heroism of their channeling or resisting it" (pp. 27–28). As gender, as sexuality, and as a battle for control over sexual energies, masculinity affords technoculture a rationalist, imperialist, and spiritual asceticism that whiteness deploys to justify its control over others who are perceived to possess none of those qualities.

The question remains: How has white masculinity become associated with ICTs? Consider the archetype of the typical computer user: a white male who carefully manages his finances and appetites (how else to explain the fact that he is middle class?). Then consider the archetype of the expert computer user (e.g., the hacker or the coder), who is in (perhaps entirely too much so) control of his sexual energies, often white, often male. Look at the composition of technology firms, many of which are nearly entirely white; consider also how many of those firms—and the venture capitalists who fund them—come under fire for sexual harassment and assault claims.

To enhance the Western technocultural matrix, antiblackness must be incorporated as the seventh node of the matrix. Doing so allows for the libidinal tensions powering chattel slavery and racial capitalism to be clearly understood as technocultural artifacts and ideological mainstays rather than as the supposedly repellent activities of individuals. This approach is responsive to de la Peña's (2006) note that discussions of technology tend to avoid "white privilege or an investment in inequalities of knowledge or access" to assess its application across generic contexts that happen to be white. By building on Afro-optimism and connecting it to Black pathos as an epistemological framework, distributed Blackness explicitly acknowledges that the political economy of racism, mediated by ICTs, is driven by the libidinal energies of antiblackness and necropolitics, and yet—and yet—Black folk persist. It becomes clear, then, that the libidinal qualities of Western technoculture *must* be revisited and revised, but not destroyed, to account for Black culture and digital practice.

The Black Technocultural Matrix (under Construction)

What is the mythos of Black technoculture? It clearly cannot just be limited to antiracism. As I have said throughout this text, racism is not the sole defining characteristic of Black identity. Neither can Black technoculture be confined to middle-class aspirations of achieving the franchise. I also hold tightly to the belief that social justice activism should not be the epitome of Black digital practice; online activism is simply the most visible and "appropriate" manifestation of online Blackness *to the mainstream*.

Unfortunately, Dinerstein's powerful arguments about technology's abstracted materialism of whiteness as a justification for dominance over humankind and the natural world (2006, p. 570) leaves little space to vivify Blackness and technology. It is especially useful to examine Orlando Patterson's (1982) concept of "social death" to understand the West's structural relationship to Blackness. Western technologies—eugenics, phrenology, social science, criminal law, and segregation—have been deployed to construct Blackness as social death, and these arrangements reify technoculture as "how to do things *to*" Black bodies and Blackness.

Wilderson (2010) accounts for technocultural libidinal energies toward Black bodies within Western arts and aesthetics, naming this phenomenon *antiblackness*. The concept has become increasingly popular among those who consider Blackness and modernity, as it accounts for how Black bodies (and Blackness itself) are constructed under and throughout Western culture. Antiblackness sees Blackness as a noncommunicable structural position in society—one that is incapable of being alienated. But in theorizing Blackness as articulated through the digital, I cannot uncritically frame Black bodies in digital spaces as social death. This is in no small measure because of the digital's communicative infrastructure—in particular, the various forms of interactivity enabled by computer-mediated communication. Moreover, the hashtag (and its sibling, the trending topic algorithm) has revealed Black sociality to such an extent that it can no longer be overlooked. I can and must acknowledge that ICTs have a "dark side" (how terrible that I cannot free myself from that metaphor!) and that those inimical artifacts and practices are often explicitly designed to achieve a particular goal: the diminishment—if not outright destruction—of nonwhites. Less clear (at least to me) are the productive qualities of antiblackness when it is applied to the digital—that is, how should we understand Black digital practice as productive, life-giving online behavior?

The "vivification" of Blackness and technology in the previous paragraphs was no accident; as I mentioned, I am an adherent of Afro-optimism. This school of thought's leading proponent, Fred Moten (2013), explicitly engages "social death," calling it the "burial ground of the subject," to provide a funereal context for Black thought—*funereal* in the sense that funerals are for the living: they are as much celebrations of life as they are recognitions of life's end. In this burial ground, Blackness is where political agency is sublimated, submerged, and enshrouded by the reality of having to live every day with death looming on the horizon. Moten's counterargument, which I find utterly compelling, is that Black life is irreducibly social (p. 739) even as it is lived in the aforementioned cemetery. The power of Moten's claim is libidinal: Black life is *lived* in the social, "which is, in any case, where and what blackness chooses to stay" (p. 741). Moten calls this "the condition of the possibility of Black thought" and names it *celebration*. For Moten, *subject* references the rational, transcendental, self-possessed being who is capable of political action—in other words, white modernity—a position that is easily transferable to this discussion of whiteness and technoculture.

Here, then, is my reconfiguration of the technocultural matrix for Blackness, with the ultimate goal of unpacking the beliefs that underpin Black (American) digital practice. Here are my suggested categories for the Black technocultural matrix:

1. Blackness
2. Intersectionality
3. America

4. Invention/style
5. Modernity
6. The future

The Black technocultural matrix neither supplants the Western technocultural version nor propounds the same ideologies of dominance and control over nonwhite bodies. Instead, I am theorizing a Black cultural relationship with technology, drawing on the Black experience in the West—an experience that is shaped by relationships with whiteness and with technology from a social and political subject position.

Blackness

> I have never felt more American than when we all hate on this mutherfucker [*sic*] together.
>
> —Dave Chappelle (2018)

My first matrix category conceives of Blackness—rather than the Black body—as an element of Black technoculture. In this unfiltered, patriotic expression, Chappelle exemplifies one of the defining characteristics of Black existence in the United States: dark, humorous critique. It evokes Black interiority, references antiblack racism, and even suggests political engagement—all from a libidinal perspective. *Blackness*, for this matrix, stands for the metaphysical and critical valences[4] of Black cultural identity, revolving around subjectivity and cultural production. My phrasing does not ignore the political and ideological aspects of Black identity but instead highlights the libidinal elements that drive those aspects of Blackness's relationship with technology. I phrase it thusly to incorporate the ratchet and the banal, qualities that are often disregarded in analyses of technology and studies of Black culture.

To return to the digital: a theory of Black cyberculture is necessary to examine how information and communication technologies afford Blackness a differently circumscribed space to luxuriate and grow—never free from white racial ideology but no longer materially coerced by it. This possibility exists *because* of the disembodiment enabled by virtuality—that is, when participating in an online space, Blackness lives as an existential "here" (Yancy, 2005) that is largely unrestricted by the fixity and pejorative reduction of the Black body that occurs offline. Online, "I am not only a point of view, but I am also a point that is viewed" (Gordon, cited in Yancy, 2005). The possibilities for communicating, performing, and apprehending Blackness in digital practice and spaces diminish the theoretical power of antiblackness. Correspondingly, arguments that Blackness is a point of noncommunicability, or social death, lose power when they are confronted with the technical and cultural visibility of Black Twitter practice and hashtags. This formulation responds but is not beholden to whiteness as the default identity of technoculture, or whiteness's ontological and axiological (e.g., the nature of existence and the philosophy of ethics and values) formulation. For example, whiteness draws on the separation of mind and body (Dyer, 1997); dominance over each is the hallmark of white superiority. In return, Dinerstein argues that whiteness's control over the Black body has led to the *colonization* of Euro-American bodies by Black music, dance, kinesthetics, and speech (2006, p. 590).

In my reformulation, Blackness reintegrates the mind and body, returning authorial control and intent over those aspects of Blackness to Black culture. The matrix quality of Blackness, then, is the communitarian enactment of intentionality across cultural aspects of Black culture. As Moten (2013) says, "Blackness is . . . irreducibly social" (p. 739). Thus Blackness in this matrix highlights how pathos—in addition to logos, or rationality—structures the Black American understanding of the world that they find themselves in. Pathos begins with the joy of embodied Black existence; it is at once a response to the effects of modernity and white supremacy on the Black psyche and a politics of the erotic engaging with "honest bodies that like to also *fuck*" (Morgan, 2015, p. 40; emphasis original). Whereas whiteness gains power from obscuring its internal differences, Blackness recognizes what makes Black folk different.

I am aware that this definition does not directly acknowledge the Middle Passage, white supremacy, or slavery as overwhelming influences on Black identity. While racism is an inexhaustible fountain of energy for whiteness, it is only part of how Blackness navigates the world. I do not deny these events' and ideologies' effects on Blackness, but their omission is meant to direct the focus to a celebration of Black life.

Intersectionality

Where masculinity is the gendered and sexual aspect of the Western technocultural matrix, *intersectionality* represents the interweaving of Blackness with multiple facets of identity, including the digital. Incorporating intersectionality signals a freeing of Blackness from the carceral fixity of the Western technocultural matrix. In discussing this element of my matrix, I recognize the brilliant Black feminists who have produced a theoretical concept for analyzing the complexity of Blackness, gender, and sexuality. While Black women theorists originally crafted intersectionality to investigate the intersecting systems of oppression affecting Black women (Collins, 2002; Crenshaw, 1990), I am here referring to intersectionality as a theory of differentiation (Brah & Phoenix, 2004; Levine-Rasky, 2011) involving social position and positioning. Brah and Phoenix (2004) argue that intersectionality, when defined by differentiation, emphasizes the "social relations, experience, subjectivity, and identity" found at the intersection of emotional and psychic dynamics as well as those of socioeconomic, political, and cultural differences (p. 83). Differentiation, then, refers to how groups define, negotiate, and challenge their positions, transforming identity from an object to a process (Levine-Rasky, 2011, p. 243). That this definition bears a resemblance to Omi and Winant's (1994) racial formation theory is no accident; both are structural perspectives on the salience of racial identity in modernity. Omi and Winant refer to racial formation projects as the tension between social structure and representation, whereas Brah and Phoenix focus on the meaning-making relationships between identities based on access to symbolic and material resources.

What does intersectionality mean for Black technoculture? My primary motivation for incorporating this concept is that Black people must constantly confront context collapse in nearly every setting in Western racial ideology—that is, their racial identity overlaps and interweaves with whatever other identity they may be inhabiting at the moment, but rarely in a manner that benefits them. Nominating intersectionality to the matrix of Black technoculture is an epistemological, methodological, and empirical imperative. From a methodological perspective, analyses of Blackness and technology should approach the standards of historical materialism; researchers *must* incorporate historical, economic, cultural, and political context, thus transforming their analysis from static observations of "Black folk doing tech" to more dynamic investigations of Black folks' relationships and positionality with technology. Doing so allows one to drill down into how tech and culture mutually constitute raced, gendered, sexual, economic, and other axes of social organization. For example, researchers who wish to study Black women's natural hair culture should take into account the aesthetic, historical, and political relationships among Black hair, older technologies, colorism in the Black community, women's bodies, patriarchy, entrepreneurship, heterosexuality, and Western culture. These interactions must be acknowledged while examining how YouTube, blogs, and online bulletin boards mediate practitioners, professionals, and a deeply engaged commenting community to build out digital spaces.

From an epistemological perspective, narratives that recount the experiences of understudied, subordinated people represent valid and reliable empirical data from which to glean patterns of use, discrimination, and belief structures. Much of the research on race and technology relies on historical archives, which are narratives of a particular type—often institutional, only occasionally personal. Historians of technology and race compellingly argue that archival sources of technology design and use rarely discuss race at all, much less feature source material from or about Black inventors, users, or practitioners. Thus intersectionality's emphasis on narratives of affected, subordinated populations as agentive data—particularly with respect to the archival capacities of digital and online media—offers researchers the unparalleled opportunity to access reflexive, banal, and political accounts of Black digital practitioners, in their own voices. This is doubly important because research on Black technology use often falls prey to technocultural deficit narratives or the aims of respectability politics instead of focusing on the everyday experiences of the Black digital.

I am aware of Black feminist scholars' arguments about other disciplines appropriating and diminishing intersectionality by applying it outside of its original generative context: Black women and the matrix of oppression. Black women could never be removed from the analyses offered here; instead, I hope to encompass and complicate Blackness across all genders and sexualities. This is not an #AllLivesMatter demurral; instead, my formulation is in line with my desire to diminish the carcerality of Western technoculture when theorizing Blackness. I use a key element of Black feminist standpoint theory—embodied cognition—to highlight how practices that are designed to valorize or demonize Black bodies can be understood as technological (see also Chun, 2011).

While some could view this application as a utopian initiative—Black transcendence, as it were—I mean to redirect intersectionality's original intent of analyzing oppression. My approach here is similar to my rationale for not allowing racism to overdetermine Black identity: oppression is not the only way to understand the contributions of intersectional identities to digital and technological practice. This move also allows me to disempower respectability as an ideological benchmark for appropriate Black practice—a benchmark that is responsible for demonizing Black women's "inappropriate" behavior on- and offline. The Black technocultural matrix thus accounts for how masculinity has come to be associated with technological prowess while encouraging analyses of Black women's technological use as only partially shaped by masculinity (as opposed to being read as "resistant" to masculinist ideals).

America: The State and the Spirit*

Where the Western technocultural matrix employs *religion* and *progress* as matrix elements, I have replaced them with *America* as both state and spirit. Before I expand on the conundrum of including America in a Black technocultural matrix, let me briefly explain why I replaced these two qualities with a reference to a problematic nation-state. Dinerstein (2006) argues that a number of factors contributed to technology's displacement of Christianity as the religion of white Western culture. Rather than viewing the universe as a creation of an ineffable, unknowable force, Western inventors from the Age of Enlightenment forward believed that their creations were uncovering the "ultimate structural principles of the universe" (p. 577). These beliefs energized European colonial and imperial endeavors as well as American narratives of the frontier. The latter centered on a "second creation" thanks to American command of agricultural and military technologies, dispossessing the "first creation" of Native American claims to the "undeveloped" land. Dinerstein continues by noting that American claims to natural resources discovered within frontier lands also drew on religious concepts; *Manifest Destiny* is a technocultural phrase denoting "the technological transformation of an 'untouched' space" (p. 578), which Americans used to justify their right to a particular geography. Through technological command, whiteness becomes the first "body" to properly use a space.

Black culture, in its guise as Black bodies and thus as one of the technologies used to domesticate the American frontier, cannot and should not make similar claims for technology as religion. This is not to say that African or African-descended populations elsewhere have not invested spiritual energies in technology; there is, however, enough evidence globally that simply investing Black resources in Western technologies often leads to rack and ruin. Returning to Baraka's (1971) thoughts about how Blackness would inform technology design and use, I argue that technology in Black technoculture is not an extension of control over the world but rather an affordance for social joy and inventive creativity.

Similarly, Black cultural beliefs in technology as "progress" must also be viewed with a suspicious eye—even those developed by Black people for Black people. For example, McMillan Cottom (2017) points out the perils that minorities and working-class people face when they assume that educational technologies, such as for-profit universities and Massive Open Online Courses (MOOCs), will improve their lives. These predatory institutions are erected primarily to enrich investors, not to educate those who can't afford traditional higher education. In chapter 2, I showed how Black folk are properly suspicious of technologies—even when they are designed for and by them—because they are concerned about being segregated or left behind. These worries are markedly different from those aired by white users of the same tech.

Why, then, is *America* an appropriate choice for the Black technocultural matrix? America as an ideal, as an institution, and as a set of racialized practices is *the* matrix for Blackness. Blackness is ineffably American—that is, it is well suited as a technological ideal for Black technoculture because America-the-nation created Blackness in order to survive and thrive. Morrison (1993) calls this "American Africanism"; American ideals inform Black community beliefs in equality, democracy, and fairness even as Black folk experience daily life leavened by the understanding that the American telos of progress depends on antiblackness. Baldwin ([1950] 1985) is best at describing this conundrum, writing about the difference between the African and the American:

> The American Negro cannot explain to the African what surely seems in himself to be a want of manliness, of racial pride, a maudlin ability to forgive. It is difficult to make clear that he is not seeking to forfeit his birthright as a Black man, but that, on the contrary, it is precisely this birthright which he is struggling to recognize and make articulate. Perhaps it now occurs to him that in this need to establish himself in relation to his past he is most American, that this depthless alienation from oneself and one's people is, in sum, the American experience. (p. 39)

This last sentence is a direct callout to Du Bois's concept of double consciousness and as such fits neatly into my argument for Blackness and technoculture. As mentioned earlier, my case for racial identity rests on the dialectic between in-group and out-group, where both groups recognize that the in-group has certain beliefs, speech, and practices. I contend that racial identity is also a national identity, an assertion that many readers will doubtlessly find obvious. But the American of African descent is, as Baldwin notes, different from the Frenchwoman of African descent in that their respective national ideals shape their relationship to the state nearly as much as their relationship with whiteness.

Black folk in America are often as enthralled by the promises of technology as any other American; however, where the West dreams of domination, Black folk dream of liberation. Black folk are also deeply aware—and thus skeptical—of the effects of Western technologies on their bodies and spirit, living as they do in areas that are zoned for toxic waste disposal, in the wake of airborne pollution and waterborne chemical effluent, or even in broadband "deserts" that have been abandoned by telecoms and the US government. As both Baldwin and Du Bois poignantly note, alienation is the birthright of the American but is always embodied by Black folk. Cyberculture researchers focusing on alienation and online identity, as Kali Tal argued back in 1996, should have always been looking to Du Bois and Black folk.

Finally, you may have noticed that *America* is followed by an asterisk. I denote it as such to signal that the United States is but one context for diasporic Blackness. For example, Brah and Phoenix (2004) note that women of African descent in the United Kingdom face similar colonial- and imperialist-bred racism from whites. They also might have more recent, viable connections with a natal country of origin, whereas many Black Americans have no clue. Similarly, people of African origin in Central and South America will have differing experiences as *mestizaje* as well as with the different (post)colonial racial regimes they grew up in. Thus this matrix is implicitly designed—like critical technocultural discourse analysis (CTDA)—to be open to a multitude of diasporic Black experiences.

Invention/Style

The matrix element *invention/style* comes directly from my Black Twitter research, but I firmly believe that invention is as essential to Black technoculture as it is to Black culture's influence in the Americas overall. Black aesthetics are intensely libidinal and performative, drawing as they do on Black sociality and the communitarian ethos of Blackness in America. These qualities also distinguish Black technological practice from Western technological practice—that is, for Black technoculture, utility and efficiency are *not* the ultimate aims. While there are indeed Black inventors, such as Sarah Goode, Granville Woods, and Mildred Kenner, who developed countless practical inventions, there are also Black artists and technologists, such as Madame CJ Walker, Grandmaster Flash, and Grand Wizard Theodore, who developed aesthetic innovations.

There is a close analog between libidinal Black technoculture and Black music genres. In describing the blues, Walcott (1972) explains that the genre is "a struggle to order that space into a distinctive and comprehensive style, a style all the more distinctive for its unstinting generosity of spirit and unfailing faithfulness to the complexities of human experience; and comprehensive because it is the product of a vision that accommodates a tragicomic sensibility" (p. 10). If this sounds nothing like the rationalistic and imperialist aims of Western and American racial ideology, that is no accident. The blues are in dialogue with Western aims not as resistance or accommodation but as relation.

Walcott continues by arguing for the blues as an insistence of the formal possibilities that are inherent in style itself. I make a similar argument for Black rapprochement with technology—that is, the expression of style in Black digital practice "embodies, abstracts, expresses and symbolizes a sense of life" (Walcott, 1972, p. 11). I return to Walcott's words because he defines *style* so much better than I could: style is "to inhabit so completely the space one *does* have, and to inhabit it so individually, that one does not need to go outward toward the corridor of time to discover possibility. For one has found it, in one's own depths" (p. 11; emphasis original). This perspective is deeply akin to that evoked in discussions about Black identity held earlier in this text. That is, the fixed perception of self that has been inflicted on Black folk by Western technoculture, or the "hail," is a record of what one should be and has been under that regime. Identity, however, is what one does after the hail. My argument is that style and invention are crucial components of Black identity; they are how Black folk negotiate the informational and institutional regimes of antiblackness.

Modernity

For Black technoculture, *modernity* is precisely the informational, capitalistic, and institutional regime of antiblackness. Surveillance and sousveillance, digital redlining (Gilliard & Culik, 2016), access to education, even voting rights are all positioned in ways that limit—if not directly injure—Black folk on the way to reifying whiteness. Respectability is a chilling example of Black aspirations to modernity in its well-intentioned paeans of hygiene, control, and assimilation. In doing so, respectability proponents extol a thinly veiled Western white argument for what Blackness should be rather than what it could be. Feagin (2013) writes, "Racial oppression and its rationalizing frame have long been central to modern Western societies, to the present day" (p. 7). Unfortunately, for Blackness there is no escaping modernity, as it is the defining frame of Western society, and its transformative effects have reshaped much of the world in the West's image. There is no return to the folkways lauded by Du Bois or to the pan-Africanism espoused by Asante, and there is no escape to postmodernity's promises of decentering global powers and bringing the margin to prominence.

In *The Black Atlantic*, Gilroy (1993) also inveighs against utopian conceptions of Blackness and modernity, arguing instead that Blackness is a counterculture for modernity. For Gilroy, the inescapability of slavery calls the entire project of modernity into question—that is, Black progress from slaves to citizens reproduces the unity of ethics and politics (which I contend for as the reassertion of pathos over logos and as intersectionality) as folk knowledge. This position refutes modernity's insistence that ontology, axiology, and aesthetics belong to distinct knowledge domains—a position privileging whiteness's Cartesian/Christian insistence on the separation of mind and body. For example, where modernity and capitalism insist that work is emancipatory and agentive, Black folk have long understood that work only signifies servitude, misery, and subordination (p. 40). Instead, Gilroy argues, Black modernity should be understood as a "vernacular variety of unhappy consciousness" (p. 58); this fits neatly into my reasoning for Black pathos as the epistemological standpoint of a libidinal economic perspective on technology. Gilroy's grounds for Blackness and modernity gain additional salience when they are read against Giddens and Pierson's (1998) contention that late modernity has transformed our world into a space where emotional communication is crucial to sustaining relationships inside and outside of marriage (p. 119).

I agree with Gilroy's (1993) assertion, however, that analyses of Black modernity "require attention to formal attributes of expressive culture and distinctive moral basis" (p. 36). This claim presages Fouché's (2006) argument for vernacular technological creativity while adding a political and civic valence. In addition, Gilroy's description of Black modernity as non-European syncopation rings true for the evaluations of Black technoculture in this text. Associating Black modernity with expressive culture, Gilroy adds,

> The particular aesthetic which the continuity of expressive culture preserves derives not from dispassionate and rational evaluation of the artistic object but from an inescapably subjective contemplation of the mimetic functions of artistic performance in the processes of struggles towards emancipation, citizenship, and eventually autonomy [emphasis mine]. Subjectivity . . . may be grounded in communication, but this form of interaction is not an equivalent and idealized exchange be-

> tween equal citizens who reciprocate their regard for each other in grammatically unified speech . . . there is no grammatical unity of speech to mediate communicative reason on the plantation. (1993, p. 57)

My arguments for the libidinal economy of Black technoculture lead me to supplement Gilroy's claims—first, by pointing out that the same expressive creativeness and subjectivity he identifies in Black music can be located in the performance and textuality of Black digital and social media practice. Second, while political motives may drive expressive culture, libidinal energies power those political moments. That is, Gilroy's "mimetic functions of artistic performance" are libidinal moments that are expressed as relations and mediated by technology.

The Future

My argument for *the future* for Black technoculture seems dishonest based on my earlier dismissal of Afrofuturism's sentiments, but "a time which is not this time but not time past" is an unwieldy phrasing. Remember, however, my claim for the *postpresent* as the temporal context for understanding how kairos and discourse build out Black discursive perspective—outside of and linked to the moment but also referring obliquely to the past and the present.

From that position, I take a linguistic approach to this matrix element—namely, that features of African American Vernacular English (AAVE) provide evidence for Black technocultural perspectives on time, modernity, and technology. The three forms I discuss briefly here bolster my claim for Black technoculture as a postpresent rather than as an Afrofuturistic technological belief system. The three grammatical features that AAVE speakers use to denote time (Rickford, 1999) are as follows:

1. The invariant *be*
2. The stressed *bin*
3. The phrase *fixin' to*

I chose linguistic forms rather than slang terms because while slang changes quickly—especially for AAVE—grammar and pronunciation are systematic features of language that persist much longer over time. These linguistic features are also class related—that is, they are much more frequently spoken by less-affluent, less-educated Black folk. However, as Spears (1998) notes, while AAVE might not be spoken by all segments of the Black community, it is commonly understood. There are often only a few generations of class differentiation in Black communities, and many who cannot or will not use these forms at work or in certain social settings will still be in contact with family and community members who use them on a daily basis. Because there is a shared understanding of these AAVE features, I am comfortable in claiming that they represent the banal, everyday speech of the community without being pejorative or assuming that Blacks are a "low class undifferentiated mass" (Du Bois, 1940). As Rickford (1999) notes, skilled AAVE speakers use these features, distinctive words, and rhetorical styles to "inform, persuade, attract, praise, celebrate, chastise, entertain, educate, get over, set apart, mark identity, reflect, refute, brag, and do all the things for which human beings use language" (p. 12).

The invariant or habitual *be* references future, conditional, or habitual or extended phenomena that are still occurring—for example, "They be on Twitter all day." It differs from standard English *be*, which only indicates that someone has done something in a particular tense. *Been*, in its unstressed form, is closely linked to the standard English forms *has been* and *have been*, but *bin* is very different. The increased emphasis marks an action or state that happened a long time ago, or in "remote time," but is in effect up to the moment of speech (Rickford & Rickford, 2000). *Bin* cannot be used with adverbial phrases marking time. *Bin* also has a performative aspect; in some cases, it may be used deceptively to indicate history with a phenomenon or object. A second performative aspect, where *been* is performed with *had*, *coulda*, or *shoulda*, marks a period that remains in effect until a time earlier than the moment of speech. Finally, *fixin' to*, which is often spoken as *finna* or *finsta*, references events that are about to happen in the immediate future.

These linguistic features indicate that Black technoculture has a different relationship with time than white Western technoculture. Western modernity prizes punctuality and efficiency; networked communication and computational platforms, even as they collapse space and time for their users, are still deeply reliant on timeliness as a means of synchronizing activities for institutional and commercial purposes. Black culture, on the other hand, can be understood as having a more flexible relationship with both the past and the postpresent, where time is relative to participation. Both *bin* and *fixin' to* indicate an elasticity of time up to a certain moment, whereas the habitual *be* indicates a timelessness to human activity.

I relate these to technoculture through Gilroy's (1993) assessment of Blackness as a counterculture of modernity. While Black culture is often in dire need of political and moral reassurance that the present is not the future, the linguistic features of AAVE indicate a comfort and willingness to live in an elastic now or, as I argued earlier, a postpresent that is not quite the future but a moment to be present within.

Coda: Research into the Black Digital

Early in the Web 2.0 era, Keith Obadike (n.d.) set up an eBay auction to sell off his Blackness as performance art. Using the platform's capacities to list the features of the "product," Obadike offered a list of situations and contexts in which his Blackness could be (and should not be) used by the purchaser. Some highlights include the following:

- This Blackness may be used to augment the blackness of those already black, especially for purposes of playing "blacker-than-thou."
- The Seller does not recommend that this Blackness be used while demanding fairness.
- The Seller does not recommend that this Blackness be used while demanding.

Although eBay quickly pulled down the auction (there were only twelve bids), Obadike's use of the e-commerce platform is one of the more notable examples of Blackness being deployed to give definition and clarity to the digital and to online spaces. While assumptions have been made that Obadike was solely auctioning off his racial and cultural identity to white folk, it is entirely feasible that he was also offering his racial authenticity to Black folk who found themselves at odds with their natal community's concept of Black identity. As such, his auction should be understood as an artifact of digital double consciousness.

While writing this text, I have consciously bounded my inquiry into cultural digital practice by focusing on Black American culture without comparing it to other diaspora cultures or to whiteness. While the public's consciousness of Black digital practice has certainly evolved since 2001, when Obadike's auction was posted, the ethos and ideals of Black technoculture have never received enough (any) attention. At best, when agitating for social or political change, Black online resistance and activism are deemed the markers of "appropriate" digital practice, but those occasions are few. This lack of serious attention is due to cultural beliefs about Black Americans as deviant versions of white Americans—a perception that has only been slightly[5] adjusted by the political and cultural prowess of Black digital practice on Twitter, Vine, YouTube, and other social media services. It's far too easy to believe, after deprecating race as a factor in internet and digital practice, that Black Americans are just Americans with less "civilized" or "sophisticated" online information needs, uses, and behaviors.

This book's concluding argument for theorizing Black technoculture, then, is meant as a corrective to deficit models of—or research into—Black digital practice. My articulation of this vision of Black technoculture is an offering to those who are interested in portraying Black digital practice from a more generous perspective as well. Black technocultural theory is a generative model one can use to ground explanations of what Black folk do in online spaces. By eschewing modernist perspectives on digital practice (e.g., brand, labor, and resistance), I offer a nuanced, comprehensive viewpoint into why Black folk use digital technologies in everyday situations. My emphasis on the everyday is intentional; I am not seeking to valorize those who are already powerful or notable in the networks that I study. While their moves are emulated or commodified, they are not definitive of the Black communities using digital media every day.

I would like to play out this succinct conclusion by returning to CTDA once more. CTDA has been invaluable in aiding my conceptualization of a Black techno- and cybercultural matrix. As a discourse analysis and interpretive method, CTDA prioritizes the belief systems of marginalized and underrepresented groups' conceptions of self with respect to their technology use. Du Bois wrote in *Dusk of Dawn*, "Lions have no historians"—an allegorical claim describing how even an apex predator has no real defense to justify its existence, certainly not against its extermination for the "benefit" of a modern society seeking to claim its territory for agriculture, industry, and exploitation. Here Du Bois offers a compelling argument to recenter Black technology use from the lion's perspective rather than from the hunter's. Black folk have long been subjected to academic and intellectual justifications for their inferiority—from Thomas Jefferson and Abraham Lincoln denying the Negro basic humanity to Oscar Lewis and Daniel Patrick Moynihan arguing that Black folk have a "culture of poverty"—even as they embody and fight for the American ideals of equality and justice that are denied to them by modernity. In my extensive reading of science and technology studies, as well as information science, library science, and information studies, I found entire texts (and disciplines) full of unexamined whiteness. Thus my research stream and this book have emerged from this perspective, where the standpoint of the culture under examination should be the reference point for inquiry.

This should not be taken as a recommendation to employ CTDA as a method, however. There are a plethora of excellent approaches—qualitative and quantitative—for analyzing digital artifacts, users, and practices. What I suggest instead for new media and internet researchers who wish to examine digital practice by nonmainstream users is to take advantage of CTDA's conceptual framework—that is, the directive to find and employ reflexive and philosophical accounts written *by* the folk using the technology under examination. Moreover, this advice is directed toward scholars of mainstream ICT users. Imagine how much more powerful internet studies would be if researchers were explicit about the whiteness of the online communities they study? If nothing else, the coders and engineers of Silicon Valley could be disabused of the notion that they are creating applications and software for "everyone" rather than for themselves. I won't hold my breath for that, however.

ACKNOWLEDGMENTS

You know who you are. Love and respect to you all.

Some portions of chapter 2 appeared in "Beyond the Pale: The Blackbird Web Browser's Critical Reception," *New Media & Society, 13*(7): 1085–1103, and are reprinted here with permission from Sage. Some research from chapter 3 was first published as "From the Blackhand Side: Twitter as a Cultural Conversation," *Journal of Broadcasting & Electronic Media, 56*(4), 529–549, and is reprinted here by permission of Taylor & Francis.

NOTES

INTRODUCTION

1 Throughout the text, I oscillate between *Black* and *African American* to refer to Black American culture. I am aware that diasporic African cultures in the Caribbean, Central America, and South America share some of the same beliefs and practices discussed here. Moreover, many African and indigenous ethnicities also have contributed values, language patterns, and aesthetics to what I am arguing here for as *Blackness*.

2 No shade to Deray Mckesson.

CHAPTER 1. DISTRIBUTING BLACKNESS

1 One of my greatest regrets is that Byron Burkhalter never revisited his 1997 research on soc.comm.african.american (moderated).

2 On September 3, 2014, the University of Southern California mistakenly announced that two white men would be leading a study of Black Twitter by reducing "Black Twitter" to "Black Twitter users who watch *Scandal*." USC's first mistake was not properly crediting the doctoral research to Dayna Chatman, the Black woman originator of the project. Their second mistake was the reduction of Black media practitioners and audiences to a homogeneous sample.

3 Is this a bug or a feature?

CHAPTER 2. INFORMATION INSPIRATIONS

1 I am aware that the internet and the World Wide Web are *not* the same. Nevertheless, this chapter uses the terms interchangeably.

2 Enactment is still a relatively unexplored concept to explore for race and new media, as few Western information/media platforms or applications are designed for users outside of whiteness.

3 See www.pewinternet.org.

4 Arnold Brown II, Frank Washington, and H. Edward Young Jr. See the website at www.laptopmag.com/articles/blackbird-the-browser-for-black-people.

5 98/Me/2000/XP/Vista.

6 The extension allowed, among other things, the customization of a page's appearance, including stripping unwanted elements or reorganizing available information.

7 For more on algorithmic discrimination in Google search results, please see Noble's (2017) groundbreaking work.
8 Digg was, at the time of the original research, a social information/news aggregator that allowed users to vote on content. It was purchased by Betaworks in 2010 and is now a curated news aggregator.
9 A bloglist is literally a list of blogs that is formatted to fit onto the side of a blog page. It is used to demonstrate affiliation with other like-minded bloggers or blogs of interest.
10 I have not updated the search for this chapter, as Blackbird has received negligible attention, use, and market share since its introduction.
11 Ars Technica was purchased by Condé Nast in 2008, several months before its coverage of Blackbird. It is part of Condé Nast Digital, along with *Wired* magazine, but is easily more enthusiast-focused than its sister technology journalism publication and website.
12 Wauters isn't Black. He also felt similarly about the Gloss browser, which was intended to target women.
13 The article's comments are no longer available online.
14 Obviously, this comment was made long before the success of Marvel's 2016 *Black Panther* movie.
15 This last sentence was apparently intended to defuse his comments by referencing a tag line from old comedic routines.

CHAPTER 3. "THE BLACK PURPOSES OF SPACE TRAVEL"

1 See Parry (2014).
2 See Florini (2019).
3 This is a reference to the pejorative news coverage of Sandra Bland's murder at the hands of police.
4 From http://twitter.com/anildash/status/969974366, @anildash.
5 From http://twitter.com/loresjoberg/status/970017179, @loresjoberg.
6 From http://twitter.com/gesteves/status/970011697, @gesteves18.
7 This article was written so recently after the introduction of the hashtag and trending topic that Wilson didn't use the now common convention of beginning a hashtag with the octothorp.
8 In 2009, Twitter's home page featured tweets in real time that were accessible without a login. Try that now.
9 Not the Nick in the tweet above.
10 This critique does not apply to the Ramsey article, however.
11 Hirsch also notes that another service, TAS (RNC 2004 Text Alert Service), developed by Nathan Freitas and UPOC, also offered Twitter-like functionality at around the same time TXTmob was deployed in 2004.
12 Users receiving tweets through this convention get a truncated portion of the message and a link to open the corresponding Twitter web page.

13 This description of Twitter's web/desktop interface is circa 2016. Twitter issued a much-derided major redesign of the web/desktop interface (there's no desktop application) in July 2019, featuring three columns and an extensive remapping of interface elements.

14 As of 2016.

15 I believe that this finding points toward an understanding of how race organizes whiteness and Twitter as well.

16 Following the fiery destruction of her apartment complex, Kimberly "Sweet" Brown uttered this iconic phrase while describing her escape from the fire.

CHAPTER 4. BLACK ONLINE DISCOURSE, PART ONE

1 I am intentionally using *frame* rather than *topoi* to suggest that these three categories are ideas that take meaning and coherence from their organization, salience, and context (Entman, 1993; Kuypers, 2010) located in the text, the communicator, the receiver, and the culture at large rather than solely in one or the other. Thus while the three concepts have powerful symbolic and thematic meaning outside of digital practice, the organizational and discursive capacity of digital practice works to frame them as powerful interpretive cues for Black online expression.

2 Black people can be prejudiced or biased, but those are individual behaviors that are unsupported by the institutional and structural behaviors of white supremacist ideology.

3 "That ho over there" is a recent gendered, misogynistic addition to ratchet's meaning. It denigrates women who are considered to be promiscuous. The reference includes an expert digital practice component: thots are accused of frequent posting of sexual or pornographic social media content for attention, along with overuse of Instagram or Snapchat visual and audio filters.

4 In addition to its status as one of the first social media networks, BlackPlanet (BP) is notable for including HTML creation tools for the users. These tools sparked a robust economy for budding graphic and web design aficionados, as BP users quickly learned to appreciate web design as a mode of Black digital expression.

5 Pew Internet defines a smartphone owner as anyone who answers yes to one or both of the following questions: "Is your phone a smartphone?" and "Does your phone operate on a smartphone platform?"

6 At the time I wrote this in 2016, smartphone screens were still averaging less than 5.0 inches (ScientiaMobile, 2018). Average screen sizes in 2019 have grown to incorporate higher-resolution displays, and now nearly 40 percent of smartphones sold in the United States have screen sizes greater than 5.5 inches (Zeb, 2018).

7 The belief about isolation can be directly traced to the smartphone's supplanting of the iPod and other MP3 players, whose primary music output was the 3.5-mm headphone jack.

8 "Government name" is AAVE for the name on your birth certificate or other government document.
9 Given my discussion of hyperlinks earlier, it's worth noting that the nickname not only is a personal reference but is often a clickable hyperlink leading to the user's account details or content (*pace* Netflix).
10 In Twitter's extensive 2019 beta testing of its mobile client, the service deprecated display names by not showing them in replies to a tweet, leaving only a machine-generated username for the reader to guess at the identity of the respondent. This practice short-circuits Black Twitter creativity for little gain, in my opinion.
11 When using Twitter as SMS, the 140 character limit still applies.
12 Twitter recently made significant changes to tweet content: tweets can now be up to 280 characters, and usernames no longer count as characters in a reply (they still count as characters in an original tweet).
13 Yes, you must say both names.
14 *Fuckboi* is a viscerally insulting term describing a man who is somehow lacking in traditional masculinity or who is "lame, who sucks, and ain't shit" (Brown, 2015).
15 I experienced something similar while giving presentations on media examples of Blackness following the aftermath of Hurricane Katrina. Informed, educated audiences would reduce or ignore my arguments for Black online authors' re- and deconstructions of Black identity to instead express their liberal (or conservative) views about the appropriateness of the actions being depicted.
16 Hate-watching is the activity of viewing media that one actively dislikes; many practitioners voice their hatred through Twitter or other social media.
17 Noble (2016) points out that algorithmic researchers admit it isn't always clear how machine-learning algorithms make connections between data points.
18 For example, Twitter has a much-derided feature displaying content "liked" (not necessarily retweeted) by one or more people that one follows.
19 This is not to say that non-Black Twitter didn't respond to the gaffe, but their responses are much tamer. They certainly didn't repost the hashtag, for example.

CHAPTER 5. BLACK ONLINE DISCOURSE, PART TWO

1 Good as in "avoiding approbation" rather than as a positive change agent.
2 Another way to understand Black cult figures (Warner, forthcoming) is the phenomenon of the "chitlin' circuit," where Black entertainers uninterested in "crossing over"—or unable to—still commanded die-hard fans and financial success by touring Black venues.
3 His concerns might have paid off; one child is a recently graduated engineer, while the other has a full scholarship to an HBCU.
4 This is how telephone companies began to describe telephone service as fax lines and DSL services were installed in businesses and residences.
5 I share this excerpt for a rather amusing reason: I presented this work to a group of mathematicians, engineers, computer scientists, and physicists during a

fellowship at Microsoft Research New England's Social Media Collective. As one might expect, the audience was 99 percent non-Black; *nobody* knew who Ayesha Curry was or why they should care. While you, dear reader, may be in the know, it is not always safe to assume that my entire audience of two will be.

6 According to Oprah, this is also a rule of Twitter: never invoke Black Twitter by name (see also Bloody Mary, Candyman, and Beetlejuice).

7 EUR stands for *Entertainment Urban Weekly*.

8 BlackVoices got its start as an AOL community portal and was particularly popular as a chat destination for many Black urban dwellers in the late 1990s.

9 In case you did forget, MSBET was a joint venture between Microsoft and BET, promoted as an online space for Black culture, entertainment, information seeking, and job hunting.

10 I was unable to retrieve my originally archived versions of these web pages from 2015, which included comments made by The Root's commenting audience. Those comments did not survive the transition to Kinja—the new publishing platform—and thus are not discussed in this analysis.

11 Many lower than mine!

12 Gold-Onwude may indeed be a Black Twitter participant but here is posting to Twitter in her capacity as a news reporter.

13 One Urban Dictionary definition uses Jesus as an MCM example: "My man crush Monday is Jesus Christ, I'll go gay for Jesus."

14 See Young (2016): "Another subsection of Black Twitter . . . a less progressive, nuance-averse demographic comprising faux-Afrocentrics and misogynists (male and female)."

CHAPTER 6. MAKING A WAY OUT OF NO WAY

1 Twitter, as always, provides a wealth of alternative examples.

2 Tricking off: spending money or resources without accruing any gain. In this case, I am name-checking these theories but not actually ingesting or incorporating them.

3 Instagram, where Black users overindex compared to their demographic census representation.

4 See the definition from *Merriam-Webster*: "the degree of attractiveness an individual, activity, or thing possesses as a behavioral goal."

5 Don't @ me.

REFERENCES

Ahmed, S. (2013). *The cultural politics of emotion* (2nd ed.). Edinburgh, Scotland: Edinburgh University Press.

Alcoff, L. M. (2000). Who's afraid of identity politics? In P. M. L. Moya & M. R. Hames-Garcia (Eds.), *Reclaiming identity: Realist theory and the predicament of postmodernism* (pp. 312–344). Oakland: University of California Press.

Alexa.com. (n.d.). Gizmodo.com traffic statistics. Retrieved from www.alexa.com

Althusser, L. (1971). Ideology and ideological state apparatuses (Notes towards an investigation). In L. Althusser, *Lenin and philosophy and other essays*. Retrieved from www.marxists.org

Anderson, B. (2006). *Imagined communities: Reflections on the origin and spread of nationalism*. New York, NY: Verso.

Anderson, M., & Hitlin, P. (2016, August 15). Social media conversations about race. Pew Internet & American Life Project. Retrieved from www.pewinternet.org

Baldwin, J. ([1950] 1985). Encounter on the Seine: Black meets brown. In J. Baldwin, *The Price of the Ticket: Collected non-fiction 1948–1985* (pp. 35–40). London, England: Michael Joseph.

Banks, A. J. (2006). *Race, rhetoric, and technology: Searching for higher ground*. New York, NY: Routledge.

Baraka, I. A. (1965). Technology and ethos. In I. A. Baraka, *Raise, race, rays, raze: Essays since 1965* (pp. 155–158). New York, NY: Random House.

Barocas, S., & Selbst, A. D. (2016). Big data's disparate impact. *California Law Review, 104*, 671–732.

Baudrillard, J. (1981). *Simulacra and simulation*. Paris, France: Éditions Galilée.

Benjamin, S. G. (2014). The uses of anger: Wanda Coleman and the poetry of Black rage. *Hecate, 40*(1), 58.

Bennett, B. (2014, December 17). I don't know what to do with good white people. Jezebel. Retrieved from https://jezebel.com

Bollen, J., Gonçalves, B., Ruan, G., & Mao, H. (2011). Happiness is assortative in online social networks. *Artificial Life, 17*(3), 237–251.

boyd, d. (2009). The not-so-hidden politics of class online. Zephoria. Retrieved from http://zephoria.org

boyd, d. (2011). White flight in networked publics? How race and class shaped American teen engagement with Myspace and Facebook. In L. Nakamura & P. Chow-White (Eds.), *Race after the internet* (pp. 203–222). New York, NY: Routledge.

boyd, d., & Ellison, N. (2007). Social network sites: Definition, history, and scholarship. *Journal of Computer-Mediated Communication, 13*(1), article 11.

Bradley, R. N. (2013a, March 19). I been on (ratchet): Conceptualizing a sonic ratchet aesthetic in Beyoncé's "Bow Down." Red Clay Scholar. Retrieved from http://redclayscholar.blogspot.com

Bradley, R. N. (2013b, July 1). To sir, with ratchety love: Listening to the (dis)respectability politics of Rachel Jeantel. Sound Studies. Retrieved from http://soundstudiesblog.com

Bragin, N. E. (2015). *Black power of hip hop dance: On kinesthetic politics*. Retrieved from ProQuest Dissertations Publishing. (3720388)

Brah, A., & Phoenix, A. (2004). Ain't I a woman? Revisiting intersectionality. *Journal of International Women's Studies, 5*(3), 75–86.

Brock, A. (2007). *Race, the internet, and the hurricane: A critical discourse analysis of Black identity online during the aftermath of Hurricane Katrina* (Doctoral dissertation). University of Illinois at Urbana-Champaign.

Brock, A. (2009). Life on the wire: Deconstructing race on the Internet. *Information, Communication & Society, 12*(3), 344–363.

Brock, A. (2011a). Beyond the pale: The Blackbird web browser's critical reception. *New Media & Society, 13*(7), 1085–1103.

Brock, A. (2011b). "When keeping it real goes wrong": Resident Evil 5, racial representation, and gamers. *Games and Culture, 6*(5), 429–452.

Brock, A. (2012). From the blackhand side: Twitter as a cultural conversation. *Journal of Broadcasting & Electronic Media, 56*(4), 529–549.

Brock, A. (2017, March). The white world: "Dusk of Dawn" as a conceptual framework for white digital practice. 12th Social Theory Forum, University of Massachusetts.

Brock, A. (2018). Critical technocultural discourse analysis. *New Media & Society, 20*(3), 1012–1030.

Brock, A., Kvasny, L., & Hales, K. (2010). Cultural appropriations of technical capital: Black women, weblogs, and the digital divide. *Information, Communication & Society, 13*(7), 1040–1059.

Brown, K. (2015, August 21). The definition of "fuckboy" is not what bad trend pieces are telling you. Jezebel. Retrieved from https://jezebel.com

Burgess, J., & Green, J. (2009). *YouTube: Online video and participatory culture*. Cambridge, England: Polity Press.

Byrne, D. N. (2007). Public discourse, community concerns, and civic engagement: Exploring Black social networking traditions on BlackPlanet.com. *Journal of Computer-Mediated Communication, 13*(1), 319–340.

Bush, V. (1945, July). As we may think. *Atlantic Monthly, 176*(1), 101–108.

Byrne, D. N. (2008). The future of (the) "race": Identity, discourse and the rise of computer-mediated public spheres. In A. Everett (Ed.), *Learning race and ethnicity: Youth and digital media*. The John D. and Catherine T. MacArthur Foundation Series on Digital Media and Learning (pp. 15–38). Cambridge, MA: MIT Press. doi:10.1162/dmal.9780262550673

Callahan, Y. (2014, September 3). USC's Black Twitter study draws criticism. The Root. Retrieved from https://thegrapevine.theroot.com

Carey, J. (1984). *Communication as culture: Essays on media and society*. London, England: Routledge.

Chappelle, D. (2018, January 3). *EQUANIMITY* [Full transcript]. Scraps from the Loft. Retrieved from http://scrapsfromtheloft.com

Chartier, D. (2008, October 15). Flock 2 browser takes flight with a few surprises. Ars Technica. Retrieved from https://arstechnica.com

Christensen, H. S. (2011). Political activities on the internet: Slacktivism or political participation by other means? *First Monday, 16*(2). doi:https://doi.org/10.5210/fm.v16i2.3336

Christians, C. (1989). A theory of normative technology. In E. F. Byrne & J. C. Pitt (Eds.), *Technological transformation*. Philosophy and Technology (Vol. 5, pp. 123–139). Dordrecht, NL: Springer.

Chun, W. H. K. (2011). Race and/as technology, or how to do things to race. In L. Nakamura & P. Chow-White (Eds.), *Race after the internet* (pp. 44–66). New York, NY: Routledge.

Cohen, C. (2004, March). Deviance as resistance: A new research agenda for the study of Black politics. *Du Bois Review: Social Science Research on Race, 1*(1), 27–45.

Collins, P. H. (2002). *Black feminist thought: Knowledge, consciousness, and the politics of empowerment*. New York, NY: Routledge.

Conger, K. (2017, August 11). Exclusive: Here's the full 10-page anti-diversity screed circulating internally at Google. Gizmodo. Retrieved from https://gizmodo.com

Cooper, B. (2012, December 31). (Un)clutching my mother's pearls, or Ratchetness and the residue of respectability. Crunk Feminist Collective. Retrieved from www.crunkfeministcollective.com

Copeland, R. (2019, August 1). Fired by Google, a Republican engineer hits back: "There's been a lot of bullying." *Wall Street Journal*. Retrieved from www.wsj.com

Cottom, T. M. (2017). *Lower ed: The troubling rise of for-profit colleges in the new economy*. New York, NY: New Press.

Crenshaw, K. (1990). Mapping the margins: Intersectionality, politics, and violence against women of color. *Stanford Law Review, 43*(6), 1241.

Daniels, J. (2009). *Cyber racism: White supremacy online and the new attack on civil rights*. Lanham, MD: Rowman & Littlefield.

Daniels, J. (2013). Race and racism in internet studies: A review and critique. *New Media & Society, 15*(5), 695–719.

Dash, A. (2008, October 22). Yo mama's so fat. Anil Dash: A Blog about Making Culture. Retrieved from http://dashes.com

Dashefsky, A., & Shapiro, H. M. (1976). Ethnic and identity. In A. Dashefsky (Ed.), *Ethnicity in society* (pp. 5–11). Chicago, IL: Rand McNally.

Davis, A. P. (2016, September 29). The good wife. The Ringer. Retrieved from www.theringer.com

Day, R. (2007). Kling and the "critical": Social informatics and critical informatics. *Journal of the American Society for Information Science and Technology, 58*(4), 575–582.

de la Peña, C. (2006). "Slow and low progress," or why American studies should do technology. *American Quarterly, 58*(3), 915–941.

de la Peña, C. (2010, October). The history of technology, the resistance of archives, and the Whiteness of race. *Technology and Culture, 51*(4), 919–937.

de Saussure, F. ([1916] 1974). *Course in general linguistics* (Wade Baskin, trans.). London, England: Fontana/Collins.

Desjardins, J. (2017, March 7). The 100 websites that rule the internet. Visual Capitalist. Retrieved from www.visualcapitalist.com

Dinerstein, J. (2006). Technology and its discontents: On the verge of the posthuman. *American Quarterly, 58*(3), 569–595.

Donath, J. S. (2002). Identity and deception in the virtual community. In M. Smith (Ed.), *Communities in cyberspace* (pp. 37–68). New York, NY: Routledge.

Douglas, N. (2009). Micah's "Black people on Twitter" theory. Too Much Nick. Retrieved from http://toomuchnick.com

Douglas, S. J. (2006). The turn within: The irony of technology in a globalized world. *American Quarterly, 58*(3), 610–638.

Du Bois, W. E. B. (1903). *The souls of Black folk: Essays and sketches*. Chicago, IL: A. G. McClurg.

Du Bois, W. E. B. (1940). *Dusk of dawn: An autobiography of a race concept*. New York, NY: Harcourt Brace.

Dyer, R. (1997). *White*. London, England: Routledge.

Ebo, B. L. (Ed.). (1998). *Cyberghetto or cybertopia? Race, class, and gender on the internet*. Westport, CT: Greenwood.

Eglash, R. (2002). Race, sex, and nerds: From Black geeks to Asian American hipsters. *Social Text, 20*(2), 49–64.

Entman, R. M. (1993). Framing: Toward clarification of a fractured paradigm. *Journal of Communication, 43*(4), 51–58.

Eromosele, D. O. (2015, December 8). Here's what's wrong with Ayesha Curry's tweet about how some women dress "these days." The Root. Retrieved from https://thegrapevine.theroot.com

Eshun, K. (2003). Future considerations of Afrofuturism. *CR: The New Centennial Review, 3*(2), 287–302. doi:10.1353/ncr.2003.0021

Evans, M. (1970). Who can be born Black? Poem Hunter. Retrieved from www.poemhunter.com

Everett, A. (2009). *Digital diaspora: A race for cyberspace*. New York, NY: SUNY Press.

Faltesek, D. (2018). *Selling social media: The political economy of social networking*. New York, NY: Bloomsbury.

Feagin, J. R. (2006). *Systemic racism: A theory of oppression*. New York, NY: Routledge.

Feagin, J., & Elias, S. (2013). Rethinking racial formation theory: A systemic racism critique. *Ethnic and Racial Studies, 36*(6), 931–960.

Florini, S. L. (2019). *Beyond hashtags: Racial politics and Black digital networks*. New York, NY: New York University Press.

Fouché, R. (2006). Say it loud, I'm Black and I'm proud: African Americans, American artifactual culture, and Black vernacular technological creativity. *American Quarterly, 58*(3), 639–661.

Fox, S., Zickuhr, K., & Smith, A. (2009). Twitter and status updating. Pew Internet & American Life Project. Retrieved from www.pewinternet.org

Fox, T. R. (2015, December 6). Ayesha Curry: Tweet sparks fantastic meltdown on Twitter. SportsGrid. Retrieved from www.sportsgrid.com

Franz, K. (2004). The open road: Automobility and racial uplift in the interwar years. In B. Sinclair (Ed.), *Technology and the African-American experience* (pp. 131–154). Cambridge, MA: MIT Press.

Freelon, D., McIlwain, C., & Clark, M. (2016). *Beyond the hashtags: #Ferguson, #Blacklivesmatter, and the online struggle for offline justice* [Research report]. Washington, DC: Center for Media & Social Impact.

Gaines, K. K. (1996). *Uplifting the race: Black leadership, politics, and culture in the twentieth century*. Chapel Hill: University of North Carolina Press.

Gallon, K. T. (2009). *Between respectability and modernity: Black newspapers and sexuality, 1925–1940*. Retrieved from ProQuest Dissertations Publishing. (3381612)

Gates, H. L. (1983). The blackness of Blackness: A critique of the sign and the signifying monkey. *Critical Inquiry, 9*(4), 685–723.

Gaunt, K. D. (2015). YouTube, twerking & you: Context collapse and the handheld co-presence of Black girls and Miley Cyrus. *Journal of Popular Music Studies, 27*(3), 244–273.

Giddens, A. (1984). *The constitution of society*. Malden, MA: Polity Press.

Giddens, A., & Pierson, C. (1998). *Conversations with Anthony Giddens*. London, England: Polity Press.

Gillespie, T. (2011, October 19). Can an algorithm be wrong? Twitter trends, the specter of censorship, and our faith in the algorithms around us. Social Media Collective Research Blog. Retrieved from http://socialmediacollective.org

Gillespie, T. (2014). The relevance of algorithms. In T. Gillespie, P. Boczkowski, & K. Foot (Eds.), *Media technologies: Essays on communication, materiality, and society* (pp. 167–193). Cambridge, MA: MIT Press.

Gilliard, C., & Culik, H. (2016). Digital redlining, access, and privacy. Common Sense Education. Retrieved from http://commonsense.org

Gilroy, P. (1993). *The Black Atlantic: Modernity and double consciousness*. Cambridge, MA: Harvard University Press.

Giroux, H. (1996). *Fugitive cultures: Race, violence, and youth*. London, England: Routledge.

Gladwell, M. (2010, September 27). Small change. *New Yorker*. Retrieved from www.newyorker.com

Gooding-Williams, R. (1998). Race, multiculturalism and democracy. *Constellations, 5*(1), 18–41.

Goffman, E. (1959). *The presentation of self in everyday life*. New York, NY: Doubleday Anchor.

Granovetter, M. S. (1973). The strength of weak ties. *American Journal of Sociology, 78*(6), 1360–1380.

Gray, K. (2016). "They're just too urban": Black gamers streaming on Twitch. In J. Daniels, K. Gregory, & T. McMillan Cottom (Eds.), *Digital sociologies* (pp. 355–369). Bristol, England: Bristol University Press.

Gray, L. (2012). Intersecting oppressions and online communities. *Information, Communication & Society, 15*(3), 411–428.

Green, V. (2001). *Race on the line: Gender, labor, and technology in the Bell system, 1880–1980*. Durham, NC: Duke University Press.

Green, V. H. (1941). *The negro motorist green book*. New York, NY: Self-published.

Greenwood, S., Perrin, P., & Duggan, M. (2016). Social media update 2016. Pew Internet & American Life Project. 11 Nov. 2016. Retrieved from www.pewinternet.org

Griffin, F. J. (2000). Black feminists and Du Bois: Respectability, protection, and beyond. *Annals of the American Academy of Political and Social Science, 568*, 28–40.

Griffin, T. (2017, January 6). Black Twitter roasted Yahoo Finance after the "Nigger Navy" typo tweet. BuzzFeed News. Retrieved from www.buzzfeednews.com

Hacking, I. (2002). *Historical ontology*. London, England: Harper University Press.

Hall, M. R. S. (2014). The negro traveller's guide to a Jim Crow south: Negotiating racialized landscapes during a dark period in United States cultural history, 1936–1967. *Postcolonial Studies, 17*(3), 307–319.

Hall, S. (1986). Gramsci's relevance for the study of race and ethnicity. *Journal of Communication Inquiry, 10*, 5–27.

Harding, S. (1992). Rethinking standpoint epistemology: What is "strong objectivity"? *Centennial Review, 36*(3), 437–470. https://jstor.org/stable/23739232

Hardt, M. (2014, September 26). How big data is unfair. Medium. Retrieved from https://medium.com

Harris, C. (1993). Whiteness as property. *Harvard Law Review, 106*, 1707–1791.

Harris, P. J. (2003). Gatekeeping and remaking: The politics of respectability in African American women's history and Black feminism. *Journal of Women's History, 15*(1), 212–220.

Harvey, S., MacCullough, B., Hughley, D. L., & Kyles, C. (Writers), & Lee, S. (Director). (2000). *The original kings of comedy* [Motion picture]. United States: Paramount Pictures.

Haythornthwaite, C. (2002). Strong, weak, and latent ties and the impact of new media. *The Information Society, 18*(5), 385–401.

Henry, A. (2006). "There's salt-water in our blood": The "Middle Passage" epistemology of two Black mothers regarding the spiritual education of their daughters. *International Journal of Qualitative Studies in Education: QSE, 19*(3), 329–345.

Herring, S. C. (2001). Computer mediated discourse. In D. Schiffrin, D. Tannen, & H. Hamilton (Eds.), *The handbook of discourse analysis* (pp. 612–634). Oxford, England: Blackwell.

Higginbotham, E. B. (1992). African-American women's history and the metalanguage of race. *Signs: Journal of Women in Culture and Society, 17*(2), 251–274.

Higginbotham, E. B. (1993). *Righteous discontent: The women's movement in the Black Baptist Church, 1880–1920*. Cambridge, MA: Harvard University Press.

Hill, J. H. (1998). Language, race, and white public space. *American Anthropologist, 100*(3), 680–689.

Hilton, S. (2010). You can tweet like this or you can tweet like that or you can tweet like us. PostBourgie. Retrieved from www.postbourgie.com

Hine, D. C. (1989). Rape and the inner lives of Black women in the Middle West. *Signs: Journal of Women in Culture and Society, 14*(4), 912–920.

Hirsch, T. (2013, October 16). TXTMob and Twitter: A reply to Nick Bilton. Public Practice. Retrieved from http://publicpractice.org/wp/?p=779

Hirsch, T., & Henry, J. (2005, April). TXTmob: Text messaging for protest swarms. In Association for Computing Machinery (ACM), *CHI '05 extended abstracts on human factors in computing systems* (pp. 1455–1458). New York, NY: ACM Digital Library. doi:http://dx.doi.org/10.1145/1056808.1056940

Hoffman, D. L., & Novak, T. P. (1998). Bridging the racial divide on the internet. *Science, 280*(5362), 390–391.

Honeycutt, C., & Herring, S. C. (2009). Beyond microblogging: Conversation and collaboration via Twitter. In R. H. Sprague Jr. (Ed.), *Proceedings of the 42nd Hawaii International Conference on System Sciences* (pp. 1–10). Piscataway, NJ: IEEE Computer Society.

Horrigan, J. (2009). Wireless internet use. Pew Internet & American Life Project. Retrieved from www.pewinternet.org

Huang, J., Thornton, K. M., & Efthimiadis, E. N. (2010, June). Conversational tagging in Twitter. In Association for Computing Machinery (ACM), *Proceedings of the 21st ACM Conference on Hypertext and Hypermedia* (pp. 173–178). New York, NY: ACM Digital Library. doi:http://dx.doi.org/10.1145/1810617.1810647

Huberman, B., Romero, D., & Wu, F. (2008). Social networks that matter: Twitter under the microscope. *First Monday, 14*(1). Retrieved from https://firstmonday.org

Hughes, E. C. ([1971] 1993). The study of ethnic relations. In E. C. Hughes (Ed.), *The sociological eye* (pp. 153–156). New Brunswick, NJ: Transaction.

Hunt, D. (2017). Race in the writers' room: How Hollywood whitewashes the stories that shape America. Hollywood Color of Change. Retrieved from https://hollywood.colorofchange.org

Hutchby, I. (2001). Technologies, texts and affordances. *Sociology, 35*(2), 441–456.

Illich, I. (1973). *Tools for conviviality*. New York, NY: Harper and Row.

Irving, D. (2016). Treading water. *Missouri Review, 39*(2), 48–67.

Isajiw, I. (1977). Olga in Wonderland: Ethnicity in technological society. *Canadian Ethnic Studies, 9*(1), 77–85.

Java, A., Song, X., Finin, T., & Tseng, B. (2009). Why we Twitter: An analysis of a microblogging community. In H. Zhang et al. (Eds.), *Advances in web mining and web usage analysis* (pp. 118–138). Berlin, Germany: Springer.

Jefferson, C. (2014, June 9). The racism beat. Medium. Retrieved from https://medium.com

Judy, R. (1994). On the question of nigga authenticity. *boundary 2*, *21*(3), 211–230.

Kendall, L. (2002). *Hanging out in the virtual pub: Masculinities and relationships online*. Berkeley: University of California Press.

Kinneavy, J. L., & Eskin, C. R. (1994). Kairos in Aristotle's rhetoric. *Written Communication*, *11*(1), 131–142. doi:10.1177/0741088394011001006

Kolko, B., Nakamura, L., & Rodman, G. (2013). *Race in cyberspace*. New York, NY: Routledge.

Krishnamurthy, B., Gill, P., & Arlitt, M. (2008). A few chirps about Twitter. In Association for Computing Machinery (ACM), *Proceedings of the first workshop on online social networks* (pp. 19–24). New York, NY: ACM Digital Library. doi:https://doi.org/10.1145/1397735.1397741

Kruse, K. M. (2018, August 20). Let's talk for a second about how we count murders, and how numbers hide the real story [Twitter status]. Retrieved from https://twitter.com

Kuypers, J. A. (2010). Framing analysis from a rhetorical perspective. In P. D'Angelo & J. A. Kuypers (Eds.), *Doing news framing analysis: Empirical and theoretical perspectives* (pp. 286–311). New York, NY: Routledge.

Labov, W. (1998). Co-existent systems in African-American vernacular English. In S. S. Mufwene, G. Bailey, J. R. Rickford, & J. Baugh (Eds.), *African-American English: Structure, history, and use* (pp. 110–153). New York, NY: Routledge.

Langlois, G. (2014). *Meaning in the age of social media*. New York, NY: Palgrave Macmillan.

Lee, H. J., & Andrejevic, M. (2013). Second-screen theory. In J. Holt & K. Swanson (Eds.), *Connected viewing: Selling, streaming & sharing media in the digital age* (p. 40). New York, NY: Routledge.

Levine-Rasky, C. (2011). Intersectionality theory applied to whiteness and middle-classness. *Social identities*, *17*(2), 239–253.

Livingstone, S. (2005). On the relation between audiences and publics. In S. Livingstone (Ed.), *Audiences and publics: When cultural engagement matters for the public sphere* (pp. 17–43). Bristol, England: Intellect Books.

Loewen, J. (2005). *Sundown towns: A hidden dimension of American racism*. New York, NY: New Press.

Lorde, A. (1984). *Sister/outsider*. New York, NY: Crossing Press.

Lucas D'Oyley, D. (2015, December 7). No, Ayesha Curry did not slut-shame women with her tweets. The Root. Retrieved from www.theroot.com

Lyotard, J. F. ([1973] 1993). *Libidinal economy* (I. H. Grant, trans.). Bloomington: Indiana University Press.

Manjoo, F. (2010, August 10). How Black people use Twitter: The latest research on race and microblogging. Slate. Retrieved from http://slate.com

Marcuse, H. (1964). *One-dimensional man: Studies in the ideology of advanced industrial society*. Boston: Beacon.

Marriott, M. (2006, March 31). Digital divide closing as Blacks turn to internet. *New York Times*. Retrieved from www.nytimes.com

Marwick, A. E., & boyd, d. (2011). I tweet honestly, I tweet passionately: Twitter users, context collapse, and the imagined audience. *New Media & Society, 13*(1), 113–140.

Marx, K. ([1852] 1972). The eighteenth brumaire of Louis Bonaparte. In S. K. Padover (Ed.), *The Karl Marx library* (Vol. 1, pp. 245–246). New York, NY: McGraw-Hill.

Marx, L. (2000). *The machine in the garden: Technology and the pastoral ideal in America*. London, England: Oxford University Press.

Massumi, B. (2002). *Parables for the virtual*. Durham, NC: Duke University Press.

Mathes, A. (2004). Folksonomies: Cooperative classification and communication through shared metadata. Adam Mathes. Retrieved from http://adammathes.com

McGahan, C. L. (2013). *Racing cyberculture: Minoritarian art and cultural politics on the internet*. New York, NY: Routledge.

McKay, T. (2019, August 6). Trump boosts fired Google engineer who proposed Richard Spencer fundraiser, suggested skinheads rebrand. Gizmodo. Retrieved from https://gizmodo.com

Meehan, E. R., Mosco, V., & Wasko, J. (1993). Rethinking political economy: Change and continuity. *Journal of Communication, 43*, 105–116. doi:10.1111/j.1460-2466.1993.tb01310.x

Melfi, T., Gigliotti, D., Chernin, P., Topping, J., Williams, P., Schroeder, A., . . . Walker, M. (2017). *Hidden figures* [Motion picture]. Los Angeles, CA: Twentieth Century Fox Home Entertainment.

Messina, C. (2007, August 25). Groups for Twitter; or a proposal for Twitter tag channels. Factory Joe. Retrieved from http://factoryjoe.com

Messina, C. (2008, January 2). Kicking off 2008 with a themeword. Factory Joe. Retrieved from http://factoryjoe.com

Miller, C. R. (1994). Opportunity, opportunism, and progress: Kairos in the rhetoric of technology. *Argumentation, 8*(1), 81–96.

Miller, D., & Slater, D. (2000). *The internet: An ethnographic approach*. Oxford, England: Berg.

Mills, C. (1997). *The racial contract*. New York, NY: Cornell University Press.

Mills, C. (1998). *Blackness visible: Essays on philosophy and race*. New York, NY: Cornell University Press.

Milner, R. M. (2016). *The world made meme: Public conversations and participatory media*. Cambridge, MA: MIT Press.

Mitchell-Kernan, C. ([1972] 1999). Signifyin', loud-talkin', and markin'. In D. Caponi (Ed.), *Signifyin(g), sanctifyin, and slam dunkin* (pp. 309–330). Amherst, MA: University of Massachusetts Press.

Mitra, A. (2001). Marginal voices in cyberspace. *New Media & Society, 3*(1), 29–48.

Mitra, A., & Watts, E. (2002). Theorizing cyberspace: The idea of voice applied to the internet discourse. *New Media & Society, 4*(4), 479–498.

Morgan, J. (2015). Why we get off: Moving towards a Black feminist politics of pleasure. *Black Scholar, 45*(4), 36–46.

Morris, S. M. (2014). *Close kin and distant relatives: The paradox of respectability in Black women's literature*. Charlottesville: University of Virginia Press.
Morris, S. M. (2016). More than human: Black feminisms of the future in Jewelle Gomez's *The Gilda stories*. *Black Scholar, 46*(2), 33–45.
Morrison, T. (1993). *Playing in the dark: Whiteness and the literary imagination*. New York, NY: Vintage.
Mosco, V. (2005). *The digital sublime: Myth, power, and cyberspace*. Cambridge, MA: MIT Press.
Mosco, V. (2009). *The political economy of communication*. London, England: Sage.
Moten, F. (2013). Blackness and nothingness (mysticism in the flesh). *South Atlantic Quarterly, 112*(4), 737–780.
Mowatt, R. A., French, B. H., & Malebranche, D. A. (2013). Black/female/body hypervisibility and invisibility. *Journal of Leisure Research, 45*(5), 644–660. doi:10.18666/jlr-2013-v45-i5-4367
Murray, J. H. (1998). *Hamlet on the holodeck: The future of narrative in cyberspace*. Cambridge, MA: MIT Press.
Myers, B. (2018, March 28). Women and minorities in tech, by the numbers. Wired. Retrieved from www.wired.com
Nakamura, L. (2002). *Cybertypes: Race, ethnicity, and identity on the internet*. New York, NY: Routledge.
Nakamura, L. (2006). Cultural difference, theory, and cyberculture studies: A case of mutual repulsion. In D. Silver & A. Massanari (Eds.), *Critical cyberculture studies* (pp. 29–36). New York: New York University Press.
Nakamura, L. (2013, December 10). Glitch racism: Networks as actors within vernacular internet theory. Culture Digitally. Retrieved from http://culturedigitally.org
Nakamura, L., & Chow-White, P. (Eds.). (2013). *Race after the internet*. New York, NY: Routledge.
Nelson, A. (2002). Introduction: Future texts. *Social Text, 71*(20.2), 1–15.
Nelson, A. (2016). *The social life of DNA: Race, reparations, and reconciliation after the genome*. New York, NY: Beacon Press.
Nelson, T. (1974). *Dream machines/computer lib*. South Bend, IN: Distributors.
Newitz, A. (2014, September 3). What happens when scientists study "Black Twitter"? Gizmodo. Retrieved from https://io9.gizmodo.com
Nielsen, J. (1993, January). User interface directions for the web. *Communications of the ACM, 42*(1), 65–72.
Nixon, R. (2011). *Slow violence and the environmentalism of the poor*. Cambridge, MA: Harvard University Press.
Noble, S. U. (2016). *Algorithms of oppression: How search engines reinforce racism*. New York: New York University Press.
Norman, D. A. (1988). *The psychology of everyday things*. New York, NY: Basic Books.
Nunley, V. L. (2011). *Keepin' it hushed: The barbershop and African American hush harbor rhetoric*. Detroit, MI: Wayne State University Press.
Nye, D. E. (1996). *American technological sublime*. Cambridge, MA: MIT Press.

Obadike, K. (n.d.). Blackness. Retrieved from https://obadike.squarespace.com

Oldenburg, R. (1999). *The great good place: Cafes, coffee shops, bookstores, bars, hair salons, and other hangouts at the heart of a community*. Cambridge, MA: Da Capo Press.

Omi, M., & Winant, H. (1994). *Racial formation in the United States: From the 1960s to the 1990s*. New York, NY: Routledge.

Ong, W. J. (1982). *Orality and literacy*. London, England: Methuen.

O'Reilly, T. (2005, September 30). What is Web 2.0? Retrieved from www.oreilly.com

O'Sullivan, D., & Byers, D. (2017, September 28). Exclusive: Fake Black activist social media accounts linked to Russian government. CNN Money. Retrieved from http://money.cnn.com

Ott, B. L. (2004). (Re)locating pleasure in media studies: Toward an erotics of reading. *Communication and Critical/Cultural Studies, 1*(2), 194–212.

Pacey, A. (1984). *The culture of technology*. Cambridge, MA: MIT Press.

Palmer, T. (2012, October 16). Where the word "ratchet" came from. The Root. Retrieved from www.theroot.com

Parham, J. (2017, October 19). Russians posing as Black activists on Facebook is more than fake news. Wired. Retrieved from www.wired.com

Parry, R. (2014). Episteme and techne. In E. N. Zalta (Ed.), *Stanford Encyclopedia of Philosophy*. Retrieved from http://plato.stanford.edu

Patterson, O. (1982). *Slavery and social death*. Cambridge, MA: Harvard University Press.

Peele, J. (Dir.). (2017). *Get out* [Video file]. Universal City, CA: Universal Pictures Home Entertainment.

Pérez-Peña, R. (2008, January 28). *Washington Post* starts an online magazine for Blacks. *New York Times*. Retrieved from www.nytimes.com

Peters, M. (2015, December 7). Steph Curry proud of wife Ayesha for staying "upbeat" through Twitter backlash. *USA Today*. Retrieved from http://ftw.usatoday.com

Phillips, W. (2015). *This is why we can't have nice things: Mapping the relationship between online trolling and mainstream culture*. Cambridge, MA: MIT Press.

Pickens, J. (2015, December 10). The respectability politricks of Ayesha Curry. *Ebony*. Retrieved from www.ebony.com

Pinch, T. J., & Bijker, W. E. (1984). The social construction of facts and artefacts: Or how the sociology of science and the sociology of technology might benefit each other. *Social Studies of Science, 14*(3), 399–441.

Porter, J. E. (2009). Recovering delivery for digital rhetoric. *Computers and Composition, 26*(4), 207–224.

Pursell, C. (2010, July). Technologies as cultural practice and production. *Technology and Culture, 51*(3), 715–722.

Rainie, L. (2016, July 14). Digital divides 2016. Pew Internet & American Life Project. Retrieved from www.pewinternet.org

Ramsey, D. X. (2015, April 10). The truth about Black Twitter. *Atlantic*. Retrieved from www.theatlantic.com

Rawls, A. W. (2000). "Race" as an interaction order phenomenon: WEB Du Bois' "double consciousness" thesis revisited. *Sociological Theory, 18*(2), 241–274.

Rhodes, J. (2016). Pedagogies of respectability: Race, media, and Black womanhood in the early 20th century. *Souls, 18*(2–4), 201–214.

Rickford, J. R. (1999). *African American Vernacular English: Features, evolution, educational implications*. Malden, MA: Blackwell.

Rickford, J. R., & Rickford, R. J. (2000). *Spoken soul: The story of Black English*. New York, NY: Wiley.

Riley, N. S. (2019, April 18). The real digital divide isn't about access to the internet. *Washington Post*. Retrieved from www.washingtonpost.com

Rock, C. (Producer), & Rock, C. (Writer). (1996). *Chris Rock: Bring the pain* [Motion picture]. New York, NY: Home Box Office.

Romanesko, J. (2008, January 28). WP Co.'s new website aims to be a "Slate for Black readers." Poynter. Retrieved from www.poynter.org

Romano, A. (2013, January 13). GitHub code search reveals coding community's hidden bigotry. Daily Dot. Retrieved from www.dailydot.com

Romano, A. (2019, March 14). A false alarm over Twitter likes and retweets caused panic—but it was justified. Vox. Retrieved from www.vox.com

The Root. (2018). The Root 100—the most influential African Americans in 2018. Retrieved from https://interactives.theroot.com

Rosen, J. (2008, July 17). When the star of the story is understanding itself. Mediashift. Retrieved from http://mediashift.org

Rosenthal, C. (2018). *Accounting for slavery: Masters and management*. Cambridge, MA: Harvard University Press.

Saadiq, R., Wiggins, D., Riley, C., Foster, D., & McElroy, T. (1988). Born not to know [YouTube video]. Retrieved from https://youtu.be/TaxUQoQ7moA

Sagolla, D. (2009). *140 characters: A style guide for the short form*. New York, NY: John Wiley & Sons.

Scheidt, L. A. (2006). Adolescent diary weblogs and the unseen audience. In D. Buckingham & R. Willett (Eds.), *Digital generations: Children, young people and new media* (pp. 193–210). Mahwah, NJ: Lawrence Erlbaum.

Schroeder, S. (2014, May 30). Is this the end of Twitter? Mashable. Retrieved from https://mashable.com

ScientiaMobile. (2018, May 8). Smartphone screen size trend. Retrieved from www.scientiamobile.com

Selwyn, N. (2004). Reconsidering political and popular understandings of the digital divide. *New Media & Society, 6*(3), 341–362.

Sexton, J. (2010). People-of-color-blindness: Notes on the afterlife of slavery. *Social Text, 28*(103), 31–56.

Shannon, C. E., & Weaver, W. ([1949] 1998). *The mathematical theory of communication*. Champaign: University of Illinois Press.

Sharpe, C. (2016). *In the wake: On Blackness and being*. Durham, NC: Duke University Press.

Shepherd, J. E. (2016, March 7). Fetty Wap fans petition for his rightful place at Nancy Reagan's funeral. Jezebel. Retrieved from https://themuse.jezebel.com
Shifman, L. (2013). *Memes in digital culture*. Cambridge, MA: MIT Press.
Sicha, C. (2009, November 11). What were Black people talking about on Twitter last night? The Awl. Retrieved from http://theawl.com
Sinclair, B. (Ed.). (2004). *Technology and the African-American experience: Needs and opportunities for study*. Cambridge, MA: MIT Press.
Smith, A. (2010a). Home broadband adoption. Pew Internet & American Life Project. Retrieved from www.pewinternet.org
Smith, A. (2010b). Mobile access 2010. Pew Internet & American Life Project. Retrieved from www.pewinternet.org
Smith, A. (2011). Twitter update 2011. Pew Internet & American Life Project. Retrieved from www.pewinternet.org
Smith, A. (2015). U.S. smartphone use in 2015. Pew Internet & American Life Project. Retrieved from www.pewinternet.org
Smith, W. A., Allen, W. R., & Danley, L. L. (2007). "Assume the position . . . you fit the description": Psychosocial experiences and racial battle fatigue among African American male college students. *American Behavioral Scientist, 51*(4), 551–578.
Smith, W. A., Yosso, T. J., & Solorzano, D. G. (2006). Challenging racial battle fatigue on historically white campuses: A critical race examination of race related stress. In C. A. Stanley (Ed.), *Faculty of color: Teaching in predominately white colleges and universities* (pp. 299–327). Bolton, MA: Anker.
Smitherman, G. (1977). *Talkin and testifyin: The language of Black America*. Detroit, MI: Wayne State University Press.
Smith-Shomade, B. E. (2004). Narrowcasting in the new world information order: A space for the audience? *Television & New Media*, 5(1), 69–81.
Solon, O. (2016, November 17). Alt-right retaliates against Twitter ban by creating "fake Black accounts." *The Guardian*. Retrieved from www.theguardian.com
Solorzano, D., Ceja, M., & Yosso, T. (2000). Critical race theory, racial microaggressions, and campus racial climate: The experiences of African American college students. *Journal of Negro Education, 69*(1), 60–73.
Spears, A. K. (1998). African-American language use: Ideology and so-called obscenity. In S. S. Mufwene, G. Bailey, J. R. Rickford, & J. Baugh (Eds.), *African-American English: Structure, history, and use* (pp. 226–250). New York, NY: Routledge.
Spears, A. K. (Ed.). (1999). *Race and ideology: Language, symbolism, and popular culture*. Detroit, MI: Wayne State University Press.
Spears, A. K. (2001). Directness in the use of African American English. *Sociocultural and Historical Contexts of African American English, 27*, 239–259.
Spinelli, M. (1996). Radio lessons for the internet. *Postmodern Culture, 6*(2).
Squires, C. R. (2002). Rethinking the black public sphere: An alternative vocabulary for multiple public spheres. *Communication Theory, 12*(4), 446–468.
Stallings, L. H. (2013). Hip hop and the Black ratchet imagination. *Palimpsest, 2*(2), 135–139.

Steele, C. K. (2016). The digital barbershop: Blogs and online oral culture within the African American community. *Social Media + Society, 2*(4). doi:10.1177/2056305116683205

Steele, C. K. (2018). Black bloggers and their varied publics: The everyday politics of Black discourse online. *Television & New Media, 19*(2), 112–127.

Straubhaar, J. (Ed.). (2012). *Inequity in the technopolis: Race, class, gender, and the digital divide in Austin*. Austin: University of Texas Press.

Sue, D. W. (2010). *Microaggressions in everyday life: Race, gender, and sexual orientation*. New York, NY: John Wiley & Sons.

Sue, D. W., Capodilupo, C. M., Torino, G. C., Bucceri, J. M., Holder, A., Nadal, K. L., & Esquilin, M. (2007). Racial microaggressions in everyday life: Implications for clinical practice. *American Psychologist, 62*(4), 271.

Sweeney, M. E. (2016, October). Emoji ethnicity update: De-coding the racial ideologies of "diverse" emoji. Paper presented at Association of Internet Researchers, Berlin, Germany.

Tal, K. (1996). The unbearable Whiteness of being: African American critical theory and cyberculture. Kali Tal. Retrieved from http://kalital.com

Tate, S. A. (2011). Playing in the dark: Being unafraid and impolite. *European Journal of Women's Studies, 18*(1), 94–96. doi:10.1177/13505068110180010703

Thompson, C. (2017, January 18). Everyday Black girl magic. Auntie Peebz: Medium. Retrieved from https://medium.com

Tiku, N. (2018, October 25). Why Netflix features Black actors in promos to Black users. Wired. Retrieved from www.wired.com

Tonnies, F. ([1887] 1999). *Community and society: Gemeinschaft and Gesellschaft*. New York, NY: Routledge.

Topolsky, J. (2016, January 29). The end of Twitter. *New Yorker*. Retrieved from www.newyorker.com

Turkle, S. (1997). *Life on the screen*. New York, NY: Simon & Schuster.

Turkle, S. (2017). *Alone together: Why we expect more from technology and less from each other*. London, England: Hachette.

Twitter.com. (n.d.). About Twitter trends. Retrieved from https://support.twitter.com

Twitter.com. (n.d.). Terms of service. Retrieved from https://twitter.com

United States National Advisory Commission on Civil Disorders. (1968). *Report of the National Advisory Commission on Civil Disorders*. New York, NY: Bantam Books.

United States vs. Microsoft Corporation, 253 F.3d 34 (D.C. Cir. 2001).

Walcott, R. (1972, December). Ellison, Gordone, Towson: Some notes on the blues, style and space. *Black World, 22*(2), 4–30.

Ward, B. (2004). *Radio and the struggle for civil rights in the South*. Gainesville: University Press of Florida.

Warner, K. J. (2015). They gon' think you loud regardless: Ratchetness, reality television, and Black womanhood. *Camera Obscura: Feminism, Culture, and Media Studies, 30*(88), 129–153.

Warner, K. J. (Forthcoming). The Black cult figure in television and film.

Weheliye, A. G. (2002). Feenin': Posthuman voices in contemporary Black popular music. *Social Text, 20*(2), 21–47.
Weheliye, A. G. (2014). *Habeas viscus: Racializing assemblages, biopolitics, and Black feminist theories of the human*. Durham, NC: Duke University Press.
White, E. F. (1990). Africa on my mind: Gender, counter discourse, and African-American nationalism. *Journal of Women's History, 2*(1), 73–97.
White, E. F. (2001). *Dark continent of our bodies: Black feminism and politics of respectability. Philadelphia*. Philadelphia, PA: Temple University Press.
Wilderson, F. (2010). *Red, White, and Black: Cinema and the structure of U.S. antagonisms*. Durham, NC: Duke University Press.
Williams, A. (2016). On Thursdays we watch *Scandal*: Communal viewing and Black Twitter. In J. Daniels, K. Gregory, & T. McMillan Cottom (Eds.), *Digital sociologies* (pp. 273–293). Bristol, England: Bristol University Press.
Wilson, C. (2009, September 9). uknowurblack. The Root. Retrieved from www.theroot.com
Wodak, R. (2001). The discourse-historical approach. In R. Wodak & M. Meyer (Eds.), *Methods of critical discourse analysis* (pp. 63–94). London, England: Sage.
Wolff, M. J. (2006). The myth of the actuary: Life insurance and Frederick L. Hoffman's *Race traits and tendencies of the American Negro. Public Health Reports, 121*, 84–91.
Womack, Y. (2013). *Afrofuturism: The world of Black sci-fi and fantasy culture*. Chicago, IL: Chicago Review Press.
Wolfram, W. (1994). On the sociolinguistic significance of obscure dialect structures: The construction in African-American vernacular English. *American Speech, 69*(4), 339–360. doi:10.2307/455854
Woolgar, S. (1991). The turn to technology in social studies of science. *Science, Technology, & Human Values, 16*(1), 20–50.
Wright, M. (2015). *Physics of Blackness: Beyond the Middle Passage epistemology*. Minneapolis: University of Minnesota Press.
Yancy, G. (2005). Whiteness and the return of the Black body. *Journal of Speculative Philosophy, 19*(4), 215–241.
Yaszek, L. (2006). Afrofuturism, science fiction, and the history of the future. *Socialism and Democracy, 20*(3), 41–60.
Young, D. (2016, June 15). How Ayesha Curry got cast as the sports world's Virgin Mary. Slate. Retrieved from https://slate.com
Zeb, Y. (2018, August 21). Top 3 most popular smartphone screen sizes in 2018 are 5.5-inch 6.0-inch and 5.1-inch—report. Research Snipers. Retrieved from www.researchsnipers.com
Zhao, D., & Rosson, M. (2009). How and why people Twitter: The role that microblogging plays in informal communication at work. In Association for Computing Machinery (ACM), *Proceedings of the ACM 2009 International Conference on Supporting Group Work* (pp. 243–252). New York, NY: ACM Digital Library. doi:https://doi.org/10.1145/1531674.1531710

INDEX

ABOUT THE AUTHOR

André Brock Jr. is an associate professor of Black Digital Media at Georgia Tech. He is an interdisciplinary scholar with an MA in English and Rhetoric from Carnegie Mellon University and a PhD in Library and Information Science from the University of Illinois at Urbana-Champaign.

His scholarship includes published articles on racial representations in videogames, Black women and weblogs, whiteness, Blackness, and digital technoculture, as well as innovative and groundbreaking research on Black Twitter. His article "From the Blackhand Side: Twitter as a Cultural Conversation" challenged social science and communication research to confront the ways in which the field, in his words, preserved "a color-blind perspective on online endeavors by normalizing whiteness and othering everyone else" and sparked a conversation that continues as Twitter in particular continues to evolve as a communication platform.

The author of numerous journal articles and book chapters, Dr. Brock's writings have appeared in prominent journals like *Media, Culture, and Society*, *New Media & Society*, *Journal of Broadcast and Electronic Media*, *Journal of Computer-Mediated Communication*, and *Information, Communication & Society*.

Dr. Brock is a charter member of the NYU Center for Critical Race and Digital Studies.